GREEK

A ROUGH GUIDE DICTIONARY PHRASEBOOK

Compiled by

LEXUS

D1550967

Credits

Compiled by Lexus with Costas Panayotakis
Lexus Series Editor: Sally Davies
Rough Guides Phrase Book Editor: Jonathan Buckley
Rough Guides Series Editor: Mark Ellingham

First edition published in 1995 by Rough Guides Ltd,
62–70 Shorts Gardens, London WC2H 9AB.
Reprinted in 1996 and 1998.
Revised in 1999.

Distributed by the Penguin Group.

Penguin Books Ltd, 27 Wrights Lane, London W8 5TZ
Penguin Books USA Inc., 375 Hudson Street, New York 10014, USA
Penguin Books Australia Ltd, 487 Maroondah Highway,
PO Box 257, Ringwood, Victoria 3134, Australia
Penguin Books Canada Ltd, Alcorn Avenue,
Toronto, Ontario, Canada M4V 1E4
Penguin Books (NZ) Ltd, 182–190 Wairau Road,
Auckland 10, New Zealand

Typeset in Bembo and Helvetica to an original design by Henry Iles.
Printed in Spain by Graphy Cems.

British Library Cataloguing in Publication Data
A catalogue for this book is available from the British Library.

ISBN 1-85828-643-3

HELP US GET IT RIGHT

Lexus and Rough Guides have made great efforts to be accurate and
informative in this Rough Guide Greek phrasebook. However, if you feel
we have overlooked a useful word or phrase, or have any other
comments to make about the book, please let us know. All contributors
will be acknowledged and the best letters will be rewarded with a free
Rough Guide phrasebook of your choice. Please write to 'Greek
Phrasebook Update', at either Shorts Gardens (London) or Hudson Street
(New York) – for full addresses see above. Alternatively you can email us at
mail@roughguides.co.uk

Online information about Rough Guides can be found at our website
www.roughguides.com

CONTENTS

Introduction

The Rough Guide Greek dictionary phrasebook is a highly practical introduction to the contemporary language. Laid out in clear A-Z style, it uses key-word referencing to lead you straight to the words and phrases you want – so if you need to book a room, just look up 'room'. The Rough Guide gets straight to the point in every situation, in bars and shops, on trains and buses, and in hotels and banks.

The main part of the Rough Guide is a double dictionary: English-Greek then Greek-English. Before that, there's a section called Basics, which sets out the fundamental rules of the language, with plenty of practical examples. You'll also find here other essentials like numbers, dates, telling the time and basic phrases.

Forming the heart of the guide, the English-Greek section gives easy-to-use transliterations of the Greek words wherever pronunciation might be a problem, and to get you involved quickly in two-way communication, the Rough Guide includes dialogues featuring typical responses on key topics – such as renting a car and asking directions. Feature boxes fill you in on cultural pitfalls as well as the simple mechanics of how to make a phone call, what to do in an emergency, where to change money, and more. Throughout this section, cross-references enable you to pinpoint key facts and phrases, while asterisked words indicate where further information can be found in The Basics.

In the Greek-English dictionary, we've given not just the phrases you're likely to hear (starting with a selection of slang and colloquialisms), but also various labels, instructions and other basic words you may come across in print or in public places.

Finally the Rough Guide rounds off with an extensive Menu Reader. Consisting of food and drink sections (each starting with a list of essential terms), it's indispensable whether you're eating out, stopping for a quick drink, or browsing through a local food market.

κaλό ταξίδι!
kalo taxithi!
have a good trip!

Basics

The Greek Alphabet

Set out below is the Greek alphabet, the names of the Greek letters, and the system of transliteration used in this book:

A, α	**a**lfa	a as in c**a**t
B, β	**vi**ta	v as in **v**et
Γ, γ	**ga**ma	y as in **y**es, except before consonants and a or o, when it's a throaty version of the g in **g**ap
Δ, δ	**the**lta	th as in **th**en
E, ε	**e**psilon	e as in g**e**t
Z, ζ	**zi**ta	z
H, η	**i**ta	i as in sk**i**
Θ, θ	**thi**ta	as the th in **th**eme (represented by th)
I, ι	**yo**ta	i as in b**i**t
K, κ	**ka**pa	k
Λ, λ	**lam**tha	l
M, μ	mi	m
N, ν	ni	n
Ξ, ξ	ksi	x
O, o	**o**mikron	o as in h**o**t
Π, π	pi	p
P, ρ	ro	r
Σ, σ, ς*	**sig**ma	s
T, τ	taf	t
Y, υ	**i**psilon	long i, indistinguishable from **i**ta
Φ, φ	fi	f
X, χ	khi	h as in **h**at or harsh ch in the Scottish word lo**ch** (represented by kh)
Ψ, ψ	psi	ps as in li**ps**
Ω, ω	om**e**ga	o as in h**o**t, indistinguishable from **o**mikron

* this letter is used only at the end of a word in lower case

9

Combinations and diphthongs:

ΑΙ, αι	e as in get
ΑΥ, αυ	av or af depending on following consonant
ΕΙ, ει	long i, exactly like ita
ΟΙ, οι	long i, exactly like ita
ΕΥ, ευ	ev or ef depending on following consonant
ΟΥ, ου	oo as in moon
ΓΓ, γγ	ng as in angle
ΓΚ, γκ	g as in goat at the beginning of a word; ng in the middle
ΜΠ, μπ	b as in bar and sometimes mb as in embassy in the middle of a word
ΝΤ, ντ	d at the beginning of a word and sometimes nd as in end in the middle
ΤΣ, τσ	ts as in hits

Pronunciation

Throughout this book Greek words have been transliterated into romanized form (see The Greek Alphabet page 9) so that they can be read as though they were English, bearing in mind the notes on pronunciation given below:

a	as in c**a**t
e	as in g**e**t
eh	represents e at end of a word; should always be pronounced as in g**e**t
g	as in **g**oat
i	as in sk**i**
kh	like the ch in the Scottish way of saying lo**ch**
o	as in h**o**t
th	as in **th**en
TH	as in **th**eme

Letters given in bold type indicate the part of the word to be stressed. When two vowels (such as 'ea') are next to each other in the pronunciation, both should be pronounced, as for example in the word: amfiTH**e**atro (amphitheatre).

Abbreviations

acc	accusative case	neut	neuter
adj	adjective	nom	nominative case
fam	familiar	pl	plural
fem	feminine	pol	polite
gen	genitive case	sing	singular
masc	masculine		

Note

An asterisk (★) next to a word in the dictionaries means that you should refer to the Basics section for further information.

Nouns and Articles

Articles

Greek nouns have one of three genders – masculine, feminine or neuter. The indefinite article (a, an) for each gender is:

masc	fem	neut
ένας	μία	ένα
enas	**mia**	**ena**

ένας άνδρας	μία γυναίκα	ένα παιδί
enas anthras	**mia yineka**	**ena pethi**
a man	a woman	a child

The definite article (the) is:

	masc	fem	neut		masc	fem	neut
sing	ο	η	το	plural	οι	οι	τα
	o	i	to		i	i	ta

ο πατέρας	οι πατεράδες
o pateras	**i paterathes**
the father	the fathers
το μωρό	τα μωρά
to moro	**ta mora**
the baby	the babies
η χώρα	οι χώρες
i khora	**i khores**
the country	the countries
η μητέρα	οι μητέρες
i mitera	**i miteres**
the mother	the mothers
ο δρόμος	οι δρόμοι
o thromos	**i thromi**
the street	the streets

το βουνό   τα βουνά
o voono   ta voona
the mountain   the mountains

Cases

There are three main cases in Greek – nominative, genitive
and accusative. The forms of articles, nouns, adjectives and
most pronouns change according to their gender, number
and case. The indefinite article (a, an) declines as follows:

sing	masc	fem	neut
nom	ένας	μία	ένα
	enas	mia	ena
gen	ενός	μιάς	ενός
	enos	mias	enos
acc	ένα(ν)*	μία	ένα
	ena(n)	mia	ena

The definite article (the) declines as follows:

sing	masc	fem	neut
nom	ο	η	το
	o	i	to
gen	του	της	του
	too	tis	too
acc	το(ν)*	τη(ν)*	το
	to(n)	ti(n)	to

*The forms έναν and τον/την should be used before nouns
beginning with a vowel.

plural	masc	fem	neut
nom	οι	οι	τα
	i	i	ta
gen	των	των	των
	ton	ton	ton
acc	τους	τις	τα
	toos	tis	ta

Nominative Case

The nominative case is used for the subject of sentences:

το δωμάτιό μου είναι μικρό
to thomatio moo ineh mikro
my room is small

ο Γιάννης διαβάζει ένα βιβλίο
o Yanis thiavazi ena vivlio
John is reading a book

Genitive Case

The genitive case is used to indicate possession and to translate 'of':

αυτό είναι το αυτοκίνητο του Γιώργου
afto ineh to aftokinito too Yorgoo
this is George's car

ο σκύλος του γείτονα
o skilos too yitona
the neighbour's dog

Accusative Case

The accusative case is used for direct objects:

μπορείτε να μας φέρετε το λογαριασμό, παρακαλώ;
boriteh na mas fereteh to logariasmo, parakalo?
could you bring us the bill, please?

έχασα το λεωφορείο
ekhasa to leoforio
I missed the bus

The accusative case is also used with some prepositions (to, from, with etc):

αυτή πήγε στην παραλία
afti piyeh stin paralia
she has gone to the beach

αυτός είναι από τη Σκωτία
aftos ineh apo ti Skotia
he comes from Scotland

αυτοί πηγαίνουν με τα πόδια
afti piyenoon meh ta pothia
they are going on foot

προτιμάμε να ταξιδεύουμε με το τρένο
protimameh na taxithevoomeh meh to treno
we prefer to travel by train

Vocative Case

Another case in Greek is the vocative case, which is used to
address someone directly. The vocative has the same endings
as the nominative case, apart from masculine nouns and
names where the final ς is dropped:

Μαρία, πού είναι ο Γιάννης;	Γιάννη, πού είναι η Μαρία;
Maria, poo ineh o Yanis?	Yani, poo ineh i Maria?
Mary, where is John?	John, where is Mary?

Noun Endings

The endings of nouns change according to whether they are
singular or plural and depending on whether they are in the
nominative, genitive or accusative cases.

Masculine Nouns

Masculine nouns usually have one of three endings:

	-ας	-ης	-ος
	ο χειμώνας	ο εργάτης	ο δάσκαλος
	the winter	the workman	the teacher
sing			
nom	ο χειμώνας	ο εργάτης	ο δάσκαλος
	o khimonas	o ergatis	o thaskalos
gen	του χειμώνα	του εργάτη	του δασκάλου
	too khimona	too ergati	too thaskaloo
acc	το χειμώνα	τον εργάτη	τον δάσκαλο
	to khimona	ton ergati	ton thaskalo

plural			
nom	οι χειμώνες	οι εργάτες	οι δάσκαλοι
	i khimones	i ergates	i thaskali
gen	των χειμώνων	των εργατών	των δασκάλων
	ton khimonon	ton ergaton	ton thaskalon
acc	τους χειμώνες	τους εργάτες	τους δασκάλους
	toos khimones	toos ergates	toos thaskaloos

A few masculine nouns end in:

-άς, -ές or -ούς

but for these only the plural differs from the above endings:

ο ψαράς	οι ψαράδες
o psaras	i psarathes
fisherman	fishermen
ο παπάς	οι παπάδες
o papas	i papathes
the priest	the priests
ο καφές	οι καφέδες
o kafes	i kafethes
the coffee	the coffees
ο καναπές	οι καναπέδες
o kanapes	i kanapethes
the couch	the couches
ο παππούς	οι παππούδες
o papoos	i papoothes
the grandfather	the grandfathers

Feminine Nouns

Feminine nouns either end in:

-α or -η

η γλώσσα	η νίκη
the tongue, the language	the victory

sing		
nom	η γλώσσα	η νίκη
	i glosa	i niki
gen	της γλώσσας	της νίκης
	tis glosas	tis nikis
acc	τη γλώσσα	τη νίκη
	ti glosa	ti niki

plural		
nom	οι γλώσσες	οι νίκες
	i gloses	i nikes
gen	των γλωσσών	των νικών
	ton gloson	ton nikon
acc	τις γλώσσες	τις νίκες
	tis gloses	tis nikes

Some irregular feminine nouns ending in -η take the plural ending -εις, for example:

η λέξη	οι λέξεις
i lexi	i lexis
the word	the words

η απόφαση	οι αποφάσεις
i apofasi	i apofasis
the decision	the decisions

Feminine nouns ending in -ος decline like masculine nouns. For example:

η έξοδος	η είσοδος
i exothos	i isothos
the exit	the entrance

Neuter Nouns

Neuter nouns have one of the following endings:

-ο, -ι or -μα

		το δέντρο the tree	το ψωμί the bread, the loaf	το όνομα the name
sing	nom	το δέντρο to thendro	το ψωμί to psomi	το όνομα to onoma
	gen	του δέντρου too thendroo	του ψωμιού too psomi-oo	του ονόματος too onomatos
	acc	το δέντρο to thendro	το ψωμί to psomi	το όνομα to onoma
plural	nom	τα δέντρα ta thendra	τα ψωμιά ta psomia	τα ονόματα ta onomata
	gen	των δέντρων ton thendron	των ψωμιών ton psomion	των ονομάτων ton onomaton
	acc	τα δέντρα ta thendra	τα ψωμιά ta psomia	τα ονόματα ta onomata

Several neuter nouns end in -ος:

το είδος to ithos the kind	τα είδη ta ithi the kinds	το μέγεθος to meyeTHos the size	τα μεγέθη ta meyeTHi the sizes

Adjectives and Adverbs

Most adjectives also change as follows according to gender and number:

masc	fem	neut	masc	fem	neut
ακριβός expensive			γλυκός sweet		
ακριβός akrivos	ακριβή akrivi	ακριβό akrivo	γλυκός glikos	γλυκιά glikia	γλυκό gliko
όμορφος beautiful			ελαφρύς light		
όμορφος omorfos	όμορφη omorfi	όμορφο omorfo	ελαφρύς elafris	ελαφριά elafria	ελαφρύ elafri

Adjective endings follow the pattern of the corresponding noun endings. Adjectives should agree with their nouns in gender, number, and case:

ο καλός φίλος
o kalos filos
the good friend

έχω μερικούς καλούς φίλους
ekho merikoos kaloos filoos
I have some good friends

η όμορφη πόλη
i omorfi poli
the beautiful town

είδαμε ένα ωραίο έργο
ithameh enah oreo ergo
we saw a good film

The most common irregular adjective is:

ο πολύς a lot of, much, many

	sing	plural
masc	ο πολύς **o polis**	οι πολλοί **i poli**
fem	η πολλή **i poli**	οι πολλές **i poles**
neut	το πολύ **to poli**	τα πολλά **ta pola**

Comparatives

The comparative is formed by putting the word πιό [**pio**] 'more' in front of the adjective:

αυτό το ξενοδοχείο είναι πιό/λιγότερο ακριβό από εκείνο
afto to xenothokhio ineh pio/ligotero akrivo apo ekino
this hotel is more/less expensive than that one

είναι πιό ήσυχα εδώ
ineh pio isikha etho
it's quieter here

Superlatives

Superlatives are formed by putting the definite article in front of the comparative:

η Ομόνοια είναι η πιό διάσημη πλατεία στην Αθήνα
i Omoni-a ineh i pio thiasimi plati-a stin ATHina
Omonia Square is the most famous square in Athens

αυτός ο δρόμος είναι ο λιγότερο επικίνδυνος
aftos o thromos ineh o ligotero epikinthinos
this road is the least dangerous

η ταβέρνα Ο Γιάννης είναι η πιο δημοφιλής ταβέρνα στη
   Μυτιλήνη
i taverna O Yanis ineh i pio thimofilis taverna sti Mitilini
the O Yanis taverna is the most popular in Mitilini

'As ... as' is translated as τόσο ... όσο:

αυτό το εστιατόριο είναι τόσο ακριβό όσο και το άλλο
afto to estiatorio ineh toso akrivo oso keh to alo
this restaurant is as expensive as that one

αυτή η πόλη δεν είναι τόσο ενδιαφέρουσα όσο νόμιζα
afti i poli then ineh toso enthiaferoosa oso nomiza
this town is not as interesting as I thought

The following common adjectives have irregular comparatives and superlatives:

κακός	χειρότερος	χείριστος
kakos	khiroteros	khiristos
bad	worse	worst
καλός	καλύτερος	κάλλιστος
kalos	kaliteros	kalistos
good	better	best
μικρός	μικρότερος	ελάχιστος
mikros	mikroteros	elakhistos
small	smaller	smallest

μεγάλος	μεγαλύτερος	μέγιστος
megalos	megaliteros	meyistos
big	bigger	biggest

λίγος	λιγότερος	ελάχιστος
ligos	ligoteros	elakhistos
few	fewer	fewest

πολύς	περισσότερος	
polis	perisoteros	
a lot of	a lot more of	

Adverbs

If the adjective ends in -ος, remove this ending and add -α to create the adverb:

adjective	adverb		adjective	adverb
καλός	καλά		ωραίος	ωραία
kalos	kala		oreos	oreh-a
good	well		nice	nicely

κακός	κακά		τυχερός	τυχερά
kakos	kaka		tikheros	tikhera
bad	badly		lucky	luckily

If the adjective ends in -ης, remove this ending and add -ως to create the adverb:

adjective	adverb
συνεχής	συνεχώς
sinekhis	sinekhos
continuous	continuously

ακριβής	ακριβώς
akrivis	akrivos
precise	precisely

διεθνής	διεθνώς
thi-eTHnis	thi-eTHnos
international	internationally

Possessive Adjectives

my	μου	moo		its	του	too
your (sing, fam)	σου	soo		our	μας	mas
his	του	too		your (pl, pol)	σας	sas
her	της	tis		their	τους	toos

Possessive adjectives do not change according to case, gender or number. They follow the noun they refer to, but note that the definite article is placed in front of the noun:

το διαβατήριό μου	τα λεφτά τους	το βιβλίο της
to thiavatirio moo	ta lefta toos	to vivlio tis
my passport	their money	her book

Pronouns

Possessive Pronouns

Possessive pronouns (mine, hers etc) are formed by placing the word δικός in front of the possessive. δικός declines like an adjective, agreeing with the object possessed in case, gender and number:

	masc	fem	neut
mine	δικός μου	δική μου	δικό μου
	thikos moo	thiki moo	thiko moo
yours (sing, fam)	δικός σου	δική σου	δικό σου
	thikos soo	thiki soo	thiko soo
his	δικός του	δική του	δικό του
	thikos too	thiki too	thiko too
hers	δικός της	δική της	δικό της
	thikos tis	thiki tis	thiko tis
its	δικός του	δική του	δικό του
	thikos too	thiki too	thiko too
ours	δικός μας	δική μας	δικό μας
	thikos mas	thiki mas	thiko mas
yours (pl, pol)	δικός σας	δική σας	δικό σας
	thikos sas	thiki sas	thiko sas
theirs	δικός τους	δική τους	δικό τους
	thikos toos	thiki toos	thiko toos

Plurals take the usual adjective endings:

αυτές είναι οι δικές μας
aftes ineh i thikes mas
these are ours

Personal Pronouns

nom	gen	acc
εγώ [ego] I	μου [moo] me	με/εμένα [meh/emena] me
εσύ [esi] you*	σου [soo] you	σε/εσένα [seh/esena] you
αυτός [aftos] he	του [too] him	τον [ton] him
αυτή [afti] she	της [tis] her	την [tin] her
αυτό [afto] it	του [too] it	το [to] it
εμείς [emis] we	μας [mas] us	μας/εμάς [mas/emas] us
εσείς [esis] you**	σας/εσάς	σας/εσάς
	[sas/esas] you	[sas/esas] you
αυτοί [afti] they (m)	τους [toos] them	τους/αυτούς [toos/aftoos] them
αυτές [aftes] they (f)	τους [toos] them	τις/αυτές [tis/aftes] them
αυτά [afta] they (n)	τους [toos] them	τα/αυτά [ta/afta] them

* εσύ is used when speaking to one person and is the familiar form generally used when speaking to family, friends and children.

** εσείς is the polite form which can be used to address one person or several people.

αυτή του έδωσε τα χρήματα
afti too ethoseh ta khrimata
she gave him the money

εγώ τους είδα να το κλέβουν
ego toos itha na to klevoon
I saw them stealing it

Where two forms are given for the accusative, the second is used after prepositions:

θα πάω μαζί με αυτές
THa pao mazi meh aftes
I will go with them

αυτό είναι ένα δώρο γιά εσένα
afto ineh ena thoro ya esena
this is a present for you

In Greek the subject pronoun (nominative) is usually omitted:

έφυγε χθές
efiyeh kh**THes**
he left yesterday

θα ήθελα να παραγγείλω
THa ithela na parangilo
I'd like to order

Although it may be retained for emphasis:

αυτή ήταν πρώτη
afti itan proti
SHE was first

εσύ φταις
esi ftes
YOU are to blame

αυτός έκλεψε το πορτοφόλι μου
aftos eklepseh to portofoli moo
HE stole my wallet

Examples using pronouns in genitive and accusative:

το πήρε από την τσάντα μου
to pireh apo tin tsanda moo
he took it from my bag

εσύ τους το έδωσες;
esi toos to **ethoses**?
did YOU give it to them?

την πήρα μαζί μου
tin pira mazi moo
I took her with me

τα αγόρασε χθες
ta agoraseh khTHes
she bought them yesterday

θα σου τον συστήσω
THa soo ton sistiso
I shall introduce you to him

την είδα
tin itha
I saw her

δε σε ακούω καλά
theh seh akoo-o kala
I cannot hear you very well

Verbs

The form of the verb given in dictionaries is usually the first person singular of the present tense. This is the basic form (equivalent to the infinitive) and the endings are either -ω (active verbs) or -μαι (passive verbs).

Although there are two categories of Greek verbs (active and passive), many verbs that are not passive in English are considered passive in Greek.

Present Tense

Present tense endings for verbs ending in -ω depend on whether or not the stress falls on the last syllable:

	stress not on last syllable	stress on last syllable	
	αγοράζω buy	πουλώ sell	μπορώ be able
I	αγοράζ-ω agorazo	πουλ-ώ poolo	μπορ-ώ boro
you	αγοράζ-εις agorazis	πουλ-άς poolas	μπορ-είς boris
he/she	αγοράζ-ει agorazi	πουλ-ά poola	μπορ-εί bori
we	αγοράζ-ουμε agorazoomeh	πουλ-άμε poolameh	μπορ-ούμε boroomeh
you	αγοράζ-ετε agorazeteh	πουλ-άτε poolateh	μπορ-είτε boriteh
they	αγοράζ-ουν agorazoon	πουλ-ούν pooloon	μπορ-ούν boroon

πόσο το πουλάς;
poso to poolas?
how much are you selling it for?

το αγοράζω για χίλιες δραχμές
to agorazo ya khili-es thrakhmes
I am buying it for 1,000 drachmas

δεν μπορεί να περπατήσει
then bori na perpatisi
he can't walk

Passive verbs ending in -μαι take the following endings:

ντώνομαι be dressed, dress (oneself)

I	ντών-ομαι	[**di**nomeh]
you	ντών-εσαι	[**di**neseh]
he/she	ντών-εται	[**di**neteh]
we	ντυν-όμαστε	[din**o**masteh]
you	ντών-εστε	[**di**nesteh]
they	ντών-ονται	[**di**nondeh]

The verbs 'to be' and 'to have' are irregular:

είμαι I am [**i**meh] είμαστε we are [**i**masteh]
είσαι you are [**i**seh] είσαστε/είστε you are [**i**sasteh/**i**steh]
είναι he/she/it is [**i**neh] είναι they are [**i**neh]

έχω I have [**e**kho] έχουμε we have [**e**khoomeh]
έχεις you have [**e**khis] έχετε you have [**e**kheteh]
έχει he/she/it has [**e**khi] έχουν they have [**e**khoon]

Past Simple Tense

To describe an action that has taken place in the past, use the past simple tense in Greek. To form this, take the basic form of the verb and add the following endings. Note that in the simple past, the stress moves back one syllable and sometimes changes have to be made to the form of the verb which comes before these endings. For example, where necessary, the letter ε is added to the beginning of the verb so that the stress can move back a syllable:

ακού-ω (I hear) κάν-ω (I do)

άκου-σ-α I heard [**a**koosa] έκαν-α I did [**e**kana]
άκου-σ-ες you heard [**a**kooses] έκανες you did [**e**kanes]
άκου-σ-ε he/she heard [**a**kooseh] έκανε he/she/it did [**e**kaneh]
ακού-σ-αμε we heard [ak**oo**sameh] εκάναμε we did [ek**a**nameh]
ακού-σ-ατε you heard [ak**oo**sateh] εκάνατε you did [ek**a**nateh]
άκου-σ-αν they heard [**a**koosan] έκαναν they did [**e**kanan]

The past tense of 'to be' and 'to have' is:

ήμουν I was [**i**moon]	ήμασταν we were [**i**mastan]
ήσουν you were [**i**soon]	ήσασταν you were [**i**sastan]
ήταν he/she/it was [**i**tan]	ήταν they were [**i**tan]

είχα I had [**i**kha]	είχαμε we had [**i**khameh]
είχες you had [**i**khes]	είχατε you had [**i**khateh]
είχε he/she/it had [**i**kheh]	είχαν they had [**i**khan]

πόσα χρήματα είχατε στην τσάντα σας;
p**o**sa khrimata **i**khateh stin ts**a**nda sas?
how much money did you have in your handbag?

επισκεφτήκατε το Αρχαιολογικό Μουσείο;
episkeft**i**kateh to Arkheoloyik**o** Moos**i**o?
did you visit the Archaeological Museum?

οι τιμές ήταν πιό φτηνές πέρυσι
i tim**e**s **i**tan pi**o** ftin**e**s p**e**risi
prices were cheaper last year

υπογράψατε στο βιβλίο;
ipogr**a**psateh sto vivl**i**o?
did you sign the book?

The Indefinite

The Greek indefinite form of the verb has no direct equivalent in English although its use often corresponds to the infinitive used after verbs such as 'to want', 'to be able to', 'can', etc, and has the following pattern:

να + basic form of verb + ending of the verb preceding it.

It must agree in person and number with the main verb preceding it:

θα μπορούσα να πληρώσω με επιταγή;
THa bor**oo**sa na plir**o**so meh epitay**i**?
could I pay by cheque?

The exception to this is the impersonal verb 'to have to', 'must' which always takes the same form πρέπει:

πρέπει να πηγαίνουμε τώρα
prepi na piyenoomeh tora
we must go now

Here is a list of some useful verbs with their indefinite and past simple in the first person:

present	indefinite	past simple	perfect
βλέπω see	να δω	είδα	έχω δει
vlepo	na tho	**itha**	ekho thi
βρίσκω find	να βρω	βρήκα	έχω βρει
vrisko	na vro	**vrika**	ekho vri
δίνω give	να δώσω	έδωσα	έχω δώσει
thino	na thoso	**ethosa**	ekho thosi
έρχομαι come	να έλθω	ήλθα	έχω έλθει
erkhomeh	na elTHo	**ilTHa**	ekho elTHi
κάνω do	να κάνω	έκανα	έχω κάνει
kano	na kano	ekana	ekho kani
λέω say	να πω	είπα	έχω πει
le-o	na po	**ipa**	ekho pi
μένω stay	να μείνω	έμεινα	έχω μείνει
meno	na mino	emina	ekho mini
παίρνω take	να πάρω	πήρα	έχω πάρει
perno	na paro	pira	ekho pari
πηγαίνω go	να πάω	πήγα	έχω πάει
piyeno	na pao	piga	ekho pa-i
πίνω drink	να πιώ	ήπια	έχω πιεί
pino	na pio	**ipia**	ekho pi-i
στέλνω send	να στείλω	έστειλα	έχω στείλει
stelno	na stilo	estila	ekho stili
τρώω eat	να φάω	έφαγα	έχω φάει
tro-o	na fa-o	efaga	ekho fa-i
ρωτώ ask	να ρωτήσω	ρώτησα	έχω ρωτήσει
roto	na rotiso	**rotisa**	ekho rotisi

αγοράζω buy agorazo	να αγοράσω na agoraso	αγόρασα agorasa	έχω αγοράσει ekho agorasi
κλείνω close klino	να κλείσω na kliso	έκλεισα eklisa	έχω κλείσει ekho klisi
κοιτάζω look kitazo	να κοιτάξω na kitaxo	κοίταξα kitaxa	έχω κοιτάξει ekho kitaxi
σταματώ stop stamato	να σταματήσω na stamatiso	σταμάτησα stamatisa	έχω σταματήσει ekho stamatisi
νομίζω think nomizo	να νομίσω na nomiso	νόμισα nomisa	έχω νομίσει ekho nomisi
γράφω write grafo	να γράψω na grapso	έγραψα egrapsa	έχω γράψει ekho grapsi

Future Tense

The simplest way to form the continuous future tense in Greek is to take the present tense forms and add the word θα in front of them:

I will be waiting	θα περιμένω	[THa perimeno]
you will ...	θα περιμένεις	[THa perimenis]
he/she will ...	θα περιμένει	[THa perimeni]
we will ...	θα περιμένουμε	[THa perimenoomeh]
you will ...	θα περιμένετε	[THa perimeneteh]
they will ...	θα περιμένουν	[THa perimenoon]

To form the simple future tense you use θα and the appropriate forms of the indefinite (without the να):

I will buy	θα αγοράσω	[THa agoraso]
you will ...	θα αγοράσεις	[THa agorasis]
he/she/it will ...	θα αγοράσει	[THa agorasi]
we will ...	θα αγοράσουμε	[THa agorasoomeh]
you will ...	θα αγοράσετε	[THa agoraseteh]
they will ...	θα αγοράσουν	[THa agorasoon]

θα σε δω το βράδυ
THa seh tho to vrathi
I'll see you tonight

Imperatives

The imperative form of the verb is used to give commands. To create the singular, familiar imperative, take the indefinite form of the verb (without the να) and change the final -ω to -ε:

κοίταξε εκεί!   πρόσεξε!
kitaxeh eki!   prosexeh!
look over there!   watch out!

Polite and plural forms of the imperative are created by changing the final -ω of the indefinite form (without the να) to -ετε or -τε :

ρωτήστε τον αστυνόμο εκεί πέρα   υπογράψτε εδώ, παρακαλώ
rotisteh ton astinomo eki pera   ipograpsteh etho, parakalo
ask the policeman over there   sign here, please

Negative imperatives are formed by placing μη or μην in front of the second person of the indefinite form (without the να) of the verb:

μην πάτε από αυτόν το δρόμο   μην πιείς αυτό το νερό
min pateh apo afton ton thromo   min pi-is afto to nero
don't go along this street   do not drink this water

Some common irregular imperatives are:

familiar	polite/plural
βρες find [vres]	βρείτε [vriteh]
δες see [thes]	δείτε [thiteh] or δέστε [thesteh]
πιές drink [pies]	πιείτε [pi-iteh] or πιέστε [pi-esteh]
πες say [pes]	πείτε [pesteh] or πέστε [pesteh]
ελα come [ela]	ελάτε [elateh]

Negatives

To form the negative, place the word δε or δεν in front of the verb:

δε μου αρέσει αυτό   δε μιλάω καλά Ελληνικά
theh moo aresi afto   theh mila-o kala Elinika
I don't like this   my Greek is not very good

δεν μπορώ να βρώ το ξενοδοχείο
then bor**o** na vro to xenothokh**i**o
I cannot find the hotel

Questions

The word order and intonation for questions in Greek are the same as in English:

πού είναι το γραφείο του ΕΟΤ, παρακαλώ;
poo **i**neh to graf**i**o too **E**-OT, parakal**o**?
where is the tourist information office, please?

Note that in questions in Greek, a semi-colon is used instead of a question mark.

Dates

To say the date, take the ordinal number, then the genitive of the month. The exception is 'the first', when you should use the ordinal number:

σήμερα είναι εικοσιεφτά Φεβρουαρίου
s**i**mera **i**neh ikosi-eft**a** Fevroo-ar**i**oo
today is the 27th of February

αύριο είναι πρώτη Ιουλίου
avrio **i**neh pr**o**ti Iool**i**-oo
tomorrow is the 1st of July

χθες ήταν τρεις Δεκεμβρίου
kh**TH**es **i**tan tris thekemvr**i**oo
yesterday was the 3rd of December

Πρωταπριλιά
protapril**i**a
1st of April

Πρωτομαγιά
protomay**a**
1st of May

Instead of saying 'nineteen ninety-five' you literally say 'one thousand, nine hundred, ninety five':

χίλια εννιακόσια ενενήντα πέντε
kh**i**lia enniak**o**sia enen**i**nta p**e**ndeh

Time

what time is it? τί ώρα είναι; [ti **o**ra ineh?]
one o'clock μία η ώρα [**mia** i **o**ra]
two o'clock δύο η ώρα [**thio** i **o**ra]
it's one o'clock είναι μία η ώρα [**i**neh mia i **o**ra]
it's two o'clock είναι δύο η ώρα [**i**neh thio i **o**ra]
it's ten o'clock είναι δέκα η ώρα [**i**neh theka i **o**ra]
five past one μία και πέντε [**mia** keh **pe**ndeh]
ten past two δύο και δέκα [**thio** keh **the**ka]
quarter past one μία και τέταρτο [**mia** keh **te**tarto]
quarter past two δύο και τέταρτο [**thio** keh **te**tarto]
twenty past ten δέκα και είκοσι [**the**ka keh **i**kosi]
half past ten δέκα και μισή [**the**ka keh mi**si**]
twenty to ten δέκα παρά είκοσι [**the**ka para **i**kosi]
quarter to two δύο παρά τέταρτο [**thio** para **te**tarto]
at half past four στις τέσσερις και μισή [stis **te**seris keh mi**si**]
at eight o'clock στις οκτώ [stis ok**to**]
14.00 δεκατέσσερις [theka-**te**seris]
17.30 δεκαεφτά και τριάντα [theka-**e**fta keh tri**a**nda]
2 am δύο η ώρα το βράδυ [**thio** i **o**ra to **vra**thi]
2 pm δύο η ώρα το μεσημέρι [**thio** i **o**ra to mesi**me**ri]
6 am έξι η ώρα το πρωί [**e**xi i **o**ra to pro-**i**]
6 pm έξι η ώρα το απόγευμα [**e**xi i **o**ra to ap**o**yevma]
noon το μεσημέρι [to mesi**me**ri]
midnight τα μεσάνυχτα [ta mes**a**nikhta]

an hour η ώρα [i **o**ra]
a minute το λεπτό [to lep**to**]
one minute ένα λεπτό [ena lep**to**]
two minutes δύο λεπτά [**thio** lep**ta**]
a second το δευτερόλεπτο [to thefter**o**lepto]
a quarter of an hour ένα τέταρτο [ena **te**tarto]
half an hour μισή ώρα [mi**si** **o**ra]
three quarters of an hour τρία τέταρτα της ώρας [**tri**a **te**tarta tis **o**ras]

Numbers

0	μηδέν	[mithen]
1	ένα	[ena]
2	δύο	[thio]
3	τρία	[tria]
4	τέσσερα	[tesera]
5	πέντε	[pendeh]
6	έξι	[exi]
7	επτά	[epta]
8	οχτώ	[okhto]
9	εννιά	[enia]
10	δέκα	[theka]
11	έντεκα	[endeka]
12	δώδεκα	[thotheka]
13	δεκατρία	[theka-tria]
14	δεκατέσσερα	[theka-tesera]
15	δεκαπέντε	[theka-pendeh]
16	δεκαέξι	[theka-exi]
17	δεκαεπτά	[theka-epta]
18	δεκαοχτώ	[theka-okhto]
19	δεκαεννιά	[theka-enia]
20	είκοσι	[ikosi]
21	εικοσιένα	[ikosi-ena]
22	εικοσιδύο	[ikosi-thio]
30	τριάντα	[trianda]
31	τριανταένα	[trianda-ena]
40	σαράντα	[saranda]
50	πενήντα	[peninda]
60	εξήντα	[exinda]
70	εβδομήντα	[evthominda]
80	ογδόντα	[ogthonda]
90	ενενήντα	[eneninda]
100	εκατό	[ekato]
110	εκατό δέκα	[ekato theka]

200	διακόσια	[thiakosia]
300	τριακόσια	[triakosia]
1,000	χίλια	[khilia]
2,000	δύο χιλιάδες	[thio khiliathes]
5,000	πέντε χιλιάδες	[pendeh khiliathes]
10,000	δέκα χιλιάδες	[theka khiliathes]
20,000	είκοσι χιλιάδες	[ikosi khiliathes]
50,000	πενήντα χιλιάδες	[peninda khiliathes]
100,000	εκατό χιλιάδες	[ekato khiliathes]
1,000,000	ένα εκατομμύριο	[ena ekatomirio]

Ordinals

Ordinal numbers decline like regular adjectives:

1st	πρώτος	[protos]
2nd	δεύτερος	[thefteros]
3rd	τρίτος	[tritos]
4th	τέταρτος	[tetartos]
5th	πέμπτος	[pemptos]
6th	έκτος	[ektos]
7th	έβδομος	[evthomos]
8th	όγδοος	[ogtho-os]
9th	ένατος	[enatos]
10th	δέκατος	[thekatos]

Basic Phrases

yes
ναί
neh

no
όχι
okhi

OK
εντάξει
endaxi

hello
χαίρετε
khereteh

good morning
καλημέρα
kalimera

good evening
καλησπέρα
kalispera

good night
καληνύχτα
kalinikhta

goodbye
αντίο
andio

hi
γειά
ya

see you
γειά, θα τα πούμε
ya, THa ta poomeh

please
παρακαλώ
parakalo

thank you
ευχαριστώ
efkharisto

yes, please
ναί, παρακαλώ
neh, parakalo

no thank you
όχι, ευχαριστώ
okhi, éfkharisto

excuse me, please (to attract attention, to get past someone)
συγγνώμη, παρακαλώ
signomi, parakalo

sorry!
συγγνώμη!
signomi!

pardon? (sorry?, what did you say?)
ορίστε;
oristeh?

what did you say?
πώς είπατε;
pos ipateh?

I don't understand
δεν καταλαβαίνω
then katalaveno

do you speak English?
μιλάτε Αγγλικά;
milateh Anglika?

I don't speak Greek
δεν μιλάω Ελληνικά
then milo Elinika

please speak more slowly
παρακαλώ, μιλάτε πιό αργά;
parakalo, milateh pio arga?

could you repeat that?
το ξαναλέτε αυτό, σας παρακαλώ;
to xanaleteh afto, sas
parakalo?

please write it down
μου το γράφετε, παρακαλώ;
moo to grafeteh, parakalo?

I would like ...
θα ήθελα ...
THa iTHela ...

can I have ...?
μπορώ να έχω ...;
boro na ekho ...?

how much is it?
πόσο κάνει;
poso kani?

cheers!
εις υγείαν!
is iyian!

where is/are the ...?
πού είναι ...;
poo ineh ...?

Conversion Tables

1 centimetre = 0.39 inches   1 inch = 2.54 cm

1 metre = 39.37 inches = 1.09 yards   1 foot = 30.48 cm

1 kilometre = 0.62 miles = 5/8 mile   1 yard = 0.91 m

                                           1 mile = 1.61 km

km	1	2	3	4	5	10	20	30	40	50	100
miles	0.6	1.2	1.9	2.5	3.1	6.2	12.4	18.6	24.8	31.0	62.1

miles	1	2	3	4	5	10	20	30	40	50	100
km	1.6	3.2	4.8	6.4	8.0	16.1	32.2	48.3	64.4	80.5	161

1 gram = 0.035 ounces   1 kilo = 1000 g = 2.2 pounds

g	100	250	500
oz	3.5	8.75	17.5

1 oz = 28.35 g
1 lb = 0.45 kg

kg	0.5	1	2	3	4	5	6	7	8	9	10
lb	1.1	2.2	4.4	6.6	8.8	11.0	13.2	15.4	17.6	19.8	22.0

kg	20	30	40	50	60	70	80	90	100
lb	44	66	88	110	132	154	176	198	220

lb	0.5	1	2	3	4	5	6	7	8	9	10	20
kg	0.2	0.5	0.9	1.4	1.8	2.3	2.7	3.2	3.6	4.1	4.5	9.0

1 litre = 1.75 UK pints / 2.13 US pints

1 UK pint = 0.57 litre   1 UK gallon = 4.55 litre
1 US pint = 0.47 litre   1 US gallon = 3.79 litre

centigrade / Celsius $°C = (°F - 32) \times 5/9$

°C	-5	0	5	10	15	18	20	25	30	36.8	38
°F	23	32	41	50	59	64	68	77	86	98.4	100.4

Fahrenheit $°F = (°C \times 9/5) + 32$

°F	23	32	40	50	60	65	70	80	85	98.4	101
°C	-5	0	4	10	16	18	21	27	29	36.8	38.3

English

→

Greek

A

a, an* enas, mia, ena
about: about 20 peripoo ikosi
  it's about 5 o'clock ineh yiro
  stis pendeh
  a film about Greece ena ergo
  ya tin Elatha
above pano apo
abroad sto exoteriko
absolutely! (I agree) apolitos!
accelerator to gazi
accept thekhomeh
accident to thistikhima
  there's been an accident
  eyineh ena thistikhima
accommodation i thiamoni
  see room
accurate akrivis
ache o ponos
  my back aches pona-i i plati
  moo
across: across the road
  apenandi sto thromo
adapter to polaplo
  (for voltage change) i briza taf
address i thi-efTHinsi
  what's your address? pia
  ineh i thi-efTHinsi soo?

Addresses are written
with the street number
after the name of the
street, e.g.

Γιάννης Παπαδόπουλος
Ελευθερίου Βενιξέλου 28
Χανιά 73100
Κρήτη

Yiannis Papadopoulos
Eleutheriou Venizelou 28
Khania 73100
Kriti

When sending mail, always use
postcodes; they can be found in
special lists in post offices. You can
write Greek addresses in the Greek
or Roman alphabet.

address book i adzenda ton
  thi-efTHinseon
admission charge timi
  isothoo
adult (man/woman) o enilikos/i
  eniliki
advance: in advance
  prokatavolika
aeroplane to a-eroplano
after meta
  after you meta apo sas
  after lunch meta apo to
  yevma
afternoon apo-yevma
  in the afternoon kata to apo-
  yevma
  this afternoon afto to apo-
  yevma
aftershave i kolonia meta to
  xirisma
aftersun cream to galaktoma
  ya ton ilio
afterwards meta
again xana
against enandion
age i ilikia
ago: a week ago prin apo mia
  evthomatha
  an hour ago prin apo mia ora

agree: I agree simfono
AIDS to AIDS
air o a-eras
 by air a-eroporikos
air-conditioning o klimatismos
airmail: by airmail
 a-eroporikos
airmail envelope o
 a-eroporikos fakelos
airport to a-erothromio
 to the airport, please sto
 a-erothromio, parakalo
airport bus to leoforio
 a-erothromi-oo
aisle seat THesi thipla sto
 thiathromo
alarm clock to xipnitiri
Albania i Alvania
Albanian (adj) Alvanikos
alcohol to alko-ol
alcoholic inopnevmatothis
all: all the boys ola ta agoria
 all the girls ola ta koritsia
 all the men oli i andres
 all the women oles i yinekes
 all of it olokliro
 all of them ola afta
 that's all, thanks afta ineh
 ola, efkharisto
allergic: I'm allergic to ... imeh
 aleryikos meh ...
allowed: is it allowed?
 epitrepeteh?
all right endaxi
 I'm all right imeh endaxi
 are you all right? (adj) iseh
 endaxi?
 (pol) esis endaxi?
almond to amigthalo

almost skhethon
alone monos
alphabet to alfavito
 see page 9
already ithi
also episis
although an keh
altogether sinolika
always panda
am*: I am imeh
am: at seven am stis efta pro
 mesimvrias
amazing (surprising)
 ekpliktikos
 (very good) thavmasios
ambulance to asTHenoforo
 call an ambulance! kalesteh
 ena asTHenoforo!

Dial 166 for an
ambulance.

America i Ameriki
American (adj) Amerikanikos
 I'm American (man/woman)
 imeh Amerikanos/
 Amerikana
among anamesa
amount to poso
 (money) ta khrimata
amp: a 13-amp fuse mia
 asfalia thekatria amper
amphitheatre to amfiTHeatro
Ancient Greece i arkhea
 Elatha
Ancient Greek ta arkhea
 Elinika
and keh

angry THimom**e**nos
animal to z**o**-o
ankle o astr**a**galos
anniversary (wedding) i ep**e**tios too g**a**moo
annoy: this man's annoying me aft**o**s o **a**ndras meh enokhl**i**
annoying enokhlitik**o**s
another **a**los, **a**li, **a**lo
  can we have another room? bor**oo**meh na **e**khoomeh **e**na **a**lo thom**a**tio?
  another beer, please **a**li m**i**a b**i**ra, parakal**o**
antibiotics to andiviotik**o**
antihistamine to andi-istaminik**o** f**a**rmako
antique: is it an antique? in**e** ant**i**ka?
antique shop to paleop**o**lio
antiseptic to andis**i**ptiko
any: have you got any bread/tomatoes? **e**kheteh psom**i**/dom**a**tes?

dialogue

> do you have any change? **e**khis kaTH**o**loo psil**a**?
> sorry, I don't have any lip**a**meh, then **e**kho kaTH**o**loo

anybody kan**i**s
  does anybody speak English? mil**a**-i kan**i**s Angl**i**ka?
  there wasn't anybody there then **i**tan kan**i**s ek**i**
anything otith**i**poteh

dialogues

> anything else? t**i**poteh **a**lo?
> nothing else, thanks t**i**poteh, efkharist**o**

> would you like anything to drink? THa TH**e**lateh na pi-**i**teh k**a**ti?
> I don't want anything, thanks then TH**e**lo t**i**poteh, efkharist**o**

apart from ekt**o**s ap**o**
apartment to thiam**e**risma
appendicitis i skoliko-ith**i**tis
appetizer to pr**o**to pi**a**to
  appetizers ta orektik**a**
aperitif to aperit**i**f
apology i sign**o**mi
apple to m**i**lo
appointment to randev**oo**

dialogue

> good afternoon, sir, how can I help you? kalisp**e**ra sas, k**i**ri-eh, pos bor**o** na sas vo-iTH**i**so?
> I'd like to make an appointment THa **i**TH**e**la na kl**i**so **e**na randev**oo**
> what time would you like? ti **o**ra TH**e**leteh?
> three o'clock tris i **o**ra

I'm afraid that's not possible; is four o'clock all right? fovameh oti afto then yineteh; boriteh stis teseris?

yes, that will be fine neh, poli kala

the name was ...? to onoma sas?

apricot to verikoko
April o Aprilios
archaeology i arkheoloyia
are*: we are imasteh
 you are isteh
 they are ineh
area i periokhi
area code o kothikos ariTHmos
arm to kheri
arrange: will you arrange it for us? THa to kanonisis ya mas?
arrival i afixi
arrive ftano
 when do we arrive? poteh ftanoomeh?
 has my fax arrived yet? eftaseh to fax moo?
 we arrived today ftasameh simera
art i tekhni
art gallery i pinakoTHiki
artist (man/woman) o kalitekhnis/i kalitekhnitha
as: as big as ... megalo san ...
 as soon as possible oso pio grigora yineteh
ashtray to tasaki, to stokhto-thokhio

ask roto
 I didn't ask for this then zitisa afto
 could you ask him to ...? boris na too pis na ...?
asleep: she's asleep kimateh
aspirin i aspirini
asthma to asTHma
astonishing ekpliktikos
at: at the hotel sto xenothokhio
 at the station sto staTHmo
 at six o'clock stis exi i ora
 at Yanni's stoo Yanni
Athens i ATHina
athletics o aTHlitismos
attractive elkistikos
aubergine i melidzana
August o Avgoostos
aunt i THia
Australia i Afstralia
Australian (adj) Afstralezikos
 I'm Australian (man/woman) imeh Afstralos/Afstraleza
automatic (adj) aftomatos
 (car) to aftomato aftokinito
automatic teller i mikhani ya metrita
autumn to fTHinoporo
 in the autumn sto fTHinoporo
avenue i leoforos
average (not good) metrio
 on average kata meson oro
awake: is he awake? ineh xipnios?
away: go away! fiyeh
 is it far away? ineh poli makria?

awful apesios
axle o axonas

B

baby to moro
baby food i pethiki trofi
baby's bottle to bibero
baby-sitter i baby-sitter
back (of body) i plati
  (back part) piso
  at the back sto piso meros
  can I have my money back?
  boro na ekho ta lefta moo
  piso?
  to come/go back epistrefo,
  yirizo piso
backache ponos stin plati
bacon to bacon
bad kakos
  a bad headache enas
  askhimos ponokefalos
badly askhima
bag i tsanda
  (suitcase) i valitsa
baggage i aposkeves
baggage check o khoros
  filaxis aposkevon
baggage claim anazitisi
  aposkevon
bakery o foornaris
balcony to balkoni
  a room with a balcony ena
  thomatio meh balkoni
bald falakros
ball (large) i bala
  (small) to balaki
ballet to baleto

banana i banana
band (musical) to singrotima
bandage o epithesmos
Bandaid® to lefkoplast
bank i trapeza

Banks are usually open
Monday to Thursday from
8 am to 2 pm, and Fridays
from 8 am to 1.30 pm Certain
branches in the major cities and
tourist centres open extra hours in
the evenings and on Saturday
mornings for exchanging money.
Usually you have to queue twice,
once to get the transaction approved
and a second time to pick up the
cash. The best rates for exchanging
money or travellers' cheques are to
be found in banks and post offices
(where there's usually less of a
queue) rather than hotels, tourist
shops etc.

bank account o trapezikos
  logariasmos
bar to bar

Bars, 'barakia' in the
plural, are a recent
transplant confined to big
cities and holiday resorts. They
range from unappealing clones of
Parisian bars to imitation British
pubs and are invariably more
expensive than cafés. They are,
however, most likely to stock a
range of foreign label beers. Some
bars and cafés close in the

afternoon but many remain open from early in the morning until late at night. In summer, the chief socializing time is rarely before 8 pm and can often start around 10 pm It is not offensive to be drunk as long as you don't annoy other people. Driving after drinking any alcohol is strictly forbidden.
see also **café**

a bar of chocolate mia sokolata
barber's to koorio
basket to kalaTHi
basketball to basketball, i kalaTHosferisi
bath to banio
 can I have a bath? boro na kano ena banio?
bathroom to lootro, to banio
 with a private bathroom meh ithiotiko lootro
bath towel i petseta too banioo
battery i bataria
bay o kolpos
be* imeh
beach i paralia
beach mat i psaTHa
beach umbrella i ombrela
beans ta fasolia
 green beans ta fasolakia
 runner beans ta fasolakia freska
 broad beans ta kookia
beard ta yenia
beautiful oreos
because epithi

because of ... exetias ...
bed to krevati
 I'm going to bed now pao ya ipno tora
bed and breakfast thomatio meh pro-ino
bedroom to ipnothomatio
beef to moskhari
beer i bira
 two beers, please thio bires, parakalo

Most bars serve foreign label beers in bottles or cans (Amstel, Heineken, Becks, etc.) You will not often find places which serve draught beer.

before prin
begin arkhizo
 when does it begin? poteh arkhizi?
beginner (man/woman) o arkharios/i arkharia
beginning: at the beginning kat arkhas
behind piso
 behind me apo piso moo
beige bez
believe pistevo
belly-dancing to tsifteteli
below apo kato
belt i zoni
bend (in road) i strofi
berth (on ship) i klini
beside: beside the ... thipla sto ...
best aristos
better kaliteros

better than ... kaliteros apo ...
are you feeling better?
esTHaneseh kalitera?
between metaxi
beyond pera apo
bicycle to pothilato
big megalos
too big poli megalo
it's not big enough then ineh
arketa megalo
bike to pothilato
(motorbike) to mikhanaki
bikini to bikini
bill o logariasmos
(US) to khartonomisma
could I have the bill, please?
boro na ekho ton
logariasmo, parakalo?
bin o skoopithotenekes
bin liners i sakoola
skoopithion
bird to pooli
biro® to stilo
birthday ta yeneTHlia
happy birthday! khronia
pola!
biscuit to biskoto
bit: a little bit ligo
a big bit ena megalo komati
a bit of ... ligo apo ...
a bit expensive ligo akrivo,
akrivootsiko
bite (by insect) to tsibima
(by dog) i thagonia
bitter (taste etc) pikros
black mavros
blanket i kooverta
bleach (for toilet) to Harpik®
bless you! ya soo!

blind tiflos
blinds ta pantzooria
blister i fooskala
blocked (road, pipe)
frakarismenos
(sink) voolomenos
block of flats i polikatikia
blond xanTHos
blood to ema
high blood pressure ipsili
pi-esi ematos
blouse i blooza
blow-dry to khtenisma
I'd like a cut and blow-dry
THa iTHela kopsimo keh
khtenisma
blue bleh
blue eyes galana matia
blusher i poothra
boarding house i pansion
boarding pass i karta
epivivaseos
boat (small) to ka-iki
(for passengers) to plio
body to soma
boil (verb) vrazo
boiled egg to vrasto avgo
boiler o vrastiras
bone to kokalo
bonnet (of car) to kapo
book to vivlio
(verb) klino
can I book a seat? boro na
kliso mia THesi?

dialogue

I'd like to book a table for
two THa iTHela na kliso

ena trapezi ya thio atoma
**what time would you like it
booked for?** ti **o**ra to
THe**le**teh?
half past seven stis efta
keh misi
that's fine end**a**xi
and your name? to **o**noma
sas, parakal**o**?

bookshop to vivliop**o**lio
bookstore to vivliop**o**lio
boot (footwear) i b**o**ta
(of car) to port-ba**ga**z
border (of country) ta s**i**nora
bored: I'm bored vari-**e**meh
boring var**e**t**o**s
**born: I was born in
Manchester** yen**i**THika sto
Manchester
I was born in 1960 yen**i**THika
to 1960 (kh**i**lia eniak**o**sia
ex**i**nda)
borrow than**i**zomeh
may I borrow ...? bor**o** na
than**i**st**o** ...?
both keh i th**i**o
bother: sorry to bother you
sign**o**mi poo sas enokhl**o**
bottle to book**a**li
a bottle of house red **e**na
book**a**li k**o**kino spit**i**ko kras**i**
bottle-opener to anikht**i**ri
bottom (of person) o k**o**los
at the bottom of the hill sto
va**TH**os too l**o**foo
at the bottom of the road sto
telos too thr**o**moo
box to koot**i**

box office to tam**i**o
boy to ag**o**ri
boyfriend o f**i**los
bra to sooti-**e**n
bracelet to vrakhi**o**li
brake to fr**e**no
(verb) fren**a**ro
brandy to koni**a**k
bread to psom**i**
white bread to **a**spro psom**i**
brown bread to m**a**vro
psom**i**
wholemeal bread to star**e**nio
psom**i**
break (verb) sp**a**o
I've broken the ... **e**spasa to ...
I think I've broken my wrist
nom**i**zo **o**ti **e**spasa ton karp**o**
moo
break down (car) pa**TH**eno
vl**a**vi
I've broken down kh**a**laseh to
aftok**i**nit**o** moo
breakdown (car) i vl**a**vi

The place where you hire
a car should give you the
telephone number for the
local Express Service in case of
breakdowns. Tourists driving their
own car with proof of AA/RAC or
similar membership are given free
road assistance from the ELPA, the
Greek equivalent, which runs
breakdown services based in
Athens, Patra, Larissa, Volos,
Ioannina, Corfu, Tripoli, Crete and
Thessaloniki. The information
number is 174. In an emergency ring

their road assistance service on 104, anywhere in the country.

breakdown service i vlaves aftokiniton
breakfast to pro-ino
break-in: I've had a break-in meh listepsan
breast to stiTHos
breathe anapneo
breeze to aeraki
bridge (over river) i yefira
brief sindomos
briefcase o khartofilakas
bright (light etc) fotinos
 bright red khtipitos kokinos
brilliant (idea, person) katapliktikos
bring ferno
 I'll bring it back later THa to fero piso argotera
Britain i Vretania
British Vretanikos
brochure to prospektoos
broken spasmenos
 it's broken ineh spasmeno
bronchitis i vronkhititha
brooch i karfitsa
broom i skoopa
brother o athelfos
brother-in-law o gambros
brown kafeh
 brown hair kastana malia
 brown eyes kastana matia
bruise i melania
brush
 (for hair) i voortsa ya ta malia
 (artist's) to pinelo
bucket o koovas

buffet car to boofeh
buggy (for child) to pethiko amaxaki
building to ktirio
bulb (light bulb) i lamba
Bulgaria i Voolgaria
Bulgarian (adj) Voolgarikos
bumper o profilaktiras
bunk i kooketa
bureau de change Sinalagma see bank
burglary i thiarixi
burn (noun) to kapsimo
 (verb) keo
burnt: this is burnt afto ineh kameno
burst: a burst pipe mia spasmeni solina
bus to leoforio
 what number bus is it to ...? ti ariTHmo ekhi to leoforio ya ...?
 when is the next bus to ...? poteh ineh to epomeno leoforio ya ...?
 what time is the last bus? ti ora ineh to telefteo leoforio?
 could you let me know when we get there? boriteh na moo to piteh, otan ftasoomeh eki?

 For city buses, tickets should be bought in advance from newspaper or cigarette kiosks. You can use the same type of ticket for buses and trolleybuses in Athens. When you get on, always validate your ticket by inserting it into the machine on the bus/trolleybus. Buses have their destination written on the front; check this carefully, rather than the number, to make sure you are not on the wrong bus. For the major inter-city lines, ticketing is now computerized, with assigned seating and sold-out vehicles common. On smaller rural/island routes, it's generally first-come, first-served with some standing allowed and tickets dispensed on the spot by a conductor.

dialogue

> **does this bus go to ...?** piyeni afto to leoforio sto ...?
>
> **no, you need a number ...** okhi, prepi na pareteh o leoforio ariTHmos ...

business i thooli-es
bus station to praktorio leoforion, o staTHmos leoforion
bus stop i stasi leoforioo
bust (sculpture) i protomi (measurement) to stiTHos
busy (restaurant etc) polisikhnastos
 I'm busy tomorrow imeh apaskholimenos avrio
but ala
butcher's o khasapis
butter to vootiro
button to koobi

buy agorazo
 where can I buy ...? poo boro na agoraso ...?
by: by bus/car meh to leoforio/aftokinito
 written by ... grameno apo ...
 by the window thipla sto paraTHiro
 by the sea konda sti THalasa
 by Thursday prin apo tin Pempti
bye yasoo

C

cabbage to lakhano
cabin (on ship) i kabina
cable car to teleferik
café i kafeteria, to kafenio

 The 'kafenio' is the traditional Greek coffee shop or café. Although its main business is Greek coffee it also serves spirits, beer, tea and soft drinks. A 'zakharoplastio' is a cross between café and patisserie and it serves coffee, alcohol, yoghurt and honey, sticky cakes etc, both to eat in and take away. A 'galaktopolio' is a type of take-away café, specializing more in dairy products (yoghurt, ice cream, custard desserts etc). These last two types of café are usually more family-oriented than a 'kafenio' and many also serve a basic continental breakfast. Usually the only edibles

sold in cafés are very sweet cakes and preserves, although some city cafés serve savoury snacks and sandwiches.
See also **bar**

cagoule to athiavrokho
cake to cake
cake shop to zakharoplastio
call fonazo
 (to phone) tilefono
 what's it called? pos to leneh?
 he/she is called ... ton/tin leneh ...
 please call a doctor seh parakalo, tilefoniseh seh ena yatro
 please give me a call at 7.30 am tomorrow seh parakalo, tilefoniseh moo avrio to pro-i stis efta keh misi
 please ask him to call me seh parakalo, pes too na moo tilefonisi
call back: I'll call back later THa xanarTHo argotera
 (phone back) THa seh paro piso
call round: I'll call round tomorrow THa peraso avrio
camcorder i mikhani lipseos
camera i fotografiki mikhani
camera shop to katastima fotografikon ithon
camp (verb) kataskinono
 can we camp here? boroomeh na

kataskinosoomeh etho?
camping gas to igra-erio

Camping gas canisters can be bought either from a hardware store, supermarkets or from campsite shops; you can't carry canisters on planes.

campsite to kambing

Official campsites range from ramshackle compounds on the islands to highly organized sites run by EOT (Greek Tourist Organization). Freelance camping is officially illegal and police crack down on people camping rough in popular tourist resorts. However, in quiet rural inland areas you may find that nobody is very bothered about it. It is always best to ask permission first in the village taverna or café before pitching a tent.

can to kooti, i konserva
 a can of beer mia bira seh kooti
can: can you ...? boriteh na ...?
 can I have ...? boro na ekho ...?
 I can't ... then boro ...
Canada o Kanathas
Canadian Kanathezikos
 I'm Canadian (man/woman) imeh Kanathos/Kanatheza

canal to kanali
cancel akirono
candies i karameles
candle to keri
canoe to kano
canoeing kano kano
can-opener to anikhtiri
cap (hat) to kapelo
(of bottle) to kapaki
car to aftokinito
by car meh to aftokinito
carafe i karafa
a carafe of house white,
please mia karafa aspro
spitiko krasi, parakalo
caravan to trokhospito
caravan site topoTHesia ya
trokhospita
carburettor to karbirater
card (birthday etc) i karta
here's my (business) card
oristeh, i karta moo
cardigan i zaketa
cardphone i tilekarta
see phone
careful prosektikos
be careful! prosekheh!
caretaker o/i epistatis
car ferry to feri-bot
car hire enikiasis aftokiniton
see rent
car park to parking
carpet to khali
(fitted) i moketa
carriage (of train) to vagoni
carrier bag i sakoola
carrot to karoto
carry metafero
carry-cot to port-beh-beh

carton i koota
carwash to plindirio
aftokiniton
case (suitcase) i valitsa
cash ta metrita
will you cash this for me?
THa moo to exaryiroseteh?
cash desk to tamio
cash dispenser i mikhani ya
metrita
cashier o/i tamias
cassette i kaseta
cassette recorder to
kasetofono
castle to kastro
casualty department Protes
Vo-iTHi-es
cat i gata
catch piano
where do we catch the bus
to ...? apo poo THa
paroomeh sto leoforio?
cathedral o kaTHethrikos
naos
Catholic (adj) kaTHolikos
cauliflower to koonoopithi
cave i spilia
ceiling to tavani
celery to selino
cellar (for wine) to kelari
cemetery to nekrotafio
Centigrade* Kelsioo
centimetre* ena ekatosto
central kendrikos
central heating i kendriki
THermansi
centre to kendro
how do we get to the city
centre? pos THa pameh sto

kendro?
cereal ta cornflakes
certainly sigoora
 certainly not fisika okhi
chair i karekla
champagne i sampania
change (money) ta resta
 (verb: money, trains) alazo
 can I change this for ...? boro
 na alaxo afto ya ...?
 I don't have any change then
 ekho psila
 can you give me change for
 a 5,000 drachma note?
 boriteh na moo khalaseteh
 pendeh khiliathes
 thrakhmes?

Kiosks may sometimes
refuse to change a 1,000
or 5,000 drachma note for
you, unless you buy something from
them.

dialogue

 do we have to change
 (trains)? prepi na
 alaxoomeh treno?
 yes, change at Corinth/no,
 it's a direct train neh,
 alaxteh stin KorinTHo/
 okhi, piyeni katefTHian

changed: to get changed
 alazo rookha
chapel to eklisaki
charge i timi, i thapani
 (verb) khreono

charge card i pistotiki karta
 see credit card
cheap ftinos
 do you have anything
 cheaper? ekheteh tipoteh
 ftinotero?
check (verb) epaliTHevo
 (US: cheque) i epitayi
 see cheque
 (US: bill) o logariasmos
 see bill
 could you check the ...,
 please? boriteh na
 elenxeteh to ..., parakalo?
checkbook to karneh
 epitagon
check-in to check-in
check in kano check-in
 where do we have to check
 in? poo prepi na kanoomeh
 check-in?
cheek (on face) to magoolo
cheerio! yasoo!
cheers! (toast) stin iya sas!, is
 iyian!
cheese to tiri
chemist's to farmakio

Greek chemists are well-
qualified to give you
advice on minor ailments;
there's generally an all-night
chemist's in bigger towns and cities;
they work on a rota system and you
generally find the address of the one
currently open on the door of any
chemist's.

cheque i epitayi

do you take cheques?
perneteh epitayes?
see **credit card**
cheque book to karneh
epitagon
cheque card i karta
epitagon
cherry to kerasi
chess to skaki
chest to stiTHos
chewing gum i tsikhla
chicken to kotopoolo
chickenpox i anemovloyia
child to pethi
  children ta pethia
child minder i dada
children's pool i pisina ton
  pethion
children's portion i pethiki
  meritha
chin to pigooni
china i porselani
Chinese (adj) Kinezikos
chips i tiganites patates
chocolate i sokolata
  milk chocolate i sokolata
  galaktos
  plain chocolate sokolata sketi
  a hot chocolate i zesti
  sokolata, mia sokolata rofima
choose thialego
Christian name to mikro
  onoma
Christmas ta khristooyena
  Christmas Eve i paramoni
  ton khristooyenon
  merry Christmas! kala
  khristooyena!
church i eklisia

cicada o tzitzikas
cider cider
cigar to pooro
cigarette to tsigaro
cigarette lighter o anaptiras
cinema o kinimatografos, to
  sinema
circle o kiklos
  (in theatre) o exostis
city i poli
city centre to kendro tis
  polis
clean (adj) kaTHaros
  can you clean these for me?
  moo pleneteh afta?
cleaning solution (for contact
  lenses) to kaTHaristiko
  thialima
cleansing lotion to galaktoma
  kaTHarismoo
clear kaTHaros
  (obvious) profanis
clever exipnos
cliff o apotomos vrakhos
climbing i orivasia
cling film to na-ilon
clinic i kliniki
cloakroom i gardaroba
clock to rolo-i
close klino

dialogue

what time do you close? ti
ora klineteh?
we close at 8 pm on
weekdays and 6 pm on
Saturdays klinoomeh stis
okto to vrathi tis

kaTHimerines keh stis exi
to apoyevma ta Savata
do you close for lunch?
klineteh ya mesimeriano
fayito?
yes, between 1 and 3.30 pm
neh, apo ti mia mekhri tis
tris keh misi

closed klistos
cloth (fabric) to ifasma
  (for cleaning etc) to pani
clothes ta rookha
clothes line i aplostra
clothes peg to mandalaki
cloud to sinefo
cloudy sinefiasmenos
clutch to debrayaz, o
  siblektis
coach (bus) to poolman
  (on train) to vagoni
coach station o staTHmos
  iperastikon leoforion
coach trip to taxithi meh
  poolman
coast i akti
  on the coast stin akti
coat (long coat) to palto
  (jacket) to sakaki
coathanger i kremastra
cockroach i katsaritha
cocoa to kakao
coconut i karitha
code (for phoning) o kothikos
  **what's the (dialling) code for
  Athens?** pios ineh o kothikos
  ya tin ATHina?
  see **dialling code**
coffee o kafes

two Greek coffees, please
thio Elinikoos kafethes,
parakalo

When you ask for a
coffee, say what kind you
want:
Eliniko   Greek/Turkish coffee
galliko   filter coffee
Nescafeh zesto/pagomeno
            hot/iced instant coffee
Other useful terms are:
sketo   unsweetened
metrio   medium-sweet
gliko   very sweet

coin to kerma
Coke® i koka-kola
cold krios
  I'm cold kriono
  I have a cold imeh
  kriomenos
collapse: **he's collapsed**
  katarefseh
collar o yakas
collect paralamvano
  I've come to collect ... ilTHa
  ya na paro ...
collect call tilefono collect
college to koleyio
colour to khroma
  **do you have this in other
  colours?** to ekheteh seh ala
  khromata?
colour film to enkhromo
  film
comb i khtena
come erkhomeh

dialogue

where do you come from?
apo poo iseh?
I come from Edinburgh
imeh apo to Ethimvoorgo

come back epistrefo
 I'll come back tomorrow THa
 epistrepso avrio
come in beno mesa
comfortable (chair) anapaftikos
 (clothes) anetos
 (room, hotel) volikos
compact disc to compact
 disc
company (business) i eteria
compartment (on train) to
 koopeh
compass i pixitha
complain paraponoomeh
complaint to parapono
 I have a complaint ekho ena
 parapono
completely telios
computer o ipolo-yistis
concert i sinavlia
concussion i thiasisi
 engefaloo
conditioner (for hair) to
 kondisioner
condom to profilaktiko
conference to sinethrio
confirm epiveveono
congratulations! sinkharitiria!
connecting flight sinthesi
 ptisis
connection (travel) i sinthesi
conscious sinesTHanomenos

constipation i thiskiliotis
consulate to proxenio
contact erkhomeh seh epafi
contact lenses i faki epafis
contraceptive (pill) to
 andisiliptiko
 (condom) to profilaktiko
convenient volikos
 that's not convenient then
 meh volevi
convent to monastiri
cook (verb) ma-yirevo
 not cooked misopsimeno
cooker i koozina
cookie to biskoto
cooking utensils ta ma-yirika
 skevi
cool throseros
Corfu i Kerkira
cork o felos
corkscrew to anikhtiri
corner: on the corner sti
 gonia
 in the corner sti gonia
cornflakes ta cornflakes
correct (right) sostos
corridor o thiathromos
cosmetics ta kalindika
cost (verb) stikhizo
 how much does it cost? poso
 kani?
cot i koonia
cotton to vamvaki
cotton wool to vamvaki
couch o kanapes
couchette i kooketa
cough o vikhas
cough medicine to farmako
 ya ton vikha

could: could you ...? boriteh na ...?

could I have ...? boro na ekho ...?

I couldn't ... then boroosa na ...

country (nation) i khora

(countryside) i exokhi

countryside i exokhi

couple (man and woman) to zevgari

a couple of ... thio apo ...

courgette to kolokiTHaki

courier o/i sinothos

course (main course etc) to piato

of course veveh-a

of course not fisika okhi

cousin (male/female) o xathelfos/i xathelfi

cow i a-yelatha

crab to kavoori

cracker to krakeraki

craft shop to ergastiri

crash i sigroosi

I've had a crash trakara

crazy trelos

cream (on milk, in cake) i krema

(lotion) i krema thermatos

(colour) krem

creche o pethikos staTHmos

credit card i pistotiki karta

Credit/charge cards are useful – indeed almost essential – for renting cars. However, most hotels, restaurants and shops prefer cash, rather than cheques or cards, so check in advance if they are accepted.

dialogue

can I pay by credit card? boro na pliroso meh pistotiki karta?

which card do you want to use? ti karta THeleteh na khrisimopi-iseteh?

yes, sir endaxi, kiri-eh

what's the number? ti ariTHmo ekhi?

and the expiry date? keh poteh ineh i imerominia lixeos?

Crete i Kriti

crisps ta tsips

crockery ta piatika

crossing (by sea) to THalasio taxithi

crossroads to stavrothromi

crowd o kosmos

crowded yematos kosmo

crown (on tooth) i korona

cruise i krooazi-era

crutches i pateritses

cry (weep) kleo

(shout) fonazo

cucumber to agoori

cup to flidzani

a cup of ..., please ena flidzani ..., parakalo

cupboard to doolapi

cure i THerapia

curly sgooros, katsaros

current to revma
curtains i koortines
cushion to maxilaraki
custom to eTHimo
Customs to Telonio
cut to kopsimo
 (verb) kovo
 I've cut myself kopika
cutlery ta makheropiroona
cycling i pothilasia
cyclist o/i pothilatis
Cyprus i Kipros

D

dad o babas
daily kaTHimerina
damage (verb) katastrefo
 damaged katastrafikeh
 I'm sorry, I've damaged this
 lipameh, to khalasa
damn! na pari i oryi!
damp (adj) igros
dance o khoros
 (verb) khorevo
 would you like to dance?
 THelis na khorepsoomeh?
dangerous epikinthinos
Danish thanos
dark (adj: colour) skotinos
 (hair) mavros
 it's getting dark skotiniazi
date*: what's the date today?
 poso ekhi o minas simera?
 let's make a date for next
 Monday as sinandiTHoomeh
 tin epomeni theftera
dates (fruit) i khoormathes

daughter i kori
daughter-in-law i nifi
dawn i avyi
 at dawn tin avyi
day i mera
 the day after tin epomeni
 mera
 the day after tomorrow
 meTHavrio
 the day before tin pro-
 igoomeni mera
 the day before yesterday
 prokhtes
 every day kaTHeh mera
 all day oli tin imera
 in two days' time meta apo
 thio meres
day trip to taxithi
 afTHimeron
dead peTHamenos, nekros
deaf koofos
deal (business) i simfonia
 it's a deal simfonisameh,
 endaxi
death o THanatos
decaffeinated coffee o kafes
 khoris kafe-ini
December o thekemvrios
decide apofasizo
 we haven't decided yet then
 ekhoomeh apofasisi akoma
decision i apofasi
deck (on ship) to katastroma
deckchair i poliTHrona, i sez
 long
deduct afero
deep vaTHis
definitely oposthipoteh
 definitely not seh kamia

periptosi
degree (qualification) to ptikhio
delay i kaTHisterisi
deliberately epitithes
delicatessen ta delicatessen
delicious nostimotatos
deliver thianemo
delivery (of mail) i thianomi, i parathosi
demotic i dimotiki
Denmark i thania
dental floss to othondiko nima
dentist o/i othondiatros

dialogue

> **it's this one here** afto etho ineh
> **this one?** afto?
> **no, that one** okhi, ekino
> **here?** etho?
> **yes** neh

dentures i masela
deodorant to aposmitiko
department to tmima
department store to megalo katastima
departure i anakhorisi
departure lounge i eTHoosa anakhoriseos
depend: it depends exartateh
it depends on ... exartateh apo ...
deposit (as security) i kataTHesi
(as part payment) i prokatavoli
description i perigrafi

dessert to glikisma
destination o pro-orismos
develop anaptiso
(a film) emfanizo

dialogue

> **could you develop these films?** boriteh na emfaniseteh afta ta film?
> **when will they be ready?** poteh THa ineh etima?
> **tomorrow afternoon** avrio to apoyevma
> **how much is the four-hour service?** poso kani i emfanisi seh teseris ores?

diabetic (man/woman) o thiavitikos/i thiavitiki
diabetic foods i thiavitiki trofi
dial (verb) kalo, perno ariTHmo
dialling code o kothikos ariTHmos

 For direct international calls from Greece, dial the country code (given below), the area code (minus the first 0), and finally the subscriber number:

UK: 0044   Australia: 0061
Ireland: 00353   New Zealand: 0064
US & Canada: 001

diamond to thiamandi
diaper i pana

diarrhoea i thiaria
diary to imerolo-yio
dictionary to lexiko
didn't
  see not
die peTHeno
diesel i dizel
diet i thi-eta
  I'm on a diet kano thi-eta
  I have to follow a special diet
  prepi na kano ithiki thi-eta
difference i thiafora
  what's the difference? pia
  ineh i thiafora?
different thiaforetikos
  this one is different afto etho
  ineh thiaforetiko
  a different table ena alo
  trapezi
difficult thiskolos
difficulty i thiskolia
dinghy to zodiak®
dining room i trapezaria
dinner (evening meal) to
  thipno
  to have dinner tro-o
  vrathino
direct (adj) kat-efTHian
  is there a direct train?
  iparkhi kat-efTHian treno
  ya ...?
direction i katefTHinsi
  which direction is it? pros ta
  poo ineh?
  is it in this direction? ineh
  pros afti tin katefTHinsi?
directory enquiries i
  plirofori-es

 The number for directory
enquiries is 131 for
Athens numbers, 132 for
other numbers in Greece and 161 for
international numbers.

dirt i vroma
dirty vromikos
disabled anapiros
  is there access for the
  disabled? iparkhi prosvasi ya
  toos anapiroos?
disappear exafanizomeh
  it's disappeared
  exafanistikeh
disappointed apogo-
  itevmenos
disappointing apogo-iteftiko
disaster i katastrofi
disco i diskotek
discount i ekptosi
  is there a discount? kaneteh
  ekptosi?
disease i arostia
disgusting a-ithiastikos
dish (meal) to piato
  (bowl) to bol
dishcloth i patsavoora
disinfectant to apolimandiko
disk (for computer) i thisketa
disposable diapers i
  khartines panes
disposable nappies i
  khartines panes
distance i apostasi
  in the distance eki kato
distilled water apestagmeno
  nero
district i sinikia

disturb enokhlo
diversion (detour) i parakampsi
diving board i anitha vootias
divorced: I'm divorced
(man/woman)
khorismenos/khorismeni
dizzy: I feel dizzy zalizomeh
do kano
what shall we do? ti THa
kanoomeh?
how do you do it? pos to
kaneteh?
will you do it for me? boriteh
na moo to kaneteh?

dialogues

how do you do? ti
kaneteh?
nice to meet you kharika
ya ti gnorimia
what do you do? ti thoolia
kaneteh?
I'm a teacher, and you?
imeh thaskalos, ki esis?
I'm a student imeh fititis
what are you doing this
evening? ti THa kaneteh
apopseh?
we're going out for a drink;
do you want to join us?
THa pameh ya ena poto –
THeleteh na elTHeteh
mazi mas?

do you want cream?
THeleteh krema?
I do, but she doesn't ego
neh, ekini, omos, okhi

doctor o/i yatros
we need a doctor
khriazomasteh enan yatro
please call a doctor seh
parakalo, kaleseh enan yatro

 Any chemist's will have a list of the nearest doctor's surgeries; if you're a citizen of an EU country, take the form E111 (obtainable from post offices in the UK) with you – this should enable you to get free treatment and pay for prescriptions at the local rate. In practice, hospital staff often meet the E111 with uncomprehending looks and you may have to request reimbursment from the NHS on your return. Some form of travel insurance is therefore advisable and is essential for non-EU citizens. In tourist areas, it should be easy to find an English-speaking doctor and the tourist police (phone 171) may be able to help with some names if you have any difficulty.

dialogue

where does it hurt? poo
ponateh?
right here akrivos etho
does that hurt more? sas
pona-i afto pio poli?
yes neh
take this to a chemist
thosteh afto seh ena
farmaki-o

document to engrafo
dog o skilos
doll i kookla
domestic flight ptisi
  esterikoo
donkey o ga-itharos
don't! mi!
  don't do that! min to kanis
  afto!
  (stop) stamata!
  see not
door i porta
doorman o THiroros
double thiplo
double bed to thiplo krevati
double room to thiplo
  thomatio
doughnut to donat
down kato
  down here etho kato
  put it down over there valeh
  to eki kato
  it's down there on the right
  vrisketeh eki kato sta thexia
  it's further down the road
  ineh ligo parakato
downmarket (restaurant etc)
  ftinos
downstairs kato
dozen mia doozina
  half a dozen misi doozina
drain o okhetos
draught beer varelisia bira
draughty: it's draughty kani
  revma
drawer to sirtari
drawing to skhethio
dreadful friktos
dream to oniro

dress to forema
dressed: to get dressed
  dinomeh
dressing (for cut) i gaza
  (for salad) to lathoxitho
dressing gown i roba
drink to poto
  (verb) pino
  a cold drink to anapsiktiko
  can I get you a drink? boro
  na seh keraso kanena poto?
  what would you like (to
  drink)? ti THa THelateh na
  pi-iteh?
  no thanks, I don't drink okhi,
  efkharisto, then pino
  I'll just have a drink of water
  THa paro monon ena potiri
  nero
drinking water to posimo nero
  is this drinking water? ineh
  posimo afto to nero?

 Although water in villages
is pure (and tastes
wonderful) because it
comes from the mountains, mineral
water is preferable to tap water in
big towns or on some of the drier
and more remote islands.

drive othiga-o
  we drove here othiyisameh
  etho
  I'll drive you home THa seh
  pao spiti

Cars have obvious advantages for getting to the more inaccessible parts of mainland Greece, but this is one of the more expensive countries in Europe to rent a car. If you drive your own vehicle to and through Greece, you'll need international third party insurance, the so-called Green Card, as well as an International Driving Licence and the registration documents. Upon arrival your passport will get a carnet stamp; this normally allows you to keep a vehicle in Greece for up to six months, exempt from road tax. Greece has the highest accident rate in Europe after Portugal, and many of the roads can be quite perilous – asphalt can turn into a dirt track without warning on the smaller routes, and railway crossings are rarely guarded. Uphill drivers insist on their right of way, as do those first to approach a one-lane bridge – headlights flashed at you mean the opposite of what they mean in the UK or North America and signify that the driver is coming through. Wearing a seatbelt is compulsory and children under 10 are not allowed to sit in the front seats. If you are involved in any kind of accident it's illegal to drive away, and you can be held at a police station for up to 24 hours. If this happens, ring your consulate immediately, in order to get a lawyer (you have this right). Don't make a statement to anyone who doesn't speak, and write, very good English. There are a limited number of express highways between Pátra, Athens, Vólos and Thessaloniki, on which tolls are levied – currently between 400dr and 700dr at each sporadically placed gate. They're nearly twice as quick as the old roads, and well worth using.

driver o/i othigos
driving licence i athia othiyiseos, to thiploma othiyiseos
drop: just a drop, please (of drink) poli ligo, parakalo
drug to farmako
  drugs (narcotics) ta narkotika
drunk (adj) meTHismenos
drunken driving methismeno othiyima

 The legal limit is 0.5% but don't drink and drive.

dry (adj) stegnos
  (wine) xiros
dry-cleaner to stegno-kaTHaristirio
duck i papia
due: he was due to arrive yesterday eprokito na ftasi khtes
  when is the train due? poteh ftani to treno?
dull (pain) exasTHenimenos
  (weather) moondos

(boring) varetos
dummy (baby's) i pipila
during kata ti thiarkia
dust i skoni
dusty skonismeno
dustbin o skoopithodenekes
duty-free (goods) ta aforolo-yita
duty-free shop to katastima aforolo-yiton
duvet to paploma

E

each kaTHeh
  how much are they each? poso ekhi to kaTHena?
ear to afti
earache: I have earache ekho pono sto afti
early noris
  early in the morning noris to pro-i
  I called by earlier perasa pro-igoomenos
earrings ta skoolarikia
east i anatoli
  in the east stin anatoli
Easter to Paskha
Easter Sunday i Kiriaki too Paskha

 Easter is by far the most important festival of the Greek year and taken much more seriously than it is anywhere in western Europe. From Wednesday of Holy Week the state radio and TV networks are given over solely to religious programmes until the following Monday. The festival is an excellent time to be in Greece, both for the beautiful and moving religious ceremonies and for the days of feasting that follow. In the week leading up to Easter Sunday you should wish people a Happy Easter 'kalo paskha'.

easy efkolos
eat tro-o
  we've already eaten, thanks fagameh ithi, efkharisto

 eating habits
Greeks don't generally eat breakfast; however, you can get a continental-style breakfast of bread, jam, yoghurt and coffee at most cafés. Greeks usually have a late lunch – between 2-3 pm The evening meal is also eaten late – between 9 and 11 pm, although it is possible to eat earlier in some more touristic establishments. Greek cuisine and restaurants are simple and straightforward. There's no snobbery about eating out.

eau de toilette i kolonia
EC i eok
economy class tooristiki THesi
egg to avgo
  hard-boiled egg avgo sfikhto
  fried egg tiganito avgo

eggplant i melidzana
either: either ... or ... i ... i ...
  either of them opio naneh
elastic to lastikho
elastic band to lastikhaki
elbow o angonas
electric ilektrikos
electrical appliances
  ilektrikes siskeves
electric fire i ilektriki somba
electrician o ilektrologos
electricity to ilektriko revma

 The supply is 220V, though anything requiring 240V will work. Most plugs are two round pins: a travel plug is useful.

elevator to asanser
else: something else kati alo
  somewhere else kapoo aloo

dialogue

would you like anything
else? THa THelateh
tipoteh alo?
no, nothing else, thanks
okhi, tipoteh alo,
efkharisto

e-mail to e-mail
embassy i presvia
emergency i ektakti anangi
  this is an emergency! ineh
  epigon!
emergency exit i exothos
kinthinoo
empty (adj) athios

end to telos
  (verb) teliono
  at the end of the street sto
  telos too thromoo
  when does it end? poteh
  telioni?
engaged (toilet, telephone)
katilimenos
  (to be married: man/woman)
aravoniasmenos/
aravoniasmeni
engine (car) i mikhani too
  aftokinitoo
England i Anglia
English ta Anglika
  I'm English (man/woman) imeh
  Anglos/Anglitha
  do you speak English?
  milateh anglika?
enjoy: to enjoy oneself
thiaskethazo

dialogue

how did you like the film?
pos soo fanikeh to ergo?
I enjoyed it very much; did
you enjoy it? moo areseh
para poli; esena soo
areseh?

enjoyable efkharistos
enlargement (of photo) i
  me-yenTHisi
enormous terastios
enough arketa
  there's not enough then
  iparkhi arketo
  it's not big enough then ineh

arketa megalo
that's enough ftani, arki
entrance i isothos
envelope o fakelos
epileptic (man/woman) o
epiliptikos/i epiliptiki
equipment o exoplismos
error to laTHos
especially ithika
essential vasikos, aparetitos
it is essential that ... ineh
aparetito na ...
EU Evropa-iki Enosi
euro to evro
Eurocheque to Eurocheque
Eurocheque card i karta
Eurocheque
Europe i Evropi
European (adj) Evropa-ikos
European Union Evropa-iki
Enosi
even: even the Greeks akoma
keh i Elines
even if ... akoma ki an ...
evening to vrathi
this evening simera to vrathi
in the evening to vrathi
evening meal to thipno
eventually telika
ever poteh

dialogue

have you ever been to
Crete? ekheteh pa-i poteh
stin Kriti?
yes, I was there two years
ago neh, imoon eki prin
apo thio khronia

every kaTHeh
every day kaTHeh mera
everyone oli
everything kaTHeh ti
everywhere pandoo
exactly! akrivos!
exam to thiagonisma
example to parathigma
for example parathigmatos
kharin
excellent exokhos
excellent! exokha!
except ektos
excess baggage to ipervaro
exchange rate sinalagmatiki
isotimia
exciting sinarpastikos
excuse me (to get past) signomi
(to get attention) parakalo
(to say sorry) meh sinkhoriteh
exhaust (pipe) i exatmisi
exhausted (tired)
exandlimenos
exhibition i ekTHesi
exit i exothos
where's the nearest exit? poo
ineh i plisi-esteri exothos?
expect perimeno
expensive akrivos
experienced embiros
explain exigo
can you explain that? boris
na moo to exiyisis?
express mail to katepigon
express train to treno express
extension (telephone) i sinthesi
tilefonoo
could you get me extension
221, please? meh sintheh-

eteh meh to 221 (thiak**o**sia
ikosi **e**na), parakal**o**?
extension lead i pro-**e**ktasi
**extra: can we have an extra
chair?** bor**oo**meh na
ekhoomeh mia kar**e**kla
ak**o**ma?
do you charge extra for that?
khre**o**neteh epipl**e**on ya af**to**?
extraordinary asini**TH**istos
extremely ipervolik**a**
eye to m**a**ti
**will you keep an eye on my
suitcase for me?** THa moo
to pros**e**kheteh?
eyebrow pencil to mol**i**vi ya
ta fr**i**thia
eye drops i stag**o**nes ya ta
m**a**tia
eyeglasses (US) ta yial**i**a
eyeliner to eyeliner
eye make-up remover to
gal**a**ktoma ka**TH**arism**oo**
eye shadow i ski**a** mati**o**n

F

face to pr**o**sopo
factory to ergost**a**sio
Fahrenheit* va**TH**m**i** Fa**re**na-it
faint (verb) lipo**TH**im**ao**
she's fainted lipo**TH**imiseh
I feel faint es**TH**anomeh
lipo**TH**im**i**a
fair (funfair) to paniy**i**ri
(trade) i ek**TH**esi
(adj) thik**e**os
fairly arket**a**

fake i apom**i**misi
Fall to f**TH**in**o**poro
see **autumn**
fall (verb) p**e**fto
she's had a fall **e**peseh
false ps**e**ftikos
family i iko-y**e**nia
famous thi**a**simos
fan (electrical) o anemist**i**ras
(hand held) i vent**a**lia
(sports) o/i opath**o**s
fan belt to vendilat**e**r
fantastic fandastik**o**s
far makri**a**

dialogue

is it far from here? **i**neh
makri**a** ap**o** eth**o**?
no, not very far **o**khi, **o**khi
keh pol**i** makri**a**
well how far? p**o**so
makri**a**, thilath**i**?
it's about 20 kilometres
ineh per**i**poo **i**kosi
khili**o**metra

fare i tim**i** too isitir**i**oo
farm to agr**o**ktima
fashionable tis m**o**thas
fast grig**o**ros
fat (person) pakh**i**s
(on meat) to l**i**pos
father o pat**e**ras
father-in-law o pe**TH**er**o**s
faucet i vr**i**si
fault to el**a**toma
sorry, it was my fault
sign**o**mi, **i**tan sf**a**lma moo

it's not my fault then fteo ego
faulty elatomatikos
favourite agapimenos
fax to fax
  (verb: person) stelno fax seh ...
  (document) stelno seh fax
February o Fevrooarios
feel esTHanomeh
  I feel hot zestenomeh
  I feel unwell then
  esTHanomeh kala
  I feel like going for a walk
  ekho orexi na pao mia volta
  how are you feeling? pos
  esTHaneseh?
  I'm feeling better
  esTHanomeh kalitera
felt-tip pen o markathoros
fence o fraktis
fender o profilaktiras
ferry to feri bot

There are three different
varieties of vessel:
medium-sized to large
ordinary ferries (which operate the
main services), hydrofoils (run by
the **Ceres "Flying Dolphins"** and
Dodecanese Hydrofoils, among
other companies), and local 'kaikia'
(small boats which in season cover
short island hops and excursions).
Costs are very reasonable on longer
journeys, though proportionately
more expensive for shorter, inter-
island connections. The most
reliable, up-to-date information is
available from the local port police
('limenarkhio'), which maintains

offices at Piraeus and on virtually all
fair-sized islands.

festival to festival
fetch pa-o na fero
  I'll fetch him THa pa-o na
  ton fero
  **will you come and fetch me
  later?** THa elTHis na meh
  paris argotera?
feverish empiretos
few: a few liyi, liyes, liga
  a few days liyes meres
fiancé o aravoniastikos
fiancée i aravoniastikia
field to khorafi
fight o agonas
figs ta sika
fill yemizo
fill in yemizo
  do I have to fill this in? prepi
  na to yemiso?
fill up yemizo telios
  fill it up, please yemisteh tin,
  parakalo
filling (in cake, sandwich) i
  yemisi
  (in tooth) to sfra-yisma
film to film

dialogue

do you have this kind of
film? ekheteh tetio film?
yes – how many
exposures? neh – meh
poses stasis?
36 trianda-exi

Fa

66

film processing i emfanisi too film
filter coffee o kafes filtroo
filter papers ta filtra ya kafeh
filthy vromeros
find vrisko
 I can't find it then to vrisko
 I've found it to vrika
find out anakalipto
 could you find out for me? boris na maTHis?
fine (weather) oreos
 (punishment) to prostimo

dialogues

 how are you? ti kanis?
 I'm fine thanks mia khara, efkharisto

 is that OK? afto ineh endaxi?
 that's fine thanks ineh mia khara, efkharisto

finger to thakhtilo
finish teliono
 I haven't finished yet then ekho teliosi akomi
 when does it finish? poteh telioni?
fire: fire! pirkaya!
 can we light a fire here? boroomeh na anapsoomeh fotia etho?
 it's on fire pireh fotia
fire alarm o sinayermos pirkayas

fire brigade i pirosvestiki ipiresia

In the event of a fire, phone 199.

fire escape i exothos pirkayas
fire extinguisher o pirosvestiras
first protos
 I was first imoon protos
 at first stin arkhi
 the first time i proti fora
 first on the left protos sta aristera
first aid i protes vo-iTHi-es
first aid kit to kooti proton vo-iTHi-on
first class (travel etc) proti THesi
first floor to proto patoma (US) to iso-yio
first name to onoma
fish to psari
fisherman o psaras
fishing village to psarokhori
fishmonger's to psarathiko
fit (attack) i prosvoli
 it doesn't fit me then moo khora-i
fitting room to thokimastirio
fix ftiakhno
 (arrange) kanonizo
 can you fix this? boris na to ftiaxis?
fizzy meh anTHrakiko
flag i simea
flannel to sfoogari

flash (for camera) to flas
flat (apartment) to thiamerisma
  (adj) epipethos
  I've got a flat tyre me epiaseh
  lastikho
flavour i gefsi
flea o psilos
flight i ptisi
flight number ariTHmos ptisis
flippers ta vatrakhopethila
flood i plimira
floor (of room) to patoma
  (of building) o orofos
  on the floor sto patoma
florist o anTHopolis
flour to alevri
flower to looloothi
flu i gripi
fluent: he speaks fluent Greek
  mila-i aptesta elinika
fly i miga
  (verb) peto
  can we fly there? boroomeh
  na pameh eki a-eroporikos?
fly in peta-o pros
fly out peta-o apo
fog i omikhli
foggy: it's foggy ekhi omikhli
folk dancing i thimotiki khori
folk music i thimotiki moosiki
follow akolooTHo
  follow me akolootha meh
food to fa-yito
food poisoning trofiki
  thilitiriasi
food shop/store to bakaliko
foot* to pothi
  on foot meh ta pothia
football (game) to pothosfero

  (ball) i bala
football match o
  pothosferikos agonas
for ya
  do you have something
  for ...? (headache/diarrhoea etc)
  ekheteh kati ya ...?

dialogues

who's the moussaka for?
ya pion ineh o moosakas?
that's for me ya mena
and this one? ki afto etho?
that's for her afto ineh ya
ekini

where do I get the bus for
Akropolis? apo poo THa
paro to leoforio ya tin
Akropoli?
the bus for Acropolis
leaves from Stathiou Street
to leoforio ya tin
Akropoli fevyi apo tin
Otho Stathioo

how long have you been
here for? poso kero iseh
etho pera?
I've been here for two
days, how about you?
vriskomeh etho pera etho
keh thio meres, esi?
I've been here for a week
vriskomeh etho pera etho
keh mia vthomatha

forehead to metopo

foreign xenos
foreigner (man/woman) o
  xenos/i xeni
forest to thasos
forget xekhno
  I forget xekhno
  I've forgotten xekhasa
fork (for eating) to pirooni
  (in road) i thiaklathosi
form (document) i etisi
formal (dress) episimos
fortnight to theka-
  penTHimero
fortunately eftikhos
forward: could you forward my
  mail? boriteh na moo
  stileteh ta gramata moo?
forwarding address i thi-
  efTHinsi apostolis
foundation cream krema
  prosopoo ya makiyaz
fountain i piyi
foyer to foyer
fracture to katagma
free elefTHeros
  (no charge) thorean
  is it free of charge? ineh
  thorean?
freeway i eTHniki othos
freezer i katapsixi
French (adj) galikos
  (language) ta galika
French fries i tiganites patates
frequent sikhnos
  how frequent is the bus to
  Corinth? kaTHeh poteh ekhi
  leoforio ya tin KorinTHo?
fresh (weather, breeze) throseros
  (fruit etc) freskos

fresh orange o freskos khimos
  portokali
Friday i Paraskevi
fridge to psiyio
fried tiganismenos
fried egg to tiganito avgo
friend (male/female) o filos/i fili
friendly filikos
from apo
  when does the next train
  from Patras arrive? poteh
  ftani to epomeno treno apo
  tin Patra?
  from Monday to Friday apo
  theftera os Paraskevi
  from next Thursday apo tin
  ali Pempti

dialogue

  where are you from? apo
  poo iseh?
  I'm from Slough imeh apo
  to Sla-oo

front to mbrostino meros
  in front mbrosta
  in front of the hotel mbrosta
  apo to xenothokhio
  at the front sto mbrostino
  meros
frost i pagonia, o pa-yetos
frozen pagomenos
frozen food i katepsiymeni
  trofi
fruit ta froota
fruit juice o khimos frooton
fry tiganizo
frying pan to tigani

full yematos
it's full of ... ineh yemato meh ...
I'm full khortasa
full board fool pansion
fun: it was fun kala itan, kanameh kefi
funeral i kithia
funny (strange) paraxenos
(amusing) astios
furniture ta epipla
further parapera
it's further down the road ineh akoma parakato

dialogue

how much further is it to Piraeus? poso ineh akomi mekhri ton Pirea?
about 5 kilometres yiro sta pendeh khiliometra

fuse i asfalia
the lights have fused ka-ikaneh ta fota
fuse box to kooti meh tis asfali-es
fuse wire to sirma asfalias
future to melon
in future sto melon

G

gallon* ena galoni
game (cards etc) to pekhnithi
(match) o agonas
(meat) to kiniyi

garage (for fuel) to venzinathiko
(for repairs) to sineryio
(for parking) to garaz

Greek garages are usually open from approx. 8 am to 8 pm; the address of those which are open at night and at weekends is usually on the door of the garage office. There will always be at least one petrol pump per district open at the weekend, but it's best to carry a full petrol can at all times.
see petrol

garden o kipos
garlic to skortho
gas to gazi
gas cylinder (camping gas) i fiali gazi
gasoline i venzini
see petrol
gas permeable lenses i imiskliri faki epafis
gas station to venzinathiko
gate i avloporta
(at airport) i exothos
gay (adj) omofilofilos
gay bar to gay bar
gears i takhitita
gearbox to kivotio takhititon
gear lever o levi-es takhititon
general yenikos
gents (toilet) i too-aleta ton anthron
genuine (antique etc) afTHendikos

German (adj) Yermanikos
 (language) ta Yermanika
German measles i eriTHra
Germany i Yermania
get (fetch) perno
 will you get me another one,
 please? THa moo paris alo
 ena, parakalo?
 how do I get to ...? pos boro
 na pao sto ...?
 do you know where I can get
 them? mipos xereteh poo
 boro na vro tetia?

dialogue

 can I get you a drink? na
 seh keraso kanena poto?
 no, I'll get this one, what
 would you like? okhi, ego
 kernao afti ti fora; ti THa
 iTHeles?
 a glass of red wine ena
 potiri kokino krasi

get back (return) epistrefo
get in (arrive) ftano
get off kateveno
 where do I get off? poo THa
 katevo?
get on (to train etc) aneveno
get out (of car etc) vyeno
get up (in the morning)
 sikonomeh
gift to thoro

It is customary to give
gifts to people on their
name days, birthdays, at

Christmas and on New Year's Eve,
and when you want to thank
someone for a favour.

gift shop katastima thoron,
 ithi thoron
gin to tzin
 a gin and tonic, please ena
 tzin meh tonik, parakalo
girl to koritsi
girlfriend i filenatha
give thino
 can you give me some
 change? boriteh na moo
 thoseteh psila?
 I gave it to him to ethosa seh
 afton
 will you give this to ...? to
 thinis afto ston ...?

dialogue

 how much do you want for
 this? posa THelis ya afto?
 10,000 drachmas theka
 khiliathes thrakhmes
 I'll give you 7,000 drachmas
 soo thino efta khiliathes

give back epistrefo, thino piso
glad efkharistimenos
glass (material) to yali
 (tumbler, wine glass) to potiri
 a glass of wine ena potiri
 krasi
glasses ta yalia
gloves ta gandia
glue i kola
go pao

we'd like to go to the ...
theloomeh na pameh sto ...

where are you going? poo
pateh?

where does this bus go? poo
pa-i afto to leoforio?

let's go! pameh

she's gone (left) efiyeh

where has he gone? poo
piyeh aftos?

I went there last week piga
eki tin perasmeni
evthomatha

hamburger to go
khamboorger ya to spiti

go away fevgo

go away! fiyeh!

go back (return) epistrefo

go down (the stairs etc)
kateveno

go in beno

go out (in the evening) v-yeno

**do you want to go out
tonight?** theleteh na pateh
exo apopseh?

go through thiaskhizo, pao
thia mesoo

go up (the stairs etc) aneveno

goat i katsika

goat's cheese to katsikisio tiri

God o THeos

goggles i maska

gold o khrisos

golf to golf

golf course to yipetho golf

good kalos

good! kala!

it's no good (product etc) afto
then ineh kalo

(not worth trying) then ofeli

goodbye ya khara, adio

good evening kalispera

Good Friday i Megali
Paraskevi

 Good Friday is a public
holiday in Greece. Post
offices, banks and some
shops close at noon, but
supermarkets and public transport
are not greatly affected.

good morning kalimera

good night kalinikhta

goose i khina

got: we've got to ... prepi
na ...

have you got any ...? ekheteh
kaTHoloo ...?

government i kivernisi

gradually siga-siga

grammar i gramatiki

gram(me) ena gramario

granddaughter i egoni

grandfather o papoos

grandmother i ya-ya

grandson o egonos

grapefruit to grapefruit

grapefruit juice o khimos
grapefruit

grapes ta stafilia

grass to khortari, to grasithi

grateful evgnomon

gravy o zomos too kreatos

great (excellent) poli kalo

that's great! iperokha!

it's a great success ineh
megali epitikhia

Great Britain i Megali
Vretania
Greece i Elatha
greedy akhortagos
Greek (adj) Elinikos
(language) ta Elinika
(man) o Elinas
(woman) i Elinitha
the Greeks i Elines
Greek coffee Elinikos kafes
Greek-Cypriot (adj)
Elinokiprios
Greek Orthodox Elinikos
OrTHothoxos
green prasinos
green card (car insurance) i
asfalia ya othiyisi sto
exoteriko
greengrocer's o manavis
grey grizos
grill i psistaria
grilled psitos sti skhara
grocer's to bakaliko
ground to ethafos
on the ground sto ethafos
ground floor to iso-yio
group to groop
guarantee i engi-isi
is it guaranteed? ineh engi-
imeno?
guest (man/woman) o
filoxenoomenos/i
filoxenoomeni
see hospitality
guesthouse i pansion

 It is difficult to find
guesthouses in less
touristy areas of Greece,
but local people may offer you
private rooms (thomatia) and food.
Between November and early April,
private rooms are closed to keep
hotels in business.

guide o/i xenagos
guidebook o tooristikos
othigos
guided tour i xenayisi
guitar i kiTHara
gum (in mouth) to oolo
gun (pistol) to pistoli
(rifle) to oplo
gym to yimnastirio

H

hair ta malia
hairbrush i voortsa ya malia, i
khtena
haircut (man's) to koorema
(woman's) to kopsimo
hairdresser's to komotirio
(men's) to koorio
hairdryer to pistolaki
hair gel o afros malion
hairgrips ta piastrakia malion
hair spray to spray ya ta malia
half misos
half an hour misi ora
half a litre miso litro
about half that peripoo to
miso apo afto
half board demi-pansion
half-bottle miso bookali
half fare miso isitirio
half price misotimis

ham to zambon
hamburger to khamboorger
hammer to sfiri
hand to kheri
handbag i tsanda
handbrake to khirofreno
handkerchief to mandili
(paper) to khartomandilo
handle to kherooli
hand luggage to sakvooa-yaz
hang-gliding i anemoporia
hangover o ponokefalos
  I've got a hangover ekho
  ponokefalo
happen simveni
  what's happening? ti
  simveni?
  what has happened? ti
  sinevi?
happy eftikhismenos
  I'm not happy about this then
  imeh efkharistimenos meh
  afto
harbour to limani
hard skliros
  (difficult) thiskolos
hard-boiled egg to sfikhto
  avgo
hard lenses i skliri faki
hardly meta vias
  hardly ever s-khethon poteh
hardware shop ta ithi
  kingalerias
hat to kapelo
hate miso
have* ekho
  can I have a ...? boro na
  ekho ena ...?
  do you have ...? ekheteh ...?

what'll you have? ti THa
piiteh?
I have to leave now prepi na
piyeno tora
do I have to ...? prepi na ...?
can we have some ...?
boroomeh na ekhoomeh
merika ...?
hayfever aler-yia sti yiri
hazelnuts to foondooki
he* aftos
  is he here? ineh etho?
head to kefali
headache o ponokefalos
headlights i provolis
headphones ta akoostika
health food shop katastima
  iyi-inon trofon
healthy iyi-is
hear akoo-o

dialogue

  can you hear me? meh
  akoos?
  I can't hear you, could you
  repeat that? then seh
  akoo-o, boris na to
  epanalavis?

hearing aid ta akoostika
heart i karthia
heart attack i karthiaki
  prosvoli
heat i zesti
heater i THermansi
  (radiator) to kalorifer
heating i THermansi
heavy varis

heel (of foot) i fterna
(of shoe) to takooni
could you heel these?
boriteh na moo valeteh
kenooryia takoonia safta?
heelbar o tsagaris
height to ipsos
helicopter to elikoptero
hello ya sas
(familiar) ya soo
(answer on phone) ebros
helmet (for motorcycle) to
kranos
help i vo-iTHia
(verb) vo-iTHo
help! vo-iTHia!
can you help me? boriteh na
meh vo-iTHiseteh?
**thank you very much for your
help** efkharisto ya ti vo-
iTHia sas
helpful exipiretikos
hepatitis i ipatititha
her*: **I haven't seen her** then
tin ekho thi
to her saftin
with her mazi tis
for her yaftin
that's her afti ineh
that's her towel afti ineh i
petseta tis
herbal tea tsa-i too voonoo
herbs ta votana
here etho
here is/are ... na ...
here you are (offering) oristeh
hers* thiko tis
that's hers afto ineh thiko tis
hey! eh!

hi! (hello) ya soo
hide (something) krivo
(oneself) krivomeh
high psilos
highchair to kareklaki
moroo
highway i eTHniki othos
hill o lofos
him*: **I haven't seen him** then
ton ekho thi
to him safton
with him mazi too
for him yafton
that's him aftos ineh
hip o gofos
hire niki-azo
for hire eniki-azonteh
where can I hire a bike? poo
boro na niki-aso ena
pothilato?
see rent
his*: **it's his car** ineh to
aftokinito too
that's his ineh thiko too
hit khtipao
hitch-hike kano otostop
hobby to khobi
hold kratao
hole i tripa
holiday i thiakopes
on holiday seh thiakopes
Holy Week i Megali
Evthomatha
home to spiti
at home (in my house etc) sto
spiti
(in my country) stin patritha
moo
we go home tomorrow

piyeno stin patritha moo
avrio
honest timios
honey to meli
honeymoon o minas too
melitos
hood (US) to kapo
hope elpizo
 I hope so etsi elpizo
 I hope not elpizo pos okhi
hopefully meh kali tikhi
horn (of car) to klaxon
horrible friktos
horse to alogo
horse riding i ipasia
hospital to nosokomio
hospitality i filoxenia
 thank you for your hospitality
 sas efkharisto ya ti filoxenia
 sas

If you are invited for a
meal, it is customary to
bring a present of sweets
or flowers for your host. You will be
treated very courteously – in some
places (especially small villages)
hospitality is still a matter of honour.
For this reason avoid offending your
hosts by being unfriendly and
unwilling to eat what you are
served. As few Greeks are
vegetarians, it is wise to warn your
host in advance if you cannot eat
certain foods.

hot zestos
 (spicy) kafteros, kaftos
 I'm hot zestenomeh

it's hot today kani poli zesti
simera
hotel to xenothokhio

 There are five hotel
categories: classes A to E,
A allegedly being the best
and E the most basic. All except the
highest category have to keep
within set price limits. Categories
assigned to establishments should
not be regarded as absolutely rigid:
some of the low-ranking places will
also have more expensive rooms
including en suite facilities, and vice
versa. You need your passport or ID
for registration.

hotel room: in my hotel room
 sto thomatio too
 xenothokhioo
hour i ora
house to spiti
house wine to krasi too
magazioo
 see wine
hovercraft to hovercraft, o
a-erolisTHitiras
how pos
 how many? posi?
 how do you do? khero poli

dialogues

 how are you? pos iseh?
 fine, thanks, and you? poli
 kala, efkharisto; ki esi?

 how much is it? poso kani

afto?
5000 drachmas pendeh khiliathes thrakhmes
I'll take it THa to paro

humid igros
humour to khioomor

Avoid jokes about politicians and political parties, Macedonia and the relationship between Greece and Turkey. It's not a good idea to joke or flirt with women you meet in villages as this could cause offence.

hungry pinasmenos
are you hungry? pinas?
hurry (verb) viazomeh
I'm in a hurry viazomeh
there's no hurry then iparkhi via
hurry up! viasoo!
hurt travmatizomeh
it really hurts pona-i poli
husband o sizigos
hydrofoil to iptameno thelfini

I

I ego
ice o pagos
with ice meh pago
no ice, thanks khoris pago, efkharisto
ice cream to pagoto
ice-cream cone to pagoto khonaki

iced coffee to frapeh
ice lolly to pagoto xilaki
idea i ithea
idiot o vlakas
if an
ignition i miza
ill arostos
I feel ill imeh arostos
illness i arostia
imitation (leather etc) i apomimisi
immediately amesos
important spootheos
it's very important ineh poli simandiko
it's not important then ineh spootheo
impossible athinaton
impressive endiposiakos
improve veltiono
I want to improve my Greek THelo na kaliterepso ta Elinika moo
in: it's in the centre ineh sto kendro
in my car mesa sto aftokinito moo
in Athens stin ATHina
in two days from now seh thio meres apo tora
in May sto Ma-io
in English sta Anglika
in Greek sta Elinika
is he in? ineh eki?
in five minutes seh pendeh lepta
inch* i intsa
include perilamvano
does that include meals? afto

perilamvani keh fayito?
is that included in the price?
perilamvaneteh stin timi?
inconvenient akatalilos, avolos
incredible apiTHanos
Indian (adj) Inthikos
indicator to flas, o thiktis
indigestion i thispepsia
indoor pool i esoteriki pisina
indoors mesa
inexpensive ftinos
  see **cheap**
inner tube (for tyre) i sabrela
infection i molinsi
infectious kolitikos
inflammation i anaflexi
informal anepisimos
information i plirofori-es
  do you have any
  information about ...?
  ekheteh tipoteh plirofori-es
  skhetika meh ...?
information desk i plirofori-es
injection i enesi
injured travmatismenos
  she's been injured khtipiseh
in-laws ta peTHerika
innocent aTHo-os
insect to endomo
insect bite to tsibima
  endomoo
  do you have anything for
  insect bites? ekheteh
  tipoteh ya tsibimata apo
  endoma?
insect repellent to AUTAN®
inside mesa
  inside the hotel mesa sto
  xenothokhio

  let's sit inside as katsoomeh
  mesa
insist epimeno
  I insist epimeno
insomnia i a-ipnia
instant coffee to neskafeh
instead andi
  give me that one instead
  thosteh moo afto sti THesi
  too aloo
  instead of ... sti THesi too ...
insulin i insoolini
insurance i asfalia
intelligent exipnos
interested: I'm interested in ...
  enthiaferomeh poli ya ...
interesting enthiaferon
  that's very interesting ineh
  poli enthiaferon
international thi-ethnis
internet to Internet
interpret thi-erminevo
interpreter o/i thi-ermineas
intersection to stavrothromi
interval (at theatre) to thi-alima
into mesa
  I'm not into ... then moo
  aresi ...
introduce sistino
  may I introduce ...? boro na
  sas sistiso ton ...?
invitation i prosklisi
invite proskalo
Ionian Sea to I-onio pelagos
Ireland i Irlanthia
Irish Irlanthos
  I'm Irish (man/woman) imeh
  Irlanthos/Irlantheza
iron (for ironing) to ilektriko

sithero
can you iron these for me?
boriteh na moo ta
sitheroseteh?
is* ineh
island to nisi
it afto
  it is ... ineh ...
  is it ...? ineh ...?
  where is it? poo ineh?
  it's him ineh aftos
  it was ... itan ...
Italian (adj) Italos
  (language) ta Italika
Italy i Italia
itch: it itches meh tro-i

J

jack (for car) o grilos
jacket to sakaki
jar to vazaki
jam i marmelatha
jammed: it's jammed ineh
  frakarismeno
January o I-anooarios
jaw to sagoni
jazz i tzaz
jealous ziliaris
jeans ta tzins
jellyfish i tsookhtra
jersey to fanelaki
jetty o molos
Jewish Evra-ikos
jeweller's to khrisokho-io
jewellery ta kosmimata
job i thoolia
jogging to jogging

to go jogging pao ya jogging
joke to astio
journey to taxithi
  have a good journey! kalo
  taxithi!
jug i kanata
  a jug of water mia kanata
  nero
juice o khimos
July o I-oolios
jump pithao
jumper to poolover
jump leads ta kalothia batarias
junction i thiastavrosi
June o I-oonios
just (only) monon
  just two mono thio
  just for me mono ya mena
  just here akrivos etho
  not just now okhi tora
  we've just arrived molis
  ftasameh

K

keep krato
  keep the change krata ta
  resta
  can I keep it? boro na to
  kratiso?
  please keep it kratisteh to,
  sas parakalo
ketchup to ketsap
kettle i booyota, o vrastiras
key to klithi
  the key for room 201, please
  to klithi ya to 201 (thiakosia
  ena), parakalo

key ring to brelok
kidneys ta nefra
kill skotono
kilo* ena kilo
kilometre* ena khiliometro
how many kilometres is it
to ...? posa khiliometra ineh
mekhri to ...?
kind (generous) evyenikos
that's very kind ineh poli
evyeniko

dialogue

which kind do you want? ti
ithos THeleteh?
I want this/that kind THelo
afto/ekino to ithos

king o vasilias
kiosk to periptero
kiss to fili
(verb) filao

 It is customary to greet
friends and relatives by
kissing them on both
cheeks. The exception to this is
when men greet each other when
they generally shake hands instead.
Foreign visitors are expected to
accept the same kind of greeting,
although you wouldn't necessarily
be expected to reciprocate – in fact
it could cause offence if a foreign
visitor were to kiss someone's wife
in greeting.

kitchen i koozina

kitchenette i koozinoola
Kleenex® ta khartomandila
knee to gonato
knickers i kilota
knife to makheri
knitwear plekta rookha
knock khtipo
knock down khtipo
he's been knocked down
khtipiTHikeh
knock over (object) anapotho-
yirizo
(pedestrian) khtipo
know (somebody) gnorizo
(something, a place) xero
I don't know then xero
I didn't know that then to
ixera
do you know where I can
find ...? mipos xereteh poo
boro na vro ...?

L

label i etiketa
ladies' (toilets) i too-aleta ton
yinekon
ladies' wear yinekia ithi
lady i kiria
lager i bira
see beer
lake i limni
lamb (meat) to arni
lamp i lamba
lane (on motorway) i loritha
(small road) i parothos
language i glosa
language course maTHimata

xenis glosas
large megalos
last telefteos
  last week i perasmeni evthomatha
  last Friday tin perasmeni Paraskevi
  last night kh-THes vrathi
  what time is the last train to Salonika? ti ora ineh to telefteo treno ya tin THesaloniki?
late arga
  sorry I'm late meh sinkhoriteh poo aryisa
  the train was late to treno ikheh kaTHisterisi
  we must go – we'll be late prepi na piyenoomeh – THa aryisoomeh
  it's getting late nikhtoni
later argotera
  I'll come back later THa yiriso argotera
  see you later adio, THa ta xanapoomeh
  later on argotera
latest o pi-o prosfatos
  by Wednesday at the latest tin Tetarti to argotero
laugh yelo
launderette to plindirio rookhon
laundromat to plindirio rookhon
laundry (clothes) i boogatha, ta aplita
  (place) to kaTHaristirio
lavatory i too-aleta

law o nomos
lawn to grasithi
lawyer o/i thikigoros
laxative to kaTHartiko
lazy tebelis
lead (electrical) o agogos
  (verb) othigo
  where does this lead to? poo othiyi afto?
leaf to filo
leaflet to thiafimistiko
leak i thiaro-i
  (verb) stazo
  the roof leaks i steyi stazi
learn maTHeno
least: not in the least katholoo
  at least toolakhiston
leather to therma
leave (bag etc) afino
  (go away) fevgo
  (forget) xekhnao
  I am leaving tomorrow fevgo avrio
  he left yesterday efiyeh kh-THes
  may I leave this here? boro nafiso afto etho?
  I left my coat in the bar afisa tin tsanda moo sto bar
  when does the bus for Athens leave? poteh fevyi to leoforio ya tin ATHina?
leeks ta prasa
left aristera
  on the left pros ta aristera
  to the left pros ta aristera
  turn left stripseh aristera
  there's none left then emineh tipoteh

left-handed aristerokhiras
left luggage (office) o khoros filaxis aposkevon
leg to pothi
lemon to lemoni
lemonade i lemonatha
lemon tea tsai meh lemoni
lend thanizo
  will you lend me your ... ? THa moo thanisis to thiko soo ...?
lens (of camera) o fakos
lesbian i lesvia
less ligotero
  less than ligotero apo
  less expensive ligotero akrivo
lesson to maTHima
let (allow) epitrepo
  will you let me know? THa moo to pis?
  I'll let you know THa soo po
  let's go for something to eat pameh na fameh kati
let off katevazo
  will you let me off at ...? THa meh katevaseteh sto ...?
letter to grama
  do you have any letters for me? ekho kanena grama?
letterbox to gramatokivotio

 Letterboxes in Greece are usually bright yellow. If you are confronted with two slots, 'esoteriko' is for domestic mail and 'exoteriko' is for overseas.

lettuce to marooli

lever o levi-es
library i vivlioTHiki
licence i athi-a
lid to kapaki
lie (tell untruth) leo psemata
lie down xaplono
life i zo-i
lifebelt i zoni asfalias
lifeguard o navagosostis
life jacket to sosivio
lift (in building) to asanser
  could you give me a lift? boriteh na meh pateh?
  would you like a lift? THeleteh na sas pao?
light to fos
  (not heavy) elafros
  do you have a light? (for cigarette) ekhis fotia?
  light green anikhto prasino
light bulb i lamba, o glombos
  I need a new light bulb khriazomeh mia kenoorya lamba
lighter (cigarette) o anaptiras
lightning i astrapi
like (verb) moo aresi
  I like it moo aresi afto
  I like going for walks moo aresi na piyeno peripato
  I like you moo aresis
  I don't like it then moo aresi afto
  do you like it? soo aresi afto?
  I'd like to go swimming THa iTHela na pao ya kolimbi
  I'd like a beer THa iTHela mia bira
  would you like a drink? THa

iTHeles ena poto?
would you like to go for a walk? THa iTHeles na pameh mia volta?
what's it like? meh ti miazi?
I want one like this THelo ena san ki afto
lime to moskholemono
lime cordial to lime
line (on paper) i grami
(phone) i tilefoniki grami
could you give me an outside line? THa moo thoseteh grami?
lips ta khilia
lip salve to vootiro kakao
lipstick to krayon
liqueur to liker
listen akoo-o
litre* ena litro
a litre of white wine ena litro aspro krasi
little mikros
just a little, thanks ligo mono, efkharisto
a little milk ligo gala
a little bit more ligo akomi
live zo
we live together sizoomeh

dialogue

where do you live? poo menis?
I live in London meno sto Lonthino

lively thrastirios
liver to sikoti

loaf i fradzola
lobby (in hotel) to saloni
lobster o astakos
local dopios
can you recommend a local wine/restaurant? boriteh na mas sistiseteh ena dopio krasi/estiatorio?
see **wine**
lock i klitharia
(verb) klithono
it's locked ineh klithomeno
lock in klithono mesa
lock out klithono apo exo
I've locked myself out klithoTHika apexo
locker (for luggage etc) i THiritha
lollipop to glifidzoori
London to LonTHino
long makris
how long will it take to fix it? poso kero THa pari ya na to ftiaxeteh?
how long does it take? posi ora kani?
a long time polis keros, poli ora
one day/two days longer mia mera/thio meres parapano
long-distance call to iperastiko tilefonima
look: I'm just looking, thanks efkharisto, vlepo mono
you don't look well then feneseh kala
look out! prosexe!
can I have a look? boro na tho?

look after prosekho, frondizo
look at kitazo
look for psakhno
 I'm looking for ... psakhno
 ya ...
look forward to perimeno
 meh khara
 I'm looking forward to it to
 perimeno pos keh pos
loose (handle etc) khalaros
lorry to fortigo
lose khano
 I've lost my way ekho
 khaTHi
 I'm lost, I want to get to ...
 ekho khaTHi, THelo na pao
 sto ...
 I've lost my (hand)bag ekhasa
 tin tsanda moo
lost property (office) to grafio
 apolesTHendon
lot: a lot, lots pola
 not a lot okhi pola
 a lot of people poli anTHropi
 a lot bigger poli megalitero
 I like it a lot moo aresi poli
lotion i losion
loud thinatos
lounge to saloni
love i agapi
 (verb) agapo
 I love Greece latrevo tin
 Elatha
lovely oreos
low khamilos
luck i tikhi
 good luck! kali tikhi!
luggage i aposkeves
luggage trolley to karotsaki ya

 tis aposkeves
lump (on body) to priximo
lunch to yevma
lungs o pnevmonas
luxurious (hotel, furnishings)
 politelis
luxury politelias

M

Macedonia i Makethonia
machine i mikhani
mad (insane) trelos
 (angry) trelos apo THimo
magazine to periothiko
maid (in hotel) i servitora
maiden name to patronimo
mail ta gramata, to
 takhithromio
 (verb) takhithromo
 is there any mail for me?
 ekho kanena grama?
 see **post**
mailbox to gramatokivotio
 see **letterbox**
main kirios
main course to kirio piato
Mainland Greece i Ipirotiki
 Elatha
main post office kendriko
 takhithromio
main road (in town) o
 kendrikos thromos
 (in country) o aftokinito-
 thromos
main switch o kendrikos
 thiakoptis
make (brand name) i marka

(verb) kano
I make it 500 drachmas
ipoloyizo oti kani pedakosi-
es thrakhmes
what is it made of? apo ti
ineh ftiagmeno?
make-up to make-up
man o andras
manager o thi-efTHindis, o
manager
can I see the manager? boro
na tho ton thi-efTHindi?
manageress i thi-efTHindria

manners
It is bad manners to
refuse someone else's
offer to pay for your share in a meal,
or their offer to pay for the wine; the
equivalent of the two-finger gesture
is a five-finger or a raised middle
finger gesture; avoid these, unless
you want to get in trouble.

manual to aftokinito meh
kanonikes takhitites
many pola
not many liga, okhi pola
map o khartis
March o Martios
margarine i margarini
market i agora
marmalade i marmelatha
married: I'm married (said by a
man/woman) imeh
pandremenos/pandremeni
are you married? (said to a
man/woman) isteh
pandremenos/pandremeni?

mascara i maskara
match (football etc) to mats, o
agonas
matches ta spirta
material (fabric) to ifasma
matter: it doesn't matter then
pirazi
what's the matter? ti
simveni?
mattress to stroma
May o Ma-ios
may: may I have another one?
THa iTHela ki alo ena?
may I come in? boro na bo?
may I see it? boro na to
tho?
may I sit here? boro na
kaTHiso etho?
maybe isos
mayonnaise i ma-yoneza
me* emena
that's for me afto ineh ya
mena
send it to me stilteh to seh
mena
me too ki ego episis
meal to fa-yito

dialogue

> **did you enjoy your meal?**
> sas areseh to fayito?
> **it was excellent, thank you**
> itan poli nostimo,
> efkharisto

mean: what do you mean? ti
eno-iteh?

dialogue

what does this word
mean? ti simeni afti i lexi?
it means ... in English
simeni ... sta Anglika

measles i ilara
meat to kreas
mechanic o mikhanikos
medicine to farmako
Mediterranean i Meso-yios
medium (adj: size) metrios
medium-dry imixiro krasi
medium-rare misopsimeno
medium-sized metrio
  meyeTHos
meet sinandao
  nice to meet you kharika
  poo sas gnorisa
  where shall I meet you? poo
  THa sas sinandiso?
meeting i sinandisi
meeting place to meros
  sinandisis
melon to peponi
men i anthres
mend thiorTHono
  could you mend this for me?
  boriteh na moo to
  ftiaxeteh?
menswear ta anthrika ithi
mention anafero
  don't mention it parakalo
menu to menoo
  may I see the menu, please?
  boro na tho to menoo,
  parakalo?
  see Menu Reader

message to minima
  are there any messages for
  me? iparkhi kanena minima
  ya mena?
I want to leave a message
  for ... thelo nafiso ena
  minima ya ...
metal to metalo
metre* to metro
microwave (oven) o foornos
  mikrokimaton, to
  microwave
midday to mesimeri
  at midday to mesimeri
middle: in the middle sti
  mesi
  in the middle of the night
  arga ti nikhta
  the middle one to meseo
midnight ta mesanikhta
  at midnight ta mesanikhta
might: I might THa boroosa
  I might not then THa
  boroosa
  I might want to stay another
  day bori na THelo na mino
  akomi mia mera
migraine i imikrania
mild (weather) eTHrios
  (taste) elafros
mile* ena mili
milk to gala
milkshake to milkshake
millimetre* ena khiliosto
minced meat o kimas
mind: never mind then pirazi
  I've changed my mind alaxa
  gnomi

dialogue

do you mind if I open the
window? seh pirazi an
anixo to paraTHiro?
no, I don't mind okhi, then
meh pirazi

mine*: it's mine ineh thiko
moo
mineral water to
emfialomeno nero
mint (sweet) i menda
minute to lepto
 in a minute seh ena lepto
 just a minute ena lepto
mirror o kaTHreftis
Miss thespinis
miss khano
 I missed the bus ekhasa to
 leoforio
missing lipi
 one of my ... is missing lipi
 ena ...
 there's a suitcase missing lipi
 mia valitsa
mist i katakhnia
mistake to laTHos
 I think there's a mistake
 nomizo oti iparkhi ena
 laTHos etho
 sorry, I've made a mistake
 meh sinkhoriteh, ekana
 laTHos
misunderstanding i parexiyisi
mix-up: sorry, there's been a
 mix-up meh sinkhoriteh,
 iparkhi ena berthema
modern modernos

modern art gallery i galeri
 modernas teknis
Modern Greek ta Nea Elinika
moisturizer i ithatiki krema
moment: I won't be a moment
 mia stigmi parakalo
monastery to monastiri
Monday i theftera
money ta lefta
month o minas
monument to mnimio
moon to fengari
moped to mikhanaki
more* perisoteros
 can I have some more water,
 please? akomi ligo nero,
 parakalo
 more expensive/interesting
 pio akrivo/enthiaferon
 more than 50 perisotero apo
 peninda
 more than that pio poli ap
 afto
 a lot more poli perisotero

dialogue

would you like some
more? THa THelateh ligo
akomi?
no, no more for me, thanks
okhi, okhi alo ya mena,
efkharisto
how about you? ki esis?
I don't want any more,
thanks then THelo alo,
efkharisto

morning to pro–i

this morning simera to pro-i
in the morning to pro-i
mosquito to koonoopi
mosquito repellent to fithaki
 ya ta koonoopia
most: I like this one most of all
 afto moo aresi pio poli apo
 ola
most of the time siniTHos
most tourists i perisoteri
 tooristes
mostly kirios
mother i mitera
motorbike i motosikleta
motorboat i varka meh
 mikhani
motorway i eTHniki othos
mountain to voono
 in the mountains pano sta
 voona
mountaineering i orivasia
mouse to pondiki
moustache to moostaki
mouth to stoma
mouth ulcer pliyi sto stoma
move metakino
 he's moved to another room
 piyeh seh alo thomatio
 could you move your car?
 boriteh na metakiniseteh to
 aftokinito sas?
 could you move up a little?
 boriteh na metakiniTHiteh
 ligo?
 where has it moved to? poo
 metaferTHikeh?
movie to film
movie theater o kinimato-
 grafos, to sinema

Mr kiri-eh
Mrs kiria
Ms thespinis
much poli
 much better/worse poli
 kalitera/khirotera
 much hotter poli pio zesta
 not much okhi poli
 not very much okhi para poli
 I don't want very much then
 THelo para poli
mud i laspi
mug (for drinking) i koopa
 I've been mugged meh
 listepsan
mum i mama
mumps i parotititha
museum to moosio

There is usually an
admission charge for both
state-run and private
museums, archaeological sites and
art galleries. Entrance to all state-
run sites and museums is free to
everyone on Sundays and public
holidays. Opening hours vary
considerably (and often change) and
you should find these out before you
go in order to avoid disappointment.
Some small museums and sites may
close for a long lunch. Churches and
monasteries are usually open to
visitors when there is no service.
Visitors are requested to be properly
dressed (long trousers for men; long
sleeves, long skirt and no trousers
for women).

mushrooms ta manitaria
music i moosiki
musician o/i moosikos
Muslim (adj) Moosoolmanikos
mussels ta mithia
must: I must ... prepi na ...
  I mustn't drink alcohol then
  prepi na pio alko-ol
mustard i moostartha
my* o/i/to ... moo
myself: I'll do it myself THa to
  kano o ithios
  by myself apo monos moo

N

nail (finger) to nikhi
  (metal) to karfi
nailbrush i voortsa ya ta
  nikhia
nail varnish to mano
name to onoma
  my name's John meh leneh
  John
  what's your name? pos seh
  leneh?
  what is the name of this
  street? pos leneh afto to
  thromo?

It is not uncommon to
hear Greeks address or
greet each other formally
by their profession: 'kalimera yatreh'
('good morning doctor'). First names
are only used between friends and
relatives. In formal situations 'kirios'
(Mr) 'kiri-eh' (Mr) or 'kiria' (Mrs/

Miss/Ms) + surname are used. It is
possible, however, to use 'kiri-eh/
kiria' + first name in semi-formal
relationships, e.g. to a neighbour
who is older than you, or a
shopkeeper you know well.

napkin i petseta
nappy i pana
narrow (street) stenos
nasty (person) apesios
  (weather, accident) askhimos
national eTHnikos
nationality i eTHnikotita
natural fisikos
nausea i naftia
navy (blue) ble maren
near konda
  is it near the city centre?
  ineh konda sto kendro tis
  polis?
  do you go near the
  Acropolis? pernateh apo tin
  Akropoli?
  where is the nearest ...? poo
  ineh to plisi-estero ...?
nearby etho konda
nearly skhethon
necessary aparetitos,
  anangeos
neck o lemos
necklace to koli-e
necktie i gravata
need: I need ...
  khriazomeh ...
  do I need to pay? khriazeteh
  na pliroso?
needle i velona
negative (film) to arnitiko

neither: neither (one) of them
kanenas apo aftoos
neither ... nor ... ooteh ...
ooteh ...
nephew o anipsios
net (in sport) to thikhti
network map o khartis
othikoo thiktioo
never poteh

dialogue

have you ever been to
Athens? ekheteh pa-i
poteh stin ATHina?
no, never, I've never been
there okhi, poteh, then
ekho pa-i poteh eki

new neos, kenooryos
news (radio, TV etc) ta nea
newsagent's to praktorio
efimerithon
newspaper i efimeritha
newspaper kiosk to periptero
meh efimerithes
New Year to neo etos

New Year's Eve and Day
are traditionally family
celebrations, although
nowadays many Greeks celebrate
both by going out to expensive
dinner dances. It is traditional to
have fireworks at midnight and cut
the cake with the lucky coin in it.

Happy New Year!
eftikhismenos o kenooryos

khronos!
New Year's Eve i
protokhronia
New Zealand i Nea Zilanthia
New Zealander: I'm a New
Zealander (man/woman) imeh
Neozilanthos/Neozilantheza
next epomenos
the next turning on the left i
epomeni strofi sta aristera
the next street on the left o
epomenos thromos sta
aristera
at the next stop stin epomeni
stasi
next week tin ali evtho-
matha
next to thipla apo
nice (food) nostimos
(looks, view etc) oreos
(person) kalos
niece i anipsia
night i nikhta
at night to vrathi
good night kalinikhta

dialogue

do you have a single room
for one night? ekheteh ena
mono thomatio ya mia
nikhta?
yes, madam malista, kiria
moo
how much is it per night?
poso kani ti mia nikhta?
it's 5000 drachmas for one
night ineh pendeh
khiliathes thrakhmes ya

mia nikhta
thank you, I'll take it
efkharisto, THa to kliso

nightclub to nait-klab
nightdress to nikhtiko
night porter o nikhterinos
THiroros
no okhi
I've no change then ekho
psila
there's no ... left then
emineh kaTHoloo ...
no way! apokli-eteh!
oh no! (upset) okh!, o okhi!
nobody kanenas
there's nobody there then
ineh kanis eki
noise i fasaria
noisy: it's too noisy ekhi poli
fasaria
non-alcoholic khoris alko-ol
none kanis
non-smoking compartment o
khoros ya mi kapnizondes
noon to mesimeri
no-one kanenas
nor: nor do I ooteh kego
normal fisiolo-yikos
north o voras
in the north sta vori-a
north of Athens vori-a tis
ATHinas
northeast o vorio-anatolikos
northwest o vorio-thitikos
northern vorios
Northern Ireland i Vorios
Irlanthia
Norway i Norviyia

Norwegian (adj) Norviyikos
nose i miti
nosebleed i emorayia sti miti
not* then
no, I'm not hungry okhi, then
pina-o
I don't want any, thank you
efkharisto, then THelo
it's not necessary then ineh
aparetito
I didn't know that then to
ixera
not that one – this one okhi
afto – to alo
note (banknote) to khartonomisma
notebook to blokaki, to
simiomatario
notepaper (for letters) to kharti
alilografias
nothing tipoteh
nothing for me, thanks
tipoteh ya mena, efkharisto
nothing else tipoteh alo
novel to miTHistorima
November o No-emvrios
now tora
number* o ariTHmos
I've got the wrong number
pira laTHos noomero
what is your phone number?
pio ineh to tilefono soo?
number plate i pinakitha
nurse (man/woman) o
nosokomos/i nosokoma
nursery slope i pista
ekmaTHisis
nut (for bolt) to paximathi
nuts to karithi

O

o'clock* i ora
occupied (toilet) katilimenos
October o Oktovrios
odd (strange) paraxenos
of* too
off (lights) klisto
  it's just off Omonia Square
  ligo pio eki apo tin Omoni-a
  we're off tomorrow
  fevgoomeh avrio
offensive (language, behaviour)
  prosvlitikos
office (place of work) to grafio
officer (said to policeman)
  astinomeh
often sikhna
  not often okhi sikhna
  how often are the buses?
  kaTHeh poteh ekhi leoforia?
oil (for car) ta lathia
  (for salad) to lathi
ointment i alifi
OK endaxi
  are you OK? iseh kala?
  is that OK with you? iseh
  efkharistimenos etsi?
  is it OK to ...? pirazi na ...?
  that's OK thanks (it doesn't
  matter) ineh endaxi,
  efkharisto
  I'm OK (nothing for me) tipoteh
  ya mena
  (I feel OK) imeh mia khara
  is this train OK for ...? afto
  ineh to treno ya ...?
  I said I'm sorry, OK? soo ipa

signomi, endaxi?
old (person) yeros
  (thing) palios

dialogue

  how old are you? poso
  khronon iseh?
  I'm twenty-five imeh
  ikosi-pendeh khronon
  and you? ki esi?

old-fashioned demodeh
old town (old part of town) i palia
  poli
  in the old town stin palia poli
olive oil to eleolatho
olives i eli-es
omelette i omeleta
on pano
  (lights) anikhto
  on the street/beach sto
  thromo/stin paralia
  is it on this road? ineh safto
  to thromo?
  on the plane mesa sto
  a-eroplano
  on Saturday to Savato
  on television stin tileorasi
  I haven't got it on me then to
  ekho mazi moo
  this one's on me (drink) ego
  kernao afti ti fora
  the light wasn't on to fos
  then itan anikhto
  what's on tonight? ti pezi
  simera?
once (one time) mia fora
  at once (immediately) amesos

one* enas, mia, ena
 the white one to aspro
one-way ticket: a one-way
 ticket to ... ena aplo ya ...
onion to kremithi
only mono
 only one mono ena
 it's only 6 o'clock ineh mono
 exi i ora
 I've only just got here molis
 eftasa
on/off switch o thiakoptis
open (adj) aniktos
 (verb: door, shop) anigo
 when do you open? poteh
 aniyeteh?
 I can't get it open then boro
 na to anixo
 in the open air stin ipeTHro
opening times ores litooryias
open ticket isitirio meh
 anikhti epistrofi
opera i opera
operation (medical) i enkhirisi
operator (telephone: man/woman)
 o tilefonitis/i tilefonitria

The number for the
international operator is
161.

opposite: the opposite
 direction stin andiTHeti
 katefTHinsi
 the bar opposite to bar
 apenandi
 opposite my hotel apenandi
 apo to xenothokhio moo
optician o optikos

or i
orange (fruit) to portokali
 (colour) portokali
orange juice i portokalatha
orchestra i orkhistra
order: can we order now? (in
 restaurant) boroomeh na
 paragiloomeh tora?
 I've already ordered, thanks
 ekho ithi paragili, efkharisto
 I didn't order this then
 paragila afto
 out of order then litooryi
ordinary kanonikos
other alos, ali, alo
 the other one to alo
 the other day tis pro-ales
 I'm waiting for the others
 perimeno toos aloos
 do you have any others?
 ekheteh tipoteh ala?
otherwise thiaforetika
our* o/i/to ... mas
ours* thikos mas
out: he's out then ineh etho
 three kilometres out of town
 tria khiliometra exo apo tin
 poli
outdoors exo
outside ... exo ...
 can we sit outside?
 borroomeh na
 kaTHisoomeh exo?
oven o foornos
over: over here etho
 over there eki, eki pera
 over 500 pano apo
 pendakosia
 it's over teliosa

overcharge: you've overcharged me meh khreosateh parapano

overcoat to palto

overlook: I'd like a room overlooking the courtyard THa iTHela ena THomatio meh THea stin avli

overnight (travel) oloniktio

overtake prosperno

owe: how much do I owe you? poso sas khrostao?

own: my own ... thiko moo ...

are you on your own? iseh monos soo?

I'm on my own imeh monos moo

owner (man/woman) o ithioktitis/i ithioktitria

P

pack (verb) ftiakhno tis valitses

a pack of ... ena paketo ...

package (parcel) to paketo

package holiday i organomeni ekthromi

packed lunch to etimo mesimeriano

packet: a packet of cigarettes ena paketo tsigara

padlock to looketo, i klitharia

page (of book) i selitha

could you page Mr ...? boriteh na fonaxeteh ton kirio ...?

pain o ponos

I have a pain here esTHanomeh ena pono etho

painful othiniros

painkillers to pafsipono

paint i boya

painting o pinakas zografikis

pair: a pair of ... ena zevgari ...

Pakistani (adj) Pakistanikos

palace to palati

pale khlomos

pale blue galazios

pan to tapsi

panties to slip, i kilotes

pants (underwear: men's) to sovrako

(women's) to slip, i kilotes

(US: trousers) to pandaloni

pantyhose to kalson

paper to kharti

(newspaper) i efimeriTHa

a piece of paper ena komati kharti

paper handkerchiefs ta khartomandila

parcel to thema

pardon (me)? (didn't understand/hear) signomi?

parents: my parents i gonis moo

parents-in-law ta peTHerika

park to parko

(verb) parkaro

can I park here? boro na parkaro etho?

parking lot to parking

part to meros

partner (boyfriend, girlfriend) o

fílos, i fíli
party (group) i omatha
 (celebration) to parti
pass (in mountains) to perasma
passenger o/i epivatis
passport to thiavatirio
past: in the past sto
 parelTHon
 just past the information
 office amesos meta to grafio
 pliroforion
path to monopati
pattern to s-khethio
pavement to pezothromio
 on the pavement sto
 pezothromio
 pavement café kafenio sto
 thromo
pay plirono
 can I pay, please? boro na
 pliroso, parakalo?
 it's already paid for ineh ithi
 pliromeno

dialogue

 who's paying? pios THa
 plirosi?
 I'll pay ego THa pliroso
 no, you paid last time, I'll
 pay okhi, esi pliroses tin
 teleftea fora, ego THa
 pliroso

payphone to tilefono meh
 kermata
peaceful irinikos
peach to rothakino
peanuts fistikia arapika

pear to akhlathi
peas ta bizelia
peculiar (taste, custom)
 paraxenos
pedestrian crossing i thiavasi
 pezon
pedestrian precinct o pezo-
 thromos
peg (for washing) to mandalaki
 (for tent) to palooki
pen to stilo
pencil to molivi
penfriend (male/female) o fílos
 thi' alilografias/i fíli thi'
 alilografias
penicillin i penikilini
penknife o soo-yias
pensioner o/i sindaxiookhos
people i anTHropi
 the other people in the hotel i
 ali anTHropi sto xeno-
 thokhio
 too many people ipervolika
 poli anTHropi
pepper (spice) to piperi
 (vegetable) i piperia
peppermint (sweet) i menda
per: per night tin vrathia
 how much per day? poso tin
 imera?
per cent tis ekato
perfect telios
perfume to aroma
perhaps isos
 perhaps not isos okhi
period (time, menstruation) i
 periothos
perm i permanand
permit i athia

person to **atomo**
personal stereo to walkman®
petrol i **venzini**

Petrol is either 3-star 'apli' (regular), 4-star 'sooper' (super) or unleaded 'amolivthi'. Most petrol stations are staffed, not self-service.
see **garage**

petrol can ena thokhio venzinis
petrol station to venzinathiko
pharmacy to farmakio
 see **chemist's**
phone to tilefono
 (verb) perno tilefono, tilefono

Phone, telegraph, fax, and telex facilities are provided by OTE (Greek Telecommunications). In the largest towns, there is sometimes an OTE branch which opens 24 hours, but most are likely to be open from 7 am to 10 or 11 pm Local calls are relatively straightforward – in many hotel lobbies or cafés you'll find red payphones which presently take a 10-drachma coin. Long-distance and international calls can be made from local branches of the OTE and from street kiosks (periptero) which have a telephone meter (o metritis) – you pay after having made the call. It is, however, preferable to make international calls from an OTE branch as a periptero can be

unreliable and the line may be bad. Reverse charge calls can only be made from branches of the OTE. Phone-cards are sold from newspaper or tobacco kiosks. All public phones in Athens now take phonecards instead of coins.
see **speak**

phone book o tilefonikos katalogos
phonecard i tilekarta
phone number o ariTHmos tilefonoo
photo i fotografia
 excuse me, could you take a photo of us? meh sinkhoriteh, THa boroosateh na mas pareteh mia fotografia?
phrase book to vivlio thialogon
piano to piano
pickpocket o portofolas
pick up: **will you be there to pick me up?** THa iseh eki na meh paris?
picnic to piknik
picture i ikona
pie i pita
 (meat) i kreatopita
 (fruit) i frootopita
piece to komati
 a piece of ... ena komati ...
pill to khapi
 I'm on the pill perno antisiliptika khapia
pillow to maxilari
pillow case i maxilaroTHiki

pin i karfitsa

pineapple o ananas

pineapple juice o khimos anana

pink roz

pipe (for smoking) i pipa, to tsibooki

(for water) o solinas

pipe cleaners kaTHaristis pipas

Piraeus o Pireas

pistachio nuts fistiki-a Eyinis

pity: it's a pity ineh krima

pizza i pitsa

place to meros

is this place taken? ineh piasmeni afti i THesi?

at your place sti THesi soo

at his place sti THesi too

plain (not patterned) monokhromo

plane to a-eroplano

by plane meh to a-eroplano

plant to fito

plaster cast o yipsos

plasters to lefkoplast

plastic plastikos

(credit cards) i pistotiki karta

plastic bag i plastiki sakoola

plate to piato

plate-smashing spasimo pi-aton

platform i platforma

which platform is for Patras, please? pia platforma ya tin Patra, parakalo?

play (in theatre) to THeatriko ergo

(verb) pezo

playground to yipetho

pleasant efkharistos

please parakalo

yes please neh, parakalo

could you please ...? THa boroosateh, parakalo, na ...?

please don't stamata, seh parakalo

pleased to meet you kharika poli

pleasure: i efkharistisi

my pleasure efkharistisi moo

plenty: plenty of ... poli/ pola ...

there's plenty of time iparkhi arketi ora

that's plenty, thanks efkharisto, arki

pliers i pensa

plug (electrical) i briza

(for car) to boozi

(in sink) i tapa

plumber o ithravlikos

pm* meta mesimvrias

poached egg to avgo poseh

pocket i tsepi

point: two point five thio koma pendeh

there's no point then iparkhi logos

points (in car) i platines

poisonous thilitiriothis

police i astinomia

call the police! kalesteh tin astinomia!

There is a separate tourist police force called 'Tooristiki Astinomia' which should be able to deal with any problems you may have. You should phone 171 for the tourist police.

policeman o astifilakas
police station to astinomiko tmima
policewoman i astinomikos
polish to verniki
polite evgenikos
polluted molismenos
pony to poni
pool (for swimming) i pisina
poor (not rich) ftokhos
  (quality) kakos
pop music i moosiki pop
pop singer o tragoothistis pop, i tragoothistria pop
population o pliTHismos
pork to khirino
port (for boats) to limani
  (drink) i mavrothafni
porter (in hotel) o akh-THoforos
portrait to portreto
posh (restaurant) akrivos
  (people) kiriles
possible thinatos
  is it possible to ...? ineh thinaton na ...?
  as ... as possible oso to thinaton ...
post (mail) ta gramata
  (verb) takhithromo
  could you post this for me?

boriteh na moo to takhithromiseteh?
postbox to gramatokivotio
postcard i kartpostal
postcode o takhithromikos kothikos
poster (for room) to poster
  (in street) i afisa
post office to takhithromio

Post office hours are approximately 8 am to 2.30 pm Monday to Friday. Some post offices in the larger cities may be open until 9 pm from Monday to Friday for postal services only. You may be asked to open a heavy envelope or registered letter in order to show its contents. Stamps can also be bought from street kiosks, but the proprietors are entitled to a 10 per cent commission and never seem to know the current international rates.

poste restante post restand
pots and pans (cooking implements) katsaroles keh tigania
potato i patata
potato chips ta tsips
pottery ta keramika
pound* (money) i lira
  (weight) i libra
power cut i thiakopi revmatos
power point o revmatothotis
practise: I want to practise my Greek THelo na exaskiso ta

Elinika moo

prawns i garithes
(larger) i karavitha
prefer: I prefer ... protimo ...
pregnant engios
prescription (for chemist) i
  sindayi
present (gift) to thoro
president (of country) o pro-
  ethros
pretty (beautiful) omorfos,
  oreos
  (quite) arketa
  it's pretty expensive ineh
  arketa akrivo
price i timi
priest o papas
prime minister o proTHi-
  poorgos
printed matter ta endipa
priority (in driving) i protereotita
prison i filaki
private ithiotikos
private bathroom to ithiotiko
  banio
probably piTHanon
problem to provlima
  no problem! kanena
  provlima!
program(me) to programa
promise: I promise
  iposkhomeh
pronounce: how is this
  pronounced? pos to proferis
  afto?
properly (repaired, locked etc)
  opos prepi
protection factor (of suntan
  lotion) o vaTHmos prostasias

Protestant o
  thiamartiromenos
public convenience i
  kinokhristi tooaleta
public holiday i thimosia aryia
pudding (dessert) to glikisma
pull travao
pullover to poolover
puncture to foo-it
purple mov
purse (for money) to portofoli
  (US: handbag) i tsanda
push sprokhno
pushchair to karotsaki
put vazo
  where can I put ...? poo boro
  na valo ...?
  could you put us up for the
  night? boriteh na mas
  filoxeniseteh ya ena vrathi?
pyjamas i pitzames

Q

quality i piotita
quarantine i karantina
quarter to tetarto
quayside: on the quayside stin
  provlita
question i erotisi
queue i oora
quick grigora
  that was quick afto itan
  grigoro
  what's the quickest way
  there? pios ineh o pio
  grigoros thromos?
  fancy a quick drink? ekhis

orexi ya ena poto sta
grigora?
quickly grigora
quiet (place, hotel) isikhos
quiet! siopi!
quince to kithoni
quite (fairly) arketa
(very) telios
that's quite right poli sosta
quite a lot arketa

R

rabbit o lagos
race (for runners, cars) i koorsa
racket i raketa
radiator (in room) to kalorifer
(of car) to psiyio aftokinitoo
radio to rathiofono
on the radio sto rathiofono
rail: by rail sithirothromikos
railway o sithirothromos
rain i vrokhi
in the rain mes tin vrokhi
it's raining vrekhi
raincoat i kabardina, to
athiavrokho
rape o viasmos
rare (steak) okhi poli psimeno
rash (on skin) to exanTHima
raspberry to vatomooro
rat o arooreos
rate (for changing money) i timi
sinalagmatos
rather: it's rather good ineh
malon kalo
I'd rather ... THa protimoosa
na ...

razor (dry) to xirafaki
(electric) i xiristiki mikhani
razor blades to xirafaki
read thiavazo
ready etimos
are you ready? (to man/woman)
iseh etimos/etimi?
I'm not ready yet then imeh
etimos akomi

dialogue

when will it be ready?
poteh THa ineh etimo?
it should be ready in a
couple of days THa prepi
na ineh etimo seh mia-
thio meres

real pragmatikos
really pragmatika
(very) poli
really! (surprise, doubt) psemata!
really? (interest) aliTHia?
rearview mirror o kaTHreftis
aftokinitoo
reasonable (prices etc) loyikos
receipt i apothixi
recently prosfata
reception (in hotel) i resepsion
(for guests) i thexiosi
at reception stin paralavi
reception desk to grafio
ipothokhis
receptionist i/o resepsionist
recognize anagnorizo
recommend: could you
recommend ...? boriteh na
moo sistiseteh ...?

record (music) o thiskos
red kokinos
red wine to kokino krasi
refund i epistrofi khrimaton
  can I have a refund? moo
  epistrefondeh khrimata?
region i periokhi
registered: by registered mail
  sistimeno
registration number o
  ariTHmos kikloforias
relative o/i singenis
religion i THriskia
remember: I don't remember
  then THimameh
  I remember THimameh
  do you remember?
  THimaseh?
rent (for apartment etc) to enikio
  (verb) niki-azo
  to/for rent eniki-azonteh

dialogue

I'd like to rent a car THa
iTHela na nikiaso ena
aftokinito
for how long? ya poso
kero?
two days ya thio meres
this is our range afti ineh i
lista mas
I'll take the ... THa paro
to ...
is that with unlimited
mileage? ineh meh
aperioristo ariTHmo
khiliometron?
it is neh, ineh

can I see your licence
please? boro na tho tin
athi-a sas, parakalo?
and your passport keh to
thiavatirio sas
is insurance included?
simperilamvaneteh i
asfalia?
yes, but you pay the first
3,000 drachmas neh, ala
esis THa pliroseteh tis
protes tris khiliathes
thrakhmes
can you leave a deposit of
1,000 drachmas? boriteh
na afiseteh ya engi-isi
khili-es thrakhmes?

rented car to enikiasmeno
aftokinito
repair i episkevi
  can you repair it? boriteh na
  to episkevaseteh?
repeat epanalamvano
  could you repeat that?
  boriteh na to
  epanalaveteh?
reservation (train, bus) to
  klisimo THesis

dialogue

I have a reservation ekho
kani mia kratisi
yes sir, what name please?
malista, kiri-eh; seh ti
onoma, parakalo?

reserve krato

dialogue

can I reserve a table for
tonight? boro na kliso ena
trapezi ya apopseh?
yes madam, for how many
people? malista, kiria
moo; ya posa atoma?
for two ya thio
and for what time? keh ya
ti ora?
for eight o'clock ya tis
okhto
and could I have your
name please? to onoma
sas, parakalo?
see alphabet page 9 for
spelling

rest: I need a rest
khriazomeh xekoorasi
the rest of the group to
ipolipo groop
restaurant to estiatorio

There are two basic types
of restaurants: the
'estiatorio' and the
taverna. Distinctions between the
two are slight but restaurants can be
more formal and more expensive
than tavernas. The latter may be
found more often in the old parts of
towns – they may have a more
limited choice of dishes and may
not display a menu. The best
strategy is to go where the Greeks
go.

rest room i too-aleta
see toilet
retired: I'm retired imeh seh
sindaxi
return: a return to ... ena
isitirio met epistrofis ya to ...
reverse charge call to
tilefonima kolekt
reverse gear i opisTHen
revolting apesios
Rhodes i Rothos
rib to plevro
rice to rizi
rich (person) ploosios
(food) varis
ridiculous yelios
right (correct) sostos
(not left) thexia
you were right ikhes thikio
that's right sosta
this can't be right afto then
bori na ineh sosto
right! endaxi!
is this the right road for ...?
ineh aftos o sostos thromos
ya ...?
on the right sta thexia
turn right stripseh thexia
right-hand drive meh thexio
timoni
ring (on finger) to thaktilithi
I'll ring you THa soo
tilefoniso
ring back THa seh paro piso
ripe (fruit) orimos
rip-off: it's a rip-off ineh listia
rip-off prices astronomikes
times
risky ripsokinthinos

river to potami
road (country) o thromos
  (in town) i othos
  is this the road for ...? ineh
  aftos o thromos ya ...?
  down the road parakato
road accident to
  aftokinitistiko thistikhima
road map o othikos khartis
roadsign i pinakitha
rob: I've been robbed meh
  listepsan
rock o vrakhos
  (music) i rok moosiki
  on the rocks (with ice) meh
  pagakia
roll (bread) to psomaki
roof i orofi, i steyi
  (flat) i taratsa
roof rack i s-khara
  aftokinitoo
room to thomatio
  (space) to meros
  in my room sto thomatio
  moo

dialogue

do you have any rooms?
ekheteh kaTHoloo
thomatia?
for how many people? ya
posa atoma?
for one/for two ya ena/ya
thio
yes, we have some
vacancies neh, ekhoomeh
elefTHera thomatia
for how many nights will it

be? ya posa vrathia to
THeleteh?
just for one night mono ya
ena vrathi
how much is it? poso
kani?
... drachmas with
bathroom and ... drachmas
without bathroom ...
thrakhmes meh mbanio
keh ... thrakhmes khoris
mbanio
can I see a room with
bathroom? boro na tho
ena thomatio meh
mbanio?
OK, I'll take it endaxi, THa
to paro

room service to servis
  thomatioo
rope to skhini
rosé (wine) to rozeh
roughly (approximately) pano-
  kato
round: it's my round ineh i sira
  moo
roundabout (for traffic) o
  kikloforiakos komvos, i
  platia
round trip ticket: a round trip
  ticket to ... ena isitirio met
  epistrofis ya to ...
route i poria
  what's the best route for ...?
  pios ineh o kaliteros thromos
  ya ...?
rubber (material) lastikho
  (eraser) i svistra, i goma

rubber band to lastikhaki
rubbish (waste) ta skoopithia
  (poor quality goods) kaki piotita
  rubbish! (nonsense) trikhes!
rucksack to sakithio
rude a-yenis
ruins ta eripia, i arkheotites
rum to roomi
  rum and coke ena roomi
  meh koka kola
run (person) trekho
  how often do the buses run?
  poso sikh-na pernoon ta
  leoforia?
  I've run out of money moo
  teliosan ta khrimata
rush hour ora ekhmis

S

sad lipimenos
saddle i sela
safe (not in danger) asfalis
  (not dangerous) akinthinos,
  avlavis
safety pin i paramana
sail to pani
sailboard to windsurf
sailboarding to windsurf
salad i salata
salad dressing to lathoxitho
sale: for sale politeh
salmon o solomos
Salonika i THesaloniki
salt to alati
same: the same o ithios
  the same as this to ithio
  opos afto

the same again, please to
  ithio xana, parakalo
  it's all the same to me to
  ithio moo kani
sand i amos
sandals ta santhalia
sandwich to sandwich
sanitary napkins i servi-etes
sanitary towels i servi-etes
sardines i sartheles
Saturday to Savato
sauce i saltsa
saucepan i katsarola
saucer to piataki
sauna i sa-oona
sausage to lookaniko
say: how do you say ... in
  Greek? pos to leneh ... sta
  Elinika?
  what did he say? ti ipeh?
  I said ... ipa ...
  he said ... ipeh ...
  could you say that again?
  boriteh na to xanapiteh?,
  boriteh na to epanalaveteh?
scarf (for neck) to kaskol
  (for head) to mandili
scenery to topio
schedule (US) to programa
scheduled flight i
  programatismeni ptisi
school to skholio
scissors: a pair of scissors to
  psalithi
scotch to skots whisky
Scotch tape® to sellotape®
Scotland i Skotia
Scottish Skotsezikos
  I'm Scottish (man/woman)

imeh Skotsezos/Skotseza
scrambled eggs ta khtipita
avga
scratch i gratzoonia
screw i vitha
screwdriver to katsavithi
scuba diving i anapnefstiki
siskevi katathiti
sea i THalasa
 by the sea konda sti THalasa
seafood ta THalasina
seafood restaurant i psaro-
taverna
seafront i paralia
 on the seafront stin paralia
seagull o glaros
search psakh-no
seashell i akhivaTHa
seasick: I feel seasick
esthanomeh naftia
 I get seasick meh piani i
THalasa
seaside: by the seaside konda
stin paralia
seat i THesi
 is this anyone's seat? ineh
kanenos afti i THesi?
seat belt i zoni asfalias
sea urchin o akhinos
seaweed ta fikia
secluded apomeros
second (of time) to theftero-
lepto
 (adj) thefteros
 just a second! mia stigmi!
second class (travel) thefteri
THesi
second floor o thefteros
orofos

(US) o tritos orofos
second-hand apo theftero
kheri
see vlepo, kitazo
 can I see? boro na tho?
 have you seen ...? ekhis
thi ...?
 see you! ta xanalemeh!
 I see (I understand) katalava
 I saw him this morning ton
itha simera to pro-i
self-catering apartment to
anexartito thiamerisma
self-service self-servis
sell poolo
 do you sell ...? poolateh ...?
Sellotape® to sellotape®
send stelno
 I want to send this to England
thelo na stilo afto stin Anglia
senior citizen o/i sindaxiookhos
separate (adj) khoristos
separated: I'm separated
(man/woman) imeh
khorismenos/khorismeni
separately (pay, travel)
xekhorista
September o Septemvrios
septic siptikos
serious sovaros
service charge (in restaurant) to
filothorima
service station to
venzinathiko
serviette i hartopetseta, i
petseta
set menu to tabl-dot
several arketi

105

Se

sew ravo
could you sew this back on?
boriteh na to rapseteh pali
sti THesi too?
sex to sex
shade: in the shade sti skia
shake: let's shake hands as
thosoomeh ta kheria
shallow (water) rikha nera
shame: what a shame! ti
krima!
shampoo to samboo-an
a shampoo and set ena
loosimo meh mizampli
share (verb: room, table etc)
mirazomeh
sharp (knife etc) kofteros
(taste, pain) thinatos
shattered (very tired)
exandlimenos
shaver i xiristiki mikhani
shaving foam o afros
xirismatos
shaving point i priza xiristikis
mikhanis
she* afti
is she here? ineh etho?
sheet (for bed) to sendoni
shelf to rafi
shellfish ta ostraka
sherry to seri
ship to plio
by ship meh plio
shirt to pookamiso
shit! skata!
shock to sok
I got an electric shock from
the ... ilektristika meh ...
shock-absorber to amortiser

shocking (behaviour, prices)
exofrenikos
shoe to papootsi
a pair of shoes ena zevgari
papootsia
shoelaces ta korthonia
papootsion
shoe polish to verniki
papootsion
shoe repairer o tsangaris
shop to magazi

 Shops are usually open
Monday to Friday from
8 am to 1.30 pm and from
5 pm to 8.30 pm (on Saturdays they
open only in the morning); however,
some may open all day, especially in
tourist areas.

shopping: I'm going shopping
pao ya psonia
shopping centre to emboriko
kendro
shop window i vitrina
shore i akti
short (person) kondos
(time) ligos
(journey) sindomos
shortcut o sindomos thromos
shorts to sorts
should: what should I do? ti
prepi na kano?
he shouldn't be long then
prepi na aryisi
you should have told me
eprepeh na moo to ikhes pi
shoulder o omos
shout (verb) fonazo

show (in theatre) to ergo
  could you show me? boriteh
  na moo thixeteh?
shower (in bathroom) to doos
  (rain) i bora
  with shower meh doos
shower gel to afrolootro
shut (verb) klino
  when do you shut? poteh
  klineteh?
  when do they shut? poteh
  klinoon?
  they're shut ineh klista
  I've shut myself out klistika
  apexo
  shut up! skaseh!
shutter (on camera) to
  thiafragma
  (on window) to exofilo, to
  pandzoori
shy dropalos
sick (ill) arostos
  I'm going to be sick (vomit)
  ekho tasi pros emeto
  see ill
side i plevra
  the other side of town i ali
  akri tis polis
side lights ta khamila fota
side salad i salata ya
  garnitoora
side street to thromaki
sidewalk to pezothromio
sight: the sights of ... ta
  axioTHeata too ...
sightseeing: we're going
  sightseeing pameh na
  thoomeh ta axioTHeata
sightseeing tour i xenayisi sta

axioTHeata
sign (roadsign etc) to sima
signal: he didn't give a signal
  then ekaneh sima
signature i ipografi
signpost i pinakitha, i tabela
silence i siopi
silk to metaxi
silly ano-itos
silver to asimi
silver foil to aloominokharto
similar omios
simple (easy) aplos
since: since yesterday apo
  kh-THes
  since I got here apo toteh
  poo irTHa etho
sing tragootho
singer (man/woman) o tragoo-
  thistis/i tragoothistria
single (man/woman) monos
  a single to ... ena aplo ya ...
  I'm single imeh elefTHeros/
  elefTHeri
single bed to mono krevati
single room to mono
  thomatio
sink (in kitchen) o nerokhitis
sister i athelfi
sister-in-law (brother's wife) i
  nifi
  (wife's sister) i kooniatha
sit: can I sit here? boro na
  kaTHiso etho?
  is anyone sitting here?
  kaTHeteh kanis etho?
sit down kaTHomeh
  sit down! katseh kato!
site to axioTHeato

(archaeological) arkheoloyikos khoros
size to meh-yeTHos
skin to therma
skindiving i katathisis
skinny kokaliaris
skirt i foosta
sky o ooranos
sleep (verb) kimameh
  did you sleep well? kimi-THikes kala?
  I need a good sleep khriazomeh ena kalo ipno
sleeper (on train) i kooketa
sleeping bag to sleeping bag
sleeping car i klinamaxa, i kooketa
sleeping pill to ipnotiko khapi
sleepy: I'm feeling sleepy nistazo
sleeve to maniki
slide (photographic) to slide
slip (under dress) to misofori
slippery glisteros
slow argos
  slow down! pio arga
slowly siga-siga
  could you say it slowly? boriteh na to piteh arga-arga?
  very slowly poli arga
small mikros
smell: it smells (smells bad) vroma-i
smile (verb) khamo-yelo
smoke o kapnos
  do you mind if I smoke? sas pirazi an kapniso?

I don't smoke then kapnizo
do you smoke? kapnizeteh?
snack: I'd just like a snack THa iTHela na fao kati prokhiyo
snake to fithi
sneeze to ftarnisma
snorkel o anapnefstiras
snow to khioni
so: it's so good ineh poli kalo
  not so fast okhi toso grigora
  so am I keh ego to ithio
  so do I keh ego episis
  so-so etsi ki etsi
soaking solution (for contact lenses) igro sindirisis fakon epafis
soap to sapooni
soap powder to aporipandiko
sober xemeTHistos
socks i kaltses
socket (electrical) i priza
soda (water) i sotha
sofa o kanapes
soft (material etc) apalos
soft-boiled egg to melato avgo
soft drink to anapsiktiko
soft lenses i malaki faki
sole i sola
  could you put new soles on these? boriteh na moo valeteh kenooryi-es soles safta?
some: can I have some water/rolls? moo thineteh ligo nero?/liga psomakia?
  can I have some? boro na paro ligo?

somebody, someone kapios
something kati
something to drink kati na
  pi-iteh
sometimes merikes fores
somewhere kapoo
son o yos
song to tragoothi
son-in-law o gambros
soon sindoma
  I'll be back soon THa yiriso
  sindoma
  as soon as possible oso to
  thinaton grigorotera
sore: it's sore ineh
  ereTHismeno
sore throat pona-i o lemos
  moo
sorry: (I'm) sorry signomi
  sorry? (didn't understand/hear)
  pardon?, signomi?
sort: what sort of ...? ti
  ithos ...?
soup i soopa
sour (taste) xinos
south notos
  south of noti-a
  in the south sto noto
  to the south noti-a
South Africa i Noti-os Afriki
South African (adj) Notio-
  afrikanos
  I'm South African (man/woman)
  imeh Notio-afrikanos/
  Notio-afrikana
southeast notio-anatolikos
southwest notio-thitikos
souvenir to enTHimio
Spain i Ispania

Spanish (adj) ispanikos
  (language) ta ispanika
spanner to klithi
spare part ta andalaktika
spare tyre i rezerva
spark plug to boozi
speak: do you speak English?
  milateh Anglika?
  I don't speak ... then milo ...

dialogue

can I speak to Costas?
boro na miliso ston Kosta,
parakalo?
who's calling? pios ton
zita-i?
it's Patricia i Patricia
I'm sorry, he's not in, can I
take a message? lipameh,
then ineh etho, boro na
too thoso kapio minima?
no thanks, I'll call back
later okhi, efkharisto, THa
xanaparo argotera
please tell him I called
parakalo, piteh too pos
tilefonisa

speciality i spesialiteh
spectacles ta yali-a
speed i takhitita
speed limit to orio takhititas
speedometer to konder
spell: how do you spell it? pos
  to grafeteh?
  see alphabet page 9
spend xothevo
spider i arakhni

spin-dryer to stegnotirio
splinter i agitha
spoke (in wheel) i aktina
spoon to kootali
sport to spor
sprain: I've sprained my ...
  straboolixa to ...
spring (season) i anixi
  (in seat etc) to elatirio
square (in town) i platia
stairs ta skalopatia, i skales
stale (bread, taste) bayatikos
stall: the engine keeps stalling
  i mikhani sinekhos stamata
stamp to gramatosimo
  see post office

dialogue

a stamp for England,
please ena gramatosimo
ya Anglia, parakalo
what are you sending? ti
THa stileteh?
this postcard afti tin karta

star to asteri
  (in film) o/i star
start i arkhi, to xekinima
  (verb) arkhizo
  when does it start? poteh
  arkhizi?
  the car won't start to
  aftokinito then xekina
starter (of car) i miza
  (food) to proto piato
starters ta orektika
starving: I'm starving
  peTHeno tis pinas

state (in country) i politia
  the States (USA) i Inomenes
  Politi-es
station o staTHmos
statue to agalma
stay: where are you staying?
  poo meneteh?
I'm staying at ... meno sto ...
I'd like to stay another two
nights THa iTHela na mino
ales thio nikhtes
steak i brizola
steal klevo
  my bag has been stolen
  klepsaneh tin tsanda moo
steep (hill) apotomos
steering to timoni
step: on the steps sta
  skalopati-a
stereo to stereofoniko
  singrotima
sterling i lira sterlina
steward (on plane) o
  a-erosinothos
stewardess i a-erosinothos
sticking plaster to lefkoplast
still: I'm still waiting akoma
  perimeno
  is he still there? ineh akoma
  eki?
  keep still! stasoo akinitos!
sting: I've been stung by ...
  meh tsibiseh ...
stockings i na-ilon kaltses
stomach to stomakhi
stomach ache o ponos sto
  stomakhi, o stomakhoponos
stone (rock) i petra
stop stamatao

please, stop here (to taxi driver etc) parakalo, stamatisteh etho

do you stop near ...? stamatateh konda ...?

stop doing that! stamata na to kanis afto!

stopover i stasi

storm i THi-ela

straight: it's straight ahead ineh olo efTHia

a straight whisky ena sketo whisky

straightaway amesos

strange (odd) paraxenos

stranger (man/woman) o xenos/i xeni

I'm a stranger here imeh xenos etho

strap to loori

strawberry i fraoola

stream to rema, to potamaki

street o thromos

on the street sto thromo

streetmap o othikos khartis

string (cord) o spangos (guitar etc) i khorthi

strong thinatos

stuck frakarismenos

the key's stuck koliseh to klithi

student o fititis, i fititria

stupid vlakas

suburb ta pro-astia

subway (US: railway) o ipo-yios

suddenly xafnika

suede to kastori

sugar i zakhari

suit (man's) to koostoomi

(woman's) to ta-yer

it doesn't suit me (jacket etc) then moo pa-i

it suits you soo pa-i

suitcase i valitsa

summer to kalokeri

in the summer to kalokeri

sun o ilios

in the sun ston ilio

out of the sun sti skia

sunbathe kano ilioTHerapia

sunblock (cream) to andiliako

sunburn to kapsimo apo ton ilio

sunburnt kamenos apo ton ilio

Sunday i Kiriaki

sunglasses ta yalia ilioo

sun lounger i shez long

sunny: it's sunny ekhi liakatha

sun roof (in car) i tzamenia skepi

sunset i thisi too ilioo

sunshade i ombrela ilioo

sunshine i liakatha

sunstroke i ili-asi

suntan to mavrisma

suntan lotion to lathi mavrismatos

suntanned iliokamenos

suntan oil to lathi mavrismatos

super katapliktikos

supermarket to supermarket

supper to thipno

supplement (extra charge) epipleon, to prosTHeto

sure: are you sure? iseh sigooros?

sure! veveos!
surname to epiTHeto
swearword i vrisia
sweater to poolover
sweatshirt i fanela
Sweden i Soo-ithia
Swedish (adj) Soo-ithikos
sweet (taste) glikos
  (dessert) to gliko
sweets i karameles
swelling to priximo
swim kolimbao
  I'm going for a swim pao ya kolibi
  let's go for a swim pameh ya kolibi
swimming costume to ma-yo
swimming pool i pisina
swimming trunks to ma-yo
switch o thiakoptis
switch off (engine) svino
  (TV, lights) klino
switch on (engine) anavo
  (TV, lights) anigo
swollen prismenos

T

table to trapezi
  a table for two ena trapezi ya thio
tablecloth to trapezomandilo
table tennis to ping-pong
table wine to epitrapezio krasi
tailback (of traffic) i oora
tailor o raftis
take (lead) perno
  (accept) thekhomeh

can you take me to the airport? boriteh na meh pateh sto a-erothromio?
do you take credit cards? thekhesteh pistotikes kartes?
fine, I'll take it endaxi THa to paro
can I take this? (leaflet etc) boro na paro afto?
how long does it take? posi ora THa pari?
it takes three hours perni tris ores
is this seat taken? ineh piasmeni i THesi?
hamburger to take away khamboorger ya to spiti
can you take a little off here? (to hairdresser) boriteh na pareteh ligo apo etho?
talcum powder i poothra talk
talk (verb) milo
tall psilos
tampons ta tampax®, ta tabon
tan to mavrisma
  to get a tan mavrizo
tank (of car) to depozito
tap i vrisi
tape (cassette) i kaseta
  (sticky) i tenia
tape measure to metro
tape recorder to magnitofono
taste i yefsi
  can I taste it? boro na to thokimaso?
taxi to taxi
  will you get me a taxi? THa moo kaleseteh ena taxi?

where can I find a taxi? poo
boro na vro ena taxi?

dialogue

> **to the airport/to the Hilton
> Hotel please** sto a-
> erothromio/sto
> xenothokhio Khilton,
> parakalo
> **how much will it be?** poso
> THa stikhisi?
> **1,500 drachmas** khili-es
> pendakosi-es thrakmes
> **that's fine, right here,
> thanks** endaxi, etho pera
> ineh, efkharisto

taxi-driver o taxidzis

 Greek taxis, especially
Athenian ones, are among
the least expensive in
Western Europe. Within city or town
limits, use of the meter is mandatory
if one is fitted. Double tariff applies
between 1 and 6 am, and outside
city or town limits at any time of the
day, and there are also surcharges
for entering a ferry harbour or
airport and for large items of
luggage. In rural areas, taxis
sometimes have no meters and you
have to agree a price. Taxi-drivers
very often charge you much more
than they should. It's a good idea to
check the official price list usually
displayed in airports for the fare
from an airport to a city centre. You
should be wary of unlicenced taxi-
drivers outside major railway
stations.

taxi rank o staTHmos taxi
tea to tsa-i
 tea for one/two please tsa-i
 ya enan/thio parakalo
teabags ta fakelakia tsa-i
teach: could you teach me?
 boris na meh maTHis?
teacher (man/woman) o
 thaskalos/i thaskala
team i omatha
teaspoon to kootalaki
tea towel i petseta koozinas
teenager o neos, i nea
telegram to tilegrafima
telephone to tilefono
 see phone
television i tileorasi
tell: could you tell him ...?
 boriteh na too piteh ...?
temperature (weather) i
 THermokrasia
 (fever) o piretos
temple (church) o na-os
tennis to tennis
tennis ball i bala too tennis
tennis court to yipetho tennis
tennis racket i raketa tennis
tent i skini
term (at university, school) i
 s-kholiki periothos
terminus (rail) to terma
terrible foveros
terrific exeretikos
than* apo
 smaller than mikroteros apo

thanks, thank you efkharisto
thank you very much
efkharisto para poli
thanks for the lift efkharisto
poo meh pirateh
no thanks okhi efkharisto

dialogue

thanks efkharisto
that's OK, don't mention it
parakalo, then kani
tipoteh

that ekinos, ekini, ekino
that one ekino
I hope that ... elpizo oti ...
that's nice ti orea!
is that ...? afto ineh ...?
that's it (that's right) akrivos
the* o, i, to; (pl) i, i, ta
theatre to THeatro
their* o/i/to ... toos
theirs* thiki toos
them* toos, tis, ta
for them ya ekinoos
with them maftoos
I gave it to them to ethosa
saftoos
who? – them pi-i? – afti
then (at that time) toteh
(after that) katopin
there eki
over there eki pera
up there eki pano
is there ...? iparkhi ...?
are there ...? iparkhoon ...?
there is ... iparkhi ...
there are ... iparkhoon ...

there you are (giving something)
oristeh
thermometer to
THermometro
Thermos flask® to THermos
these afti, aftes, afta
can I have these? boro na
ekho afta?
Thessaly i THesalia
they* afti, aftes, afta
thick pakhis
(stupid) khazos
thief (man/woman) o kleftis/i
kleftra
thigh to booti
thin leptos
(person) athinatos
thing to pragma
my things ta pragmata moo
think skeptomeh
(believe) nomizo
I think so etsi nomizo
I don't think so then nomizo
I'll think about it THa to
skepto
third party insurance asfalia ya
khrisi apo tritoos
thirsty: I'm thirsty thipso
this aftos, afti, afto
this one afto etho
this is my wife apo etho i
yineka moo
is this ...? ineh ...?
those ekini, ekines, ekina
which ones? – those pi-a? –
afta
Thrace i THraki
thread i klosti
throat o lemos

throat pastilles pastili-es
lemoo
through thiamesoo
  does it go through ...? (train,
  bus) perna-i apo to ...?
throw (verb) rikhno
throw away (verb) peto
thumb o andikhiras
thunderstorm i kateyitha, i
  THi-ela
Thursday i Pempti
ticket to isitirio

dialogue

  a return to Athens ena
  isitirio epistrofis ya tin
  ATHina
  coming back when? poteh
  ineh i epistrofi?
  today/next Tuesday
  simera/tin epomeni Triti
  that will be 2,000
  drachmas thio khiliathes
  thrakhmes, parakalo

ticket office (bus, rail) i
  THiritha
tide i paliri-a
tie (necktie) i gravata
tight (clothes etc) stenos
  it's too tight ineh poli steno
tights to kalson
till mekhri
time* o khronos
  (occasion) i fora
  what's the time? ti ora ineh?
  this time afti ti fora
  last time tin perasmeni fora

next time tin epomeni fora
  four times teseris fores
timetable to programa
tin (can) i konserva
tinfoil to asimokharto
tin-opener to anikhtiri
tiny mikroskopikos
tip (to waiter etc) to filothorima

 There are no specific
rules on how large a tip
you should leave in a
restaurant, and tipping is not
regarded as essential. In most
restaurants and tavernas a
service charge is included. Look
for the word 'to filothorima' το
φιλοδώρημα on the menu which
indicates whether the service
charge is included. You are expected
to tip cinema- or theatre-attendants.
It is not usual to tip taxi-drivers; they
usually round up the fare if the
amount of change is small and often
claim that they have no change!

tired koorasmenos
  I'm tired imeh koorasmenos
tissues ta khartomandila
to: to Salonica/London ya tin
  THesaloniki/to Lonthino
  to Greece/England ya tin
  Elatha/Anglia
  to the post office sto
  takhithromio
toast (bread) to tost
today simera
toe to thakhtilo too pothioo
together mazi

we're together (in shop etc) imasteh mazi

can we pay together? boroomeh na plirosoomeh mazi?

toilet i too-aleta

where is the toilet? poo ineh i too-aleta?

I have to go to the toilet prepi na pao stin too-aleta

Public toilets are rare in Greece, especially in less touristy places, but are sometimes found in parks or squares. You will have to take advantage of toilets in restaurants and bars or toilets at railway/bus stations and in museums etc. Throughout Greece you place used paper in the adjacent wastebaskets, not in the bowl.

toilet paper kharti iyias
tomato i domata
tomato juice to domatozoomo, o domatokhimos
tomato ketchup to ketsap
tomorrow avrio
tomorrow morning avrio to pro-i

the day after tomorrow methavrio

toner (cosmetic) to tonotiko
tongue i glosa
tonic (water) to tonik
tonight apopseh
tonsillitis i amigthalititha

too (excessively) poli
(also) episis
too hot poli kafto
too much para poli
me too kego episis
tooth to thondi
toothache o ponothondos
toothbrush i othondovoortsa
toothpaste i othondokrema
top: on top of ... pano apo ...
at the top stin korifi
top floor to retire
topless yimnostiTHi
torch o fakos
total to sinolo
tour i peri-iyisi, i xenayisi
is there a tour of ...? iparkhi peri-iyisi ya ...?
tour guide o/i xenagos
tourist (man/woman) o tooristas/i tooristria
tourist information office Grafio Pliroforion E-OT
tour operator to taxithiotiko grafio
towards pros
towel i petseta
town i poli
in town stin poli
just out of town akrivos exo apo tin poli
town centre to kendro tis polis
town hall to thimarkhio
toy to pekh-nithi
track (US) i platforma
see platform
tracksuit i aTHlitiki forma
traditional parathosiakos

traffic i kikloforia
traffic jam i kikloforiaki simforisi
traffic lights ta fanaria tis trokheas
trailer (for carrying tent etc) i rimoolka
(US: caravan) to trokhospito
trailer park topoTHesia ya trokhospita
train to treno
by **train** meh treno

dialogue

> is this the train for ...? afto ineh to treno ya ...?
> **sure** neh
> no, you want that platform there okhi, THa pateh seh ekini tin platforma eki

trainers (shoes) ta aTHlitika papootsia
train station o sithiro-thromikos staTHmos
tram to tram
translate metafrazo
could you translate that? boriteh na metafraseteh afto?
translation i metafrasi
translator o/i metafrastis
trashcan o skoopithodenekes
travel taxithevo
we're travelling around taxithevoomeh triyiro
travel agent's to taxithiotiko grafio
traveller's cheque i

taxithiotiki epitayi
tray o thiskos
tree to thendro
tremendous tromeros
trendy modernos
trim: just a trim please (to hairdresser) ligo konditera, parakalo
trip (excursion) to taxithi
I'd like to go on a trip to ... THa iTHela na pao ena taxithi stin ...
trolley to trolley, to karotsaki
trolleybus to trolley
see **bus**
trouble o belas
I'm having trouble with ... ekho provlimata meh ...
sorry to trouble you meh sinkhoriteh poo sas vazo seh mbela
trousers to pandaloni
true aliTHinos
that's not true then ineh aliTHia
trunk (US: of car) to port-bagaz
trunks (swimming) to mayo
try prospaTHo, thokimazo
can I have a try? boro na thokimaso?
try on provaro
can I try it on? boro na to thokimaso pano moo?
T-shirt to bloozaki
Tuesday i Triti
tuna o tonos
tunnel i siraga
Turkey i Toorkia
Turkish (adj) Toorkikos

Turkish coffee Toorkikos kafes, Elinikos kafes
  see coffee
Turkish-Cypriot (adj) Toorkiko-Kipriakos
turn: turn left/right stripseh aristera/thexia
  where do I turn off? poo strivo?
turn off: can you turn the heating off? boris na klisis ti THermansi/to kalorifer?
turn on: can you turn the heating on? boris na anixis ti THermansi/to kalorifer?
turning (in road) i strofi
TV i tileorasi
tweezers to tsimbithaki
twice thio fores
  twice as much ta thipla
twin beds thio krevatia
twin room to thomatio meh thio krevatia
twist: I've twisted my ankle stramboolixa ton astragalo moo
type to ithos
  a different type of ... ena alo ithos apo ...
typical kharaktiristikos
tyre to lastikho

U

ugly askhimos
UK to Inomeno Vasili-o
ulcer to elkos
umbrella i ombrela

uncle o THios
unconscious anesTHitos
under apo kato
  (less than) ligotero apo
underdone (meat) misopsimenos
underground (railway) o ipoyios
underpants to sovrako, to slip
understand: I understand katalaveno
  I don't understand then katalaveno
  do you understand? katalavenis?
unemployed anergos
United States i Inomenes Politi-es
university to panepistimio
unleaded petrol i amolivthi venzini
unlimited mileage aperiorista khiliometra
unlock xeklithono
unpack anigo tis valitses
until mekhri
unusual asiniTHistos
up pano
  (upwards) pros ta pano
  up there eki pano
  he's not up yet (not out of bed) then sikoTHikeh akomi
  what's up? (what's wrong?) ti yineteh?
upmarket (restaurant etc) akrivos
upset stomach o stomakhoponos
upside down ta pano kato

upstairs pano
urgent epigon
us* mas
  with us meh mas
  for us ya mas
use khrisimopi-o
  may I use ...? boro na
  khrisimopi-iso ...?
useful khrisimos
usual siniTHismenos
  the usual (drink etc) to
  siniTHismeno

V

vacancy: do you have any
  vacancies? (hotel) ekheteh
  elefTHera thomatia?
vacation i thiakopes
  see holiday
vaccination o emvoliasmos
vacuum cleaner i ilektriki
  skoopa
valid (ticket etc) engiros
  how long is it valid for? ya
  poso is-khi-i?
valley i kilatha
valuable (adj) politimos
  can I leave my valuables
  here? boro na afiso ta timalfi
  moo etho?
value i axia
van to trokhospito
vanilla i vanilia
  a vanilla ice cream ena
  pagoto vanilia
vary: it varies metavaleteh
vase to vazo

veal to moskhari
vegetables ta lakhanika
vegetarian o/i khortofagos
vending machine o aftomatos
  politis
very poli
  very little for me poli ligo ya
  mena
  I like it very much moo aresi
  para poli
vest (under shirt) to fanelaki
via thia mesoo
video (film) i video-tenia
  (video recorder) to video
view i THea
villa i vila
village to khorio
vinegar to xithi
vineyard to ambeli
visa i viza
visit (verb) episkeptomeh
  I'd like to visit ... THa iTHela
  na episkefto ...
vital: it's vital that ... ineh
  vasiko na ...
vodka i votka
voice i foni
volleyball to volley-ball, i
  khirosferisi
voltage i tasis
  see electricity
vomit (verb) kano emeto

W

waist i mesi
waistcoat to yileko
wait perimeno

wait for me perimeneh meh!

don't wait for me mi meh perimenis

can I wait until my wife gets here? boro na paragilo otan elTHi i yineka moo?

can you do it while I wait? na perimeno na to kaneteh?

could you wait here for me? boriteh na meh perimeneteh na yiriso?

waiter o servitoros

waiter! garson!

waitress i garsona, i servitora

waitress! sas parakalo!

wake: can you wake me up at 5.30? boriteh na meh xipniseteh stis pendeh keh misi?

wake-up call tilefonima ya xipnima

Wales i Oo-alia

walk: is it a long walk? ineh poli perpatima?

it's only a short walk ekhi ligo perpatima

I'll walk THa perpatiso

I'm going for a walk pao ena peripato

Walkman® to walkman®

wall o tikhos

wallet to portofoli

wander: I like just wandering around moo aresi na khazevo triyiro

want: I want a ... THelo ena ...

I don't want any ... then THelo ...

I want to go home THelo na pao spiti moo

I don't want to then THelo

he wants to ... THeli na ...

what do you want? ti THelis?

ward (in hospital) o THalamos

warm zestos

I'm so warm zestenomeh arketa

was*: I was ... imoon ...

he/she/it was ... itan ...

wash (verb) pleno

(oneself) plenomeh

can you wash these? boriteh na plineteh afta?

washer (for bolt etc) i rothela

washhand basin o niptiras

washing (clothes) i boogatha

washing machine to plindirio

washing powder i skoni plindirioo, to aporipandiko

washing-up liquid to sapooni piaton

wasp i sfinga

watch (wristwatch) to rolo-i

will you watch my things for me? boriteh na prosekheteh ta pragmata moo?

watch out! prosekheh!

watch strap to looraki roloyioo

water to nero

may I have some water? moo thineteh ligo nero?

waterproof (adj) athi-avrokhos

waterskiing to THalasio ski

wave (in sea) to kima

way: could you tell me the way

to ...? boriteh na moo piteh
pos THa pa-o sto ..?
it's this way apo etho ineh
it's that way apo eki ineh
is it a long way to ...? ineh
makri-a ya to ...?
no way! apokli-eteh!

dialogue

could you tell me the way
to ...? boriteh na moo
thixeteh to thromo ya ...?
go straight on until you
reach the traffic lights
piyeneteh olo isia mekhri
na ftaseteh sta fanaria
turn left stripsteh aristera
take the first on the right
parteh ton proto thromo
sta thexia
see where

we* emis
weak athinatos
weather o keros

dialogue

what's the weather
forecast? ti ipeh to theltio
keroo?
it's going to be fine THa
ineh kalos keros
it's going to rain THa vrexi
it'll brighten up later THa
anixi o keros argotera

wedding o gamos

wedding ring i vera
Wednesday i Tetarti
week i evthomatha
a week (from) today seh mia
evthomatha apo simera
a week (from) tomorrow
seh mia evthomatha apo
avrio
weekend to Savatokiriako
at the weekend to
Savatokiriako
weight to varos
weird paraxenos
weirdo o trelaras
welcome: welcome to ... kalos
ilTHateh sto ...
you're welcome (don't mention
it) parakalo
well: I don't feel well then
esTHanomeh kala
she's not well ekini then
ineh kala
you speak English very well
milateh poli kala Anglika
well done! bravo
this one as well ki afto
episis
well well! (surprise) ya thes!

dialogue

how are you? ti kanis?
very well, thanks poli kala,
efkharisto
and you? ki esi?

well-done (meat)
kalopsimenos
Welsh Oo-alos

I'm Welsh (man/woman) imeh
Oo-alos/Oo-ali
were*: we were imasteh
you were isasteh/isteh
they were itan
west thitikos
in the west sta thitika
West Indian (adj) apo tis
thitikes Inthi-es
wet vregmenos
what? ti?
what's that? ti ineh ekino?
what should I do? ti prepi na
kano?
what a view! ti THea!
what bus do I take? ti
leoforio prepi na paro?
wheel i rotha
wheelchair i anapiriki
poliTHrona
when? poteh?
when we get back otan
yirisoomeh
when's the train/ferry? poteh
fevyi to treno/to karavi?
where? poo?
I don't know where it is then
xero poo ineh

dialogue

where is the cathedral?
poo ineh o kaTHethrikos
naos?
it's over there ineh eki
pera
could you show me where
it is on the map? boriteh
na moo thixeteh sto

kharti poo ineh?
it's just here ineh akrivos
etho
see way

which: which bus? pio
leoforio?

dialogue

which one? pio?
that one ekino
this one? afto?
no, that one okhi, ekino

while: while I'm here oso imeh
etho
whisky to whisky
white aspros
white wine to aspro krasi
who? pios?
who is it? pios ineh?
the man who ... o anTHropos
poo ...
whole: the whole week oli tin
evthomatha
the whole lot ola
whose: whose is this? pianoo
ineh afto?
why? yati?
why not? yati okhi?
wide platis
wife: my wife i sizigos moo
will: will you do it for me? THa
moo to kanis afto?
wind o anemos
window to paraTHiro
near the window konda sto
paraTHiro

in the window (of shop) sti vitrina
window seat i THesi sto paraTHiro
windscreen to parbriz
windscreen wiper o ialokaTHaristiras
windsurfing to windsurfing
windy: it's so windy ekhi poli a-era
wine to krasi
can we have some more wine? boroomeh na ekhoomeh ligo krasi akoma?

Both estatoria and tavernas will usually offer you a choice of bottled wines, and some (mainly tavernas) may have their own house variety, kept in barrels and served out in metal jugs. If you want house wine, ask for 'khima krasi/retsina'. Retsina – pine-resinated wine, a slightly acquired taste – is invariably better straight from the barrel. Not as many tavernas keep wine from the barrel these days, but always ask whether they have wine 'varelisio' or 'khima' – both mean, in effect, 'from the barrel'.

wine list o katalogos ton krasion
winter o khimonas
in the winter ton khimona
winter holiday i khimerines thiakopes
wire to sirma

(electric) to ilektriko kalothio
wish: best wishes poles efkhes
with meh
I'm staying with ... meno meh ...
without khoris
witness o/i martiras
will you be a witness for me? THa iseh martiras moo?
woman i yineka

women
Many women travel by themselves about Greece without being harassed or feeling intimidated. Most of the hassle you are likely to get is from a small minority of Greeks who migrate to the main resorts and towns in summer in pursuit of 'fun-loving' tourists. In remote mountains and inland areas, you may feel more uncomfortable travelling alone. The intensely traditional Greeks may have trouble understanding why you are unaccompanied, and might not welcome your presence in their exclusively male 'kafenia' – often the only place where you can get a drink. Because of the machismo of the majority of Greek men, foreign women should be careful when dealing with approaches; flirting can often lead to unpleasant misunderstandings.

wonderful THavmasios

won't*: it won't start then THa
xekinisi
wood (material) to xilo
woods (forest) to thasos
wool to mali
word i lexi
work i thoolia
  it's not working then
  thoolevi
  I work in ... ergazomeh
  seh ...
world o kosmos
worry: I'm worried
  stenokhori-emeh
worry beads to kombolo-i
worse: it's worse ineh
  khirotera
worst o khiroteros
worth: is it worth a visit? axizi
  mia episkepsi?
**would: would you give this
  to ...?** boriteh na thoseteh
  afto ston ...?
wrap: could you wrap it up?
  boriteh na to tilixeteh?
wrapping paper to kharti
  peritiligmatos
  (for presents) kharti ya thora
wrist o karpos
write grafo
  could you write it down?
  boriteh na moo to
  grapseteh?
  how do you write it? pos to
  grafeteh?
writing paper to kharti
  alilografias
wrong: it's the wrong key afto
  ineh laTHos klithi

the bill's wrong o logariasmos
ineh laTHos
sorry, wrong number
signomi, laTHos noomero
sorry, wrong room signomi,
laTHos thomatio
**there's something wrong
with ...** iparkhi kapio laTHos
meh ...
what's wrong? ti simveni?

X

X-ray i aktinografia

Y

yacht to yot
yard* i yartha
  (courtyard, backyard) i avli
year o khronos
yellow kitrinos
yes neh
yesterday kh-THes
yesterday morning kh-THes
  to pro-i
  the day before yesterday
  prokh-THes
yet akomi

dialogue

has it arrived yet? akomi
then eftaseh?
no, not yet okhi, okhi
akomi
you'll have to wait a little

longer yet THa prepi na perimeneteh akomi ligo

yoghurt to ya-**oo**rti
you* (fam) esi
  (pl or polite) esis
  I'll see you later THa seh tho argotera
  this is for you afto ineh ya sas
  with you mazi sas
young neos
your* (fam) o/i/to ... soo
  (pl or polite) o/i/to ... sas
  your camera i fotografiki mikhani soo/sas
yours (fam) thiko soo
  (pl or polite) thiko sas
youth hostel o xenonas neon

Z

zero mithen
zip to fermoo-ar
  could you put a new zip in? boriteh na valeteh ena kenoor-yio fermoo-ar?
zip code o takhithromikos kothikos
zoo o zo-oloyikos kipos

Greek

→

English

Colloquial Greek

The following are words or expressions you might well hear. You shouldn't be tempted to use any of the stronger ones unless you are sure of your audience.

άντε γαμήσου [**andeh** gam**i**soo] fuck off!

βλάκα [vl**aka**] idiot, blockhead

βρωμο... [vrom**o**] bloody ...

γαμώ το! [gam**o** to] fuck!

γκόμενα [**go**mena] bird, chick

γουστάρω [goost**a**ro] I feel like it

δεν πειράζει [den pir**a**zi] it doesn't matter

είσαι; [**i**seh] do you want to?

έλα [**e**la] come on!, move!

θαυμάσια! [THavm**a**sia] great!

in [in] fashionable

καμάκι [kam**a**ki] stud, Don Juan

κερατάς [ker**a**t**a**s] bastard

μαλάκα [mal**a**ka] wanker

μου τα'πρηξες [moo t**a**prixes] you're getting on my tits, you're getting up my nose

μπάτσος [b**a**tsos] cop

Παναγία μου [Pan**a**y**i**a moo] my God!

πούστης [**poo**stis] faggot, poofter

πουτάνα [poot**a**na] whore

πώ πώ! [po po] bloody hell!

ρε Κώστα [reh K**o**sta] Kostas, my old pal

ρε μαλάκα [reh mal**a**ka] you stupid wanker

σκάσε! [sk**a**seh] shut up!

σκατά! [skat**a**] shit!

στ'αρχίδια μου [star**khi**dia moo] I don't give a fuck

τζάμπα [tz**a**mba] dirt cheap

τί γίνεται; [ti y**i**neteh] how is it going?

τί να κάνουμε; [ti na k**a**noomeh] what can you do?

τύφλα στο μεθύσι [**ti**fla sto meTH**i**si] pissed (drunk)

A

αγάπη (η) [agapi (i)] love

αγαπημένος [agapimenos] favourite

αγαπώ [agapo] love (verb)

αγγίζω [angizo] touch (verb)

ΑΓΓΛΙΑ Αγγλία (η) [Anglia (i)] England

Αγγλίδα (η) [Anglitha (i)] Englishwoman

ΑΓΓΛΙΚΑ Αγγλικά (τα) [Anglika (ta)] English

ΑΓΓΛΙΚΟΣ Αγγλικός [Anglikos] English

άγγλος (ο) [Anglos (o)] Englishman

αγελάδα (η) [ayelatha (i)] cow

αγενής [ayenis] rude

άγκυρα (η) [angira (i)] anchor

αγκώνας (ο) [angonas (o)] elbow

ΑΓΝΟ ΠΑΡΘΕΝΟ ΜΑΛΛΙ αγνό παρθένο μαλλί pure new wool

ΑΓΟΡΑ αγορά (η) [agora (i)] market

αγοράζω [agorazo] buy (verb)

αγόρι (το) [agori (to)] boy

άγριος [agrios] wild, fierce

αγρόκτημα (το) [agroktima (to)] farm

αγρότης (ο) [agrotis (o)] farmer

αγώνας (ο) [agonas (o)] fight, struggle; game

άδεια (η) [athia (i)] licence; permission

άδεια οδηγήσεως (η) [athia othiyiseos (i)] driving licence

άδειος [athios] empty, vacant

αδελφή (η) [athelfi (i)] sister

ΑΔΕΛΦΟΙ αδελφοί brothers

αδελφός (ο) [athelfos (o)] brother

ΑΔΙΕΞΟΔΟ αδιέξοδο cul-de-sac, dead end

αδύνατος [athinatos] impossible; weak

Α.Ε. public limited company

ΑΕΡΑΝΤΛΙΑ αεραντλία (η) air pump

αέρας (ο) [aeras (o)] air; wind; choke

ΑΕΡΟΔΡΟΜΙΟ αεροδρόμιο (το) [aerothromio (to)] airport

ΑΕΡΟΛΙΜΗΝ αερολιμήν (ο) [aerolimin (o)] airport

αεροπλάνο (το) [aeroplano (to)] plane

αεροπορική εταιρεία (η) [aeroporiki eteria (i)] airline

ΑΕΡΟΠΟΡΙΚΩΣ αεροπορικώς [aeroporikos] by air; by air mail

ΑΕΡΟΣΥΝΟΔΟΣ αεροσυνοδός (ο/η) [aerosinothos (o/i)] steward, stewardess

ΑΘΗΝΑ Αθήνα (η) [ATHina (i)] Athens

αθλητής (ο) [aTHlitis (o)] athlete

ΑΘΛΗΤΙΚΑ αθλητικά (τα) [aTHlitika (ta)] sports shop

αθλητικά παπούτσια (τα) [aTHlitika papootsia (ta)] trainers

ΑΘΛΗΤΙΚΕΣ ΕΓΚΑΤΑΣΤΑΣΕΙΣ αθλητικές εγκαταστάσεις sporting facilities αθλητική φόρμα (η) [aTHlitikí forma (i)] tracksuit

ΑΘΛΗΤΙΚΟ ΚΕΝΤΡΟ αθλητικό κέντρο (το) [aTHlitikó kendro (to)] sports centre

αθώος [aTHoos] innocent

ΑΙΓΑΙΟ Αιγαίο (το) [E-yeo (to)] Aegean

ΑΙΘΟΥΣΑ ΤΡΑΝΖΙΤ αίθουσα τράνζιτ transit lounge

αίμα (το) [ema (to)] blood

αιμορραγώ [emoragó] bleed

αισθάνομαι [esTHanomeh] feel (verb)

ΑΙΤΗΣΗ αίτηση (η) [etisi (i)] application form; application

αιτία (η) [etia (i)] cause; reason

εξ αιτίας ... [exetias ...] because of ...

αιώνας (ο) [eonas (o)] century

ΑΚΑΤΑΛΛΗΛΟ ακατάλληλο adults only

Α΄ ΚΑΤΗΓΟΡΙΑΣ Α΄ κατηγορίας first class

ακολουθώ [akolooTHó] follow

ακόμα, ακόμη [akoma, akomí] still; yet; even; also

ακουστικά (τα) [akoostiká (ta)] hearing aid; headphones

ΑΚΟΥΣΤΙΚΟ ακουστικό (το) [akoostikó (to)] receiver

ακούω [akoo-o] hear; listen

άκρη (η) [akri (i)] edge; end; tip

ΑΚΡΙΒΕΣ ΑΝΤΙΤΙΜΟ ΜΟΝΟ ακριβές αντίτιμο μόνο exact fare only

ακριβός [akrivos] expensive

ακροατήριο (το) [akroatírio (to)] audience

ΑΚΡΥΛΙΚΟ ακρυλικό [akrilikó] acrylic

ΑΚΤΗ ακτή (η) [akti (i)] beach; coast, shore

ακυρώνω [akirono] cancel

ΑΛΒΑΝΙΑ Αλβανία (η) [Alvania (i)] Albania

αληθινός [aliTHinos] true; real

αλλά [alla] but

ΑΛΛΑΓΗ ΛΑΔΙΩΝ αλλαγή λαδιών oil change

αλλάζω [allazo] change (verb)

αλλάζω ρούχα [allazo rookha] change one's clothes

ΑΛΛΕΡΓΙΑ αλλεργία (η) [alleryía (i)] allergy

ΑΛΛΕΡΓΙΑ ΣΤΗ ΓΥΡΗ αλλεργία στη γύρη [alleryía sti yíri] hay fever

αλλεργικός σε [alleryikos seh] allergic to

άλλη [ali] other; else

άλλη μία [ali mia] another

άλλο [alo] other; else; another

όχι άλλο [okhi alo] no more

άλλο ένα [alo ena] another

άλλος [alos] other; else

άλλος ένας [alos enas] another

αλλού [aloo] elsewhere

αλμυρός [almiros] salty

άλογο (το) [alogo (to)] horse

ΑΛΟΙΦΗ αλοιφή (η) [alifi (i)] ointment

αλουμινόχαρτο (το) [aloominokharto (to)] aluminium foil

ΑΛΣΟΣ άλσος (το) [alsos (to)] wooded park, grove

αλτ! [alt!] stop!

αλυσίδα (η) [alisitha (i)] chain

ΑΜΑΞΑ άμαξα (η) [amaxa (i)]
coach, car (on train)

ΑΜΑΞΙ αμάξι (το) [amaxi (to)]
car (on train)

ΑΜΑΞΟΣΤΟΙΧΙΑ
αμαξοστοιχία (η) [amaxostikhia
(i)] train

Αμερικανίδα (η) [Amerikanitha (i)]
American (woman)

Αμερικανικός [Amerikanikos]
American (adj)

Αμερικανός (ο) [Amerikanos (o)]
American (man)

ΑΜΕΡΙΚΗ Αμερική (η)
[Ameriki (i)] America

ΑΜΕΣΟΣ ΔΡΑΣΙΣ άμεσος
δράσις emergencies

αμέσως [amesos] immediately

αμμόλοφοι (οι) [amolofi (i)] sand
dunes

άμμος (η) [amos (i)] sand

αμορτισέρ (το) [amortiser (to)]
shock-absorber

αμπέλι (το) [ambeli (to)]
vineyard

αμπέρ (το) [amper] amp

ΑΜΠΟΥΛΕΣ αμπούλες
ampoules

αν [an] if

ΑΝΑΒΡΑΖΟΝΤΑ ΔΙΣΚΙΑ
αναβράζοντα δισκία
effervescent tablets

ανάβω [anavo] light (verb)

αναγκαίος [anangeos] necessary

ανάγκη [anangi] need

αναγνωρίζω [anagnorizo]
recognize, acknowledge,
admit

ανακατεύω [anakatevo] mix
(verb)

ΑΝΑΚΟΙΝΩΣΗ ανακοίνωση
(η) [anakinosi (i)]
announcement

ΑΝΑΚΛΗΣΙΣ ανάκλησις (η)
[anaklisis (i)] withdrawal

ΑΝΑΛΗΨΗ ανάληψη
withdrawal(s) (of money)

αναμείνατε στο ακουστικό
[anaminateh sto akoostiko] hold
the line please

ανάμεσα [anamesa] among;
between

αναπαύομαι [anapavomeh] rest,
relax

ανάπαυση (η) [anapafsi (i)] rest

αναπαυτικός [anapaftikos]
comfortable

αναπηρική πολυθρόνα (η)
[anapiriki polithrona (i)]
wheelchair

ανάπηρος [anapiros] disabled

αναπνέω [anapneo] breathe

αναποδογυρίζω [anapothoyirizo]
knock over

αναπτήρας (ο) [anaptiras (o)]
lighter

αναπτύσσω [anaptiso] develop;
explain

ανατολή (η) [anatoli (i)] east;
dawn

ανατολή του ήλιου (η) [anatoli
too ilioo (i)] sunrise

ΑΝΑΧΩΡΕΙ ΚΑΘΗΜΕΡΙΝΑ
ΓΙΑ ... αναχωρεί καθημερινά
γιά ... departs daily to ...

ΑΝΑΧΩΡΗΣΕΙΣ αναχωρήσεις
departures

ΑΝΑΧΩΡΗΣΗ αναχώρηση (η)
[anakhorisi (i)] departure

ΑΝΑΨΥΚΤΗΡΙΟ αναψυκτήριο
refreshments

άνδρας (ο) [anthras (o)] man

ΑΝΔΡΙΚΑ ανδρικά (τα)
[anthrika (ta)] menswear

ΑΝΔΡΙΚΑ ΕΙΔΗ ΚΑΙ
ΑΞΕΣΟΥΑΡ ανδρικά είδη και
αξεσουάρ men's fashions and
accessories

ΑΝΔΡΙΚΑ ΕΝΔΥΜΑΤΑ
ανδρικά ενδύματα [anthrika
enthimata] menswear

ΑΝΔΡΙΚΑ ΕΣΩΡΟΥΧΑ
ανδρικά εσώρουχα [anthrika
esorookha] men's underwear

ΑΝΔΡΙΚΑΙ ΚΟΜΜΩΣΕΙΣ
ανδρικαί κομμώσεις [anthrikeh
komosis] men's hairdresser

ΑΝΔΡΙΚΑ ΥΠΟΔΗΜΑΤΑ
ανδρικά υποδήματα [anthrika
ipothimata] men's footwear

ΑΝΔΡΙΚΑ ΥΠΟΚΑΜΙΣΑ
ανδρικά υποκάμισα [anthrika
ipokamisa] men's shirts

ΑΝΔΡΩΝ ανδρών gents'
(toilet), men's room

ανεβαίνω [aneveno] get in (car);
get up; go up

ΑΝΕΛΚΥΣΤΗΡΑΣ
ανελκυστήρας (ο) [anelkistiras
(o)] lift, elevator

ΑΝΕΜΙΣΤΗΡΑΣ ανεμιστήρας
(ο) [anemistiras (o)] fan

άνεμος (ο) [anemos (o)] wind

ΑΝΕΞΑΡΤΗΤΟ ΔΙΑΜΕΡΙΣΜΑ
ανεξάρτητο διαμέρισμα (το)
[anexartito thiamerisma (to)] self-

catering apartment

ανεξάρτητος [anexartitos]
independent

άνεργος [anergos] unemployed

ανήκω [aniko] belong

ανησυχώ [anisikho] be anxious,
be worried

ανησυχώ για [anisikho ya]
worry about

ανηψιά (η) [anipsia (i)] niece

ανηψιός (ο) [anipsios (o)]
nephew

ΑΝΘΟΠΩΛΕΙΟ ανθοπωλείο
(το) [anтнopolio (to)] florist's

άνθρωποι (οι) [anтнropi (i)]
people

αν και [an keh] although

ΑΝΟΔΟΣ άνοδος (η) [anothos
(i)] ascent, way up

ανοίγω [anigo] open (verb);
switch on

ανοίγω τις βαλίτσες [anigo tis
valitses] unpack

ΑΝΟΙΚΤΑ ανοικτά [anikta]
open

ΑΝΟΙΚΤΟ ΑΠΟ ... ΩΣ ...
ανοικτό από ... ως ... [anikto
apo ... os ...] open from ...
to ...

ΑΝΟΙΚΤΟΝ ανοικτόν [anikton]
open (adj)

ανοικτός [aniktos] open (adj);
on (light)

άνοιξη (η) [anixi (i)] spring
(season)

ανοιχτήρι (το) [anikhtiri (to)] tin
opener; corkscrew

ΑΝΟΙΧΤΟ ανοιχτό [anikhto]
open; light (colour)

ΑΝΤΑΛΛΑΚΤΙΚΑ
ανταλλακτικά (τα) spare parts
ΑΝΤΑΛΛΑΚΤΙΚΑ
ΑΥΤΟΚΙΝΗΤΩΝ
ανταλλακτικά αυτοκινήτων (τα)
auto spares
ανταλλάσω [andalaso]
exchange (verb)
άντε! [andeh!] come on!
αντέχω [andekho] endure,
tolerate
αντί [andi] instead of
ΑΝΤΙΒΙΟΤΙΚΟ αντιβιοτικό
(το) [andiviotiko (to)] antibiotic
ΑΝΤΙ-ΙΣΤΑΜΙΝΙΚΟ
ΦΑΡΜΑΚΟ αντι-ισταμινικό
φάρμακο (το) [andi-istaminiko
farmako (to)] antihistamine
αντίκα (η) [andika (i)] antique
ΑΝΤΙΚΕΣ αντίκες [andikes]
antiques
αντίο [andio] goodbye
αντιπαθητικός [andipaTHitikos]
obnoxious
ΑΝΤΙΠΡΟΣΩΠΕΙΑ
ΑΥΤΟΚΙΝΗΤΩΝ
αντιπροσωπεία αυτοκινήτων
(η) [andiprosopia aftokiniton (i)]
car dealer
ΑΝΤΙΠΡΟΣΩΠΟΣ
αντιπρόσωπος (ο) [andiprosopos
(o)] agent
αντιπυρετικό [andipiretiko] anti-
fever
ΑΝΤΙΣΗΠΤΙΚΟ αντισηπτικό
(το) [andisiptiko (to)] antiseptic
ΑΝΤΙΣΥΛΛΗΠΤΙΚΟ
αντισυλληπτικό (το)
[andisiliptiko (to)] contraceptive

ΑΝΤΙΣΥΛΛΗΠΤΙΚΟ ΧΑΠΙ
αντισυλληπτικό χάπι (το)
[andisiliptiko khapi (to)]
contraceptive pill
ΑΝΤΙΤΙΜΟ (ΔΙΑΔΡΟΜΗΣ)
αντίτιμο (διαδρομής) (το)
[anditimo (thiathromis) (to)] fare
ΑΝΤΙΦΛΕΓΜΩΔΕΣ
αντιφλεγμώδες anti-
inflammation
αντλία (η) [andlia (i)] pump
ΑΝΤΛΙΑ ΒΕΝΖΙΝΗΣ αντλία
βενζίνης petrol/gas pump
ΑΝΤΛΙΑ ΝΤΙΖΕΛ αντλία
ντίζελ diesel pump
ΑΝΩ άνω [ano] up
ΑΞΕΣΟΥΑΡ ΑΥΤΟΚΙΝΗΤΩΝ
αξεσουάρ αυτοκινήτων (τα)
auto accessories
άξονας (ο) [axonas (o)] axle
ΑΠΑΓΟΡΕΥΕΤΑΙ
απαγορεύεται it is
prohibited
ΑΠΑΓΟΡΕΥΕΤΑΙ Η ΕΙΣΟΔΟΣ
απαγορεύεται η είσοδος no
entry, no admission
ΑΠΑΓΟΡΕΥΕΤΑΙ Η
ΚΑΤΑΠΟΣΙΣ απαγορεύεται η
κατάποσις do not swallow
ΑΠΑΓΟΡΕΥΕΤΑΙ Η
ΚΑΤΑΣΚΗΝΩΣΗ
απαγορεύεται η κατασκήνωση
no camping
ΑΠΑΓΟΡΕΥΕΤΑΙ Η
ΚΟΛΥΜΒΗΣΗ απαγορεύεται
η κολύμβηση no swimming
ΑΠΑΓΟΡΕΥΕΤΑΙ Η ΛΗΨΙΣ
ΔΙΑ ΤΟΥ ΣΤΟΜΑΤΟΣ
απαγορεύεται η λήψις διά του

στόματος not to be taken
orally
ΑΠΑΓΟΡΕΥΕΤΑΙ Η
ΣΤΑΘΜΕΥΣΗ απαγορεύεται
η στάθμευση no parking
ΑΠΑΓΟΡΕΥΕΤΑΙ Η ΣΤΑΣΗ
απαγορεύεται η στάση no
waiting, no stopping
ΑΠΑΓΟΡΕΥΕΤΑΙ Η
ΧΟΡΗΓΗΣΗ ΑΝΕΥ
ΣΥΝΤΑΓΗΣ ΙΑΤΡΟΥ
απαγορεύεται η χορήγηση
άνευ συνταγής ιατρού available
on prescription only
ΑΠΑΓΟΡΕΥΕΤΑΙ Ο
ΓΥΜΝΙΣΜΟΣ απαγορεύεται ο
γυμνισμός nudism prohibited
ΑΠΑΓΟΡΕΥΟΝΤΑΙ ΟΙ
ΚΑΤΑΔΥΣΕΙΣ απαγορεύονται
οι καταδύσεις no diving
ΑΠΑΓΟΡΕΥΕΤΑΙ ΤΟ
ΚΑΜΠΙΝΓΚ απαγορεύεται το
κάμπινγκ no camping
ΑΠΑΓΟΡΕΥΕΤΑΙ ΤΟ
ΚΑΠΝΙΖΕΙΝ απαγορεύεται το
καπνίζειν no smoking
ΑΠΑΓΟΡΕΥΕΤΑΙ ΤΟ
ΚΑΠΝΙΣΜΑ απαγορεύεται το
κάπνισμα no smoking
ΑΠΑΓΟΡΕΥΕΤΑΙ ΤΟ
ΚΥΝΗΓΙ απαγορεύεται το
κυνήγι no hunting
ΑΠΑΓΟΡΕΥΕΤΑΙ ΤΟ
ΠΡΟΣΠΕΡΑΣΜΑ
απαγορεύεται το προσπέρασμα
no overtaking, no passing
ΑΠΑΓΟΡΕΥΕΤΑΙ ΤΟ
ΨΑΡΕΜΑ απαγορεύεται το
ψάρεμα no fishing

ΑΠΑΓΟΡΕΥΜΕΝΗ ΠΕΡΙΟΧΗ
απαγορευμένη περιοχή
restricted area
απαγορευμένος [apagorevmenos]
forbidden
απαίσιος [apesios] appalling
απαιτώ [apeto] demand (verb)
απαλός [apalos] soft
απαντάω [apandao] answer
(verb)
απάντηση (η) [apandisi (i)]
answer
απέvταρος [apendaros] broke
απίθανος [apiTHanos] incredible
ΑΠΛΗ ΒΕΝΖΙΝΗ απλή
βενζίνη (η) [apli venzini (i)]
two-star petrol/gas
ΑΠΛΗ ΔΙΑΔΡΟΜΗ απλή
διαδρομή (η) [apli thiathromi (i)]
single/one-way fare
ΑΠΛΟ ΕΙΣΙΤΗΡΙΟ απλό
εισιτήριο (το) [aplo isitirio (to)]
single/one-way ticket
απλός [aplos] simple
απλώνω [aplono] stretch (verb)
από [apo] from; since; than
από το ... στο ... [apo to ... sto ...]
from ... to ...
από κάτω [apo kato] below,
under
από πάνω [apo pano] over,
above
αποβιβάζομαι [apovivazomeh]
land (verb)
απογειώνομαι [apoyionomeh]
take off (verb)
απόγευμα (το) [apoyevma (to)]
afternoon
το απόγευμα [to apoyevma] in

the afternoon

ΑΠΟΓΕΥΜΑΤΙΝΗ
ΠΑΡΑΣΤΑΣΗ απογευματινή
παράσταση (η) [apoyevmatini
parastasi (i)] matinee

απογοητευμένος [apogo-
itevmenos] disappointed

ΑΠΟΔΕΙΞΗ απόδειξη (η)
[apothixi (i)] receipt, evidence

ΑΠΟ ΔΕΥΤΕΡΟ ΧΕΡΙ από
δεύτερο χέρι [apo theftero kheri]
second-hand

ΑΠΟΛΥΜΑΝΤΙΚΟ
απολυμαντικό (το) [apolimandiko
(to)] disinfectant

ΑΠΟΣΚΕΥΕΣ αποσκευές (οι)
[aposkeves (i)] luggage,
baggage

ΑΠΟΣΜΗΤΙΚΟ αποσμητικό
(το) [aposmitiko (to)] deodorant

ΑΠΟΣΤΟΛΕΑΣ αποστολέας
[apostoleas] sender

απότομος [apotomos] steep

απότομος βράχος (ο) [apotomos
vrakhos (o)] cliff

αποφασίζω [apofasizo] decide

απόψε [apopseh] tonight

ΑΠΡΙΛΙΟΣ Απρίλιος (ο)
[Aprilios (o)] April

Α´ ΠΡΟΒΟΛΗΣ α´ προβολής
major cinema/movie
theater

απρόσμενος [aprosmenos]
surprising

ΑΠΩΛΕΣΘΕΝΤΑ
ΑΝΤΙΚΕΙΜΕΝΑ
απωλεσθέντα αντικείμενα
[apolesτHenda adikimena] lost
property

αράχνη (η) [arakhni (i)] spider

αργά [arga] late; slowly

αργίες (οι) [aryies (i)] public
holidays

αργός [argos] slow

αργότερα [argotera] later

αργώ [argo] arrive late; go
slowly

ΑΡΙΘΜΟΣ αριθμός (ο)
[ariτHmos (o)] number

ΑΡΙΘΜΟΣ ΘΕΣΕΩΣ αριθμός
θέσεως [ariτHmos τHeseos] seat
number

αριστερά [aristera] left

αριστερόχειρας [aristerokhiras]
left-handed

αρκετά [arketa] enough; quite

αρκετοί [arketi] several

αρνητικό (το) [arnitiko (to)]
negative

αρουραίος (ο) [arooreos (o)] rat

αρραβωνιασμένος
[aravoniasmenos] engaged (to be
married)

αρραβωνιαστικιά (η)
[aravoniastikia (i)] fiancée

αρραβωνιαστικός (ο)
[aravoniastikos (o)] fiancé

αρρενωπός [arenopos] manly;
macho

αρρώστια (η) [arostia (i)] disease

άρρωστος [arostos] ill, sick

ΑΡΤΟΠΟΙΕΙΟ αρτοποιείο (το)
[artopi-io (to)] bakery

αρχαιολογία (η) [arkheoloyia (i)]
archaeology

αρχαίος [arkheos] ancient

αρχαιότητες (οι) [arkheotites (i)]
ruins

αρχάρια (η) [arkharia (i)] beginner

αρχάριος (ο) [arkharios (o)] beginner

αρχή (η) [arkhi (i)] beginning

αρχίζω [arkhizo] begin

αρχιτέκτων (ο/η) [arkhitekton (o/i)] architect

άρωμα (το) [aroma (to)] perfume

ΑΣΑΝΣΕΡ ασανσέρ (το) [asanser (to)] lift, elevator

ασετόν (το) [aseton (to)] nail varnish remover

ΑΣΗΜΕΝΙΟΣ ασημένιος [asimenios] silver

ΑΣΗΜΙΚΑ ασημικά (τα) [asimika (ta)] silver(ware)

ΑΣΘΕΝΟΦΟΡΟ ασθενοφόρο (το) [asтHenoforo (to)] ambulance

ΑΣΘΜΑ άσθμα (το) [asтHma (to)] asthma

ΑΣΠΙΡΙΝΗ ασπιρίνη (η) [aspirini (i)] aspirin

άσπρος [aspros] white

άστατος [astatos] changeable

αστείο (το) [astio (to)] joke

αστείος [astios] funny, amusing

αστέρι (το) [asteri (to)] star

αστράγαλος (ο) [astragalos (o)] ankle

ΑΣΤΥΝΟΜΙΑ αστυνομία (η) [astinomia (i)] police

ΑΣΤΥΝΟΜΙΚΟ ΤΜΗΜΑ αστυνομικό τμήμα (το) [astinomiko tmima (to)] police station

αστυφύλακας (ο) [astifilakas (o)] policeman

αστυνομικός (η) [astinomikos (i)] policewoman

ΑΣΦΑΛΕΙΑ ασφάλεια (η) [asfalia (i)] fuse; insurance

ΑΣΦΑΛΕΙΑΙ ασφάλειαι [asfali-eh] insurance

ασφαλής [asfalis] safe

άσχημα [askhima] badly

άσχημος [askhimos] ugly

ατζέντα (η) [atzenda (i)] address book

ατμόπλοιο (το) [atmoplio (to)] steamer

άτομο (το) [atomo (to)] person

ΑΥΓΟΥΣΤΟΣ Αύγουστος (ο) [Avgoostos (o)] August

αυθεντικός [afтHendikos] genuine

αύριο [avrio] tomorrow

Αυστραλέζα (η) [Afstraleza (i)] Australian (woman)

Αυστραλέζικος [Afstralezikos] Australian (adj)

ΑΥΣΤΡΑΛΙΑ Αυστραλία (η) [Afstralia (i)] Australia

Αυστραλός (ο) [Afstralos (o)] Australian (man)

αυτά, αυτές [afta, aftes] these; they; them

αυτή [afti] she; this (one)

αυτής [aftis] of her

αυτί (το) [afti (to)] ear

αυτό [afto] it; this

αυτό εδώ [afto etho] this one

αυτοί [afti] these; they

ΑΥΤΟΚΙΝΗΤΟ αυτοκίνητο (το) [aftokinito (to)] car

αυτόματος [aftomatos] automatic (adj)

αυτό που [afto poo] what

αυτός [aftos] he; this (one)

αυτός ο ίδιος [aftos o ithios] himself

αυτού [aftoo] of him, of it

αυτούς [aftoos] them

ΑΥΤ/ΤΟ αυτ/το car

αυτών [afton] of them

αφεντικό (το) [afendiko (to)] boss

ΑΦΕΤΗΡΙΑ αφετηρία (η) [afetiria (i)] terminus

αφήνω [afino] leave (verb)

ΑΦΙΞΕΙΣ αφίξεις arrivals

ΑΦΙΞΗ άφιξη (η) [afixi (i)] arrival

αφίσα (η) [afisa (i)] poster

ΑΦΟΙ. αφοί. bros.

ΑΦΟΡΟΛΟΓΗΤΑ αφορολόγητα (τα) [aforoloyita (ta)] duty-free

αφροδίσιο νόσημα (το) [afrothisio nosima (to)] VD

ΑΦΡΟΣ ΞΥΡΙΣΜΑΤΟΣ αφρός ξυρίσματος (ο) [afros xirismatos (o)] shaving foam

αφρός (ο) [afros (o)] surf

αχθοφόρος (ο) [akhthoforos (o)] doorman

αχινός (ο) [akhinos (o)] sea urchin

Β
▬

ΒΑΓΟΝΙ βαγόνι (το) [vagoni (to)] coach, car (train)

ΒΑΓΚΟΝ-ΛΙ βαγκόν-λι [vagon-li] sleeper, sleeping car

βάζο (το) [vazo (to)] vase

βάζω [vazo] put

ΒΑΘΙΑ ΝΕΡΑ βαθιά νερά deep water

βάθος: στο βάθος [sto vaтнos] in the background; at the bottom

βαθύς [vaтнis] deep

βαλβίδα (η) [valvitha (i)] valve

βαλίτσα (η) [valitsa (i)] bag, suitcase

ΒΑΜΒΑΚΕΡΟ βαμβακερό (το) [vamvakero (to)] cotton

βαρετός [varetos] boring

ΒΑΡΚΑ βάρκα (η) [varka (i)] small boat; dinghy

βάρκα με κουπιά [varka meh koopia] rowing boat

βάρκα με μηχανή [varka meh mikhani] motorboat

ΒΑΡΟΣ βάρος (το) [varos (to)] weight

βαρύς [varis] heavy; rich (food)

βασιλιάς (ο) [vasilias (o)] king

βασίλισσα (η) [vasilisa (i)] queen

ΒΑΦΗ βαφή (η) [vafi (i)] hair dye

βάφω [vafo] paint; tint (verb)

βγάζω φωτογραφία [vgazo fotografia] photograph (verb)

βγαίνω [vgeno] go out

ΒΓΑΛΤΕ ΤΗΝ ΚΑΡΤΑ βγάλτε την κάρτα remove the card

βέβαια [veveh-a] of course

βελόνα (η) [velona (i)] needle

βελτιώνω [veltiono] improve

ΒΕΝΖΙΝΑΔΙΚΟ βενζινάδικο (το) [venzinathiko (to)] petrol station, gas station

ΒΕΝΖΙΝΗ βενζίνη (η) [venzini (i)] petrol, gas(oline)

βεντιλατέρ (το) [vendilater (to)] fan belt

ΒΕΡΝΙΚΙ ΠΑΠΟΥΤΣΙΩΝ βερνίκι παπουτσιών (το) [verniki papootsion (to)] shoe polish

ΒΗΧΑΣ βήχας (ο) [vikhas (o)] cough

βήχω [vikho] cough (verb)

βιάζομαι [viazomeh] hurry (verb)

βιάσου! [viasoo!] hurry up!

βιασμός (ο) [viasmos (o)] rape

βιβλίο (το) [vivlio (to)] book

βιβλίο διαλόγων [vivlio thialogon] phrase book

ΒΙΒΛΙΟΘΗΚΗ βιβλιοθήκη (η) [vivlioTHiki (i)] library

ΒΙΒΛΙΟΠΩΛΕΙΟ βιβλιοπωλείο (το) [vivliopolio (to)] bookshop, bookstore

ΒΙΔΑ βίδα (η) [vitha (i)] screw

ΒΙΖΑ βίζα (η) [viza (i)] visa

βίλλα (η) [vila (i)] villa

βίντεο (το) [video (to)] video

ΒΙΤΑΜΙΝΕΣ βιταμίνες (οι) [vitamines (i)] vitamins

Β΄ ΚΑΤΗΓΟΡΙΑΣ Β΄ κατηγορίας second class

βλάβη (η) [vlavi (i)] breakdown (car)

βλάκας (ο) [vlakas (o)] idiot; stupid

βλέπω [vlepo] see

βοήθεια (η) [voiTHia (i)] help

βοηθώ [vo-iTHo] help (verb)

βόμβα (η) [vomva (i)] bomb

Βόρειος Ιρλανδία (η) [vorios Irlanthia (i)] Northern Ireland

ΒΟΥΛΓΑΡΙΑ Βουλγαρία (η) [voolgaria (i)] Bulgaria

Βουλγαρικός [voolgarikos] Bulgarian (adj)

βουλιάζω [vooliazo] sink (verb)

ΒΟΥΛΚΑΝΙΖΑΤΕΡ βουλκανιζατέρ [voolkanizater] tyre repairs

βουνό (το) [voono (to)] mountain

βούρτσα (η) [voortsa (i)] brush

βουτάω [vootao] dive (verb)

Β΄ ΠΡΟΒΟΛΗΣ β΄ προβολής local cinema/movie theater

βράδυ (το) [vrathi (to)] evening

το βράδυ [to vrathi] in the evening

βραδυά (η) [vrathia (i)] evening

ΒΡΑΔΥΝΗ ΠΑΡΑΣΤΑΣΗ βραδυνή παράσταση evening performance

βράζω [vrazo] boil (verb)

βράχια (τα) [vrakhia (ta)] rocks; cliffs

βραχιόλι (το) [vrakhioli (to)] bracelet

βράχος (ο) [vrakhos (o)] rock

ΒΡΕΤΑΝΝΙΑ Βρεταννία (η) [vretania (i)] Britain

Βρεταννίδα (η) [vretanitha (i)] Briton (woman)

Βρεταννικός [vretanikos] British

Βρεταννός (ο) [vretanos (o)] Briton (man)

βρέχει [vrekhi] it's raining

βρίσκω [vrisko] find (verb)

βροντή (η) [vrondi (i)] thunder

βροχή (η) [vrokhi (i)] rain

βρύση (η) [vrisi (i)] tap, faucet

βρώμικος [**vromikos**] dirty
βυζαίνω [**vizeno**] breastfeed
βυθός (ο) [**viTHos** (o)] bottom (of sea)

Γ

γάιδαρος (ο) [**gaitharos** (o)] donkey
ΓΑΛΑΚΤΟΠΩΛΕΙΟ γαλακτοπωλείο (το) [**galaktopolio** (to)] shop/take-away café selling dairy products
ΓΑΛΑΚΤΩΜΑ ΚΑΘΑΡΙΣΜΟΥ γαλάκτωμα καθαρισμού (το) [**galaktoma kaTHarismoo** (to)] cleansing lotion
ΓΑΛΛΙΑ Γαλλία (η) [**galia** (i)] France
Γαλλικός [**galikos**] French (adj)
γάμος (ο) [**gamos** (o)] wedding
γαμπρός (ο) [**gambros** (o)] bridegroom; son-in-law; brother-in-law
γάντια (τα) [**gandia** (ta)] gloves
γάτα (η) [**gata** (i)] cat
γειά σου! [**yia soo!**] hello!; bless you!; cheers!
γείτονας (ο) [**yitonas** (o)] neighbour
γελοίο [**yelio**] ridiculous
γελώ [**yelo**] laugh (verb)
γεμάτος [**yematos**] full
γεμίζω [**yemizo**] fill (verb)
γενέθλια (τα) [**yeneTHlia** (ta)] birthday

γένια (τα) [**yenia** (ta)] beard
γενναίος [**yeneos**] brave
ΓΕΡΜΑΝΙΑ Γερμανία (η) [**Yermania** (i)] Germany
Γερμανικός [**Yermanikos**] German (adj)
γέρος [**yeros**] old (person)
ΓΕΥΜΑ γεύμα (το) [**yevma** (to)] meal
γεύση (η) [**yefsi** (i)] flavour; taste
ΓΕΦΥΡΑ γέφυρα (η) [**yefira** (i)] bridge
ΓΗΠΕΔΟ γήπεδο (το) [**yipetho** (to)] football pitch
ΓΗΠΕΔΟ ΤΕΝΝΙΣ γήπεδο τέννις [**yipetho tenis**] tennis court
για [**ya**] for
για μένα [**ya mena**] for me
γιαγιά (η) [**yaya** (i)] grandmother
ΓΙΑ ΕΞΩΤΕΡΙΚΗ ΧΡΗΣΗ ΜΟΝΟΝ για εξωτερική χρήση μόνον for external use only
ΓΙΑ ΕΣΩΤΕΡΙΚΗ ΧΡΗΣΗ ΜΟΝΟΝ για εσωτερική χρήση μόνον for internal use only
γιακάς (ο) [**yakas** (o)] collar
γιατί; [**yati?**] why?
ΓΙΑ ΤΟ ΣΠΙΤΙ για το σπίτι [**ya to spiti**] to take away, to go (food)
ΓΙΑΤΡΟΣ γιατρός (ο/η) [**yatros** (o/i)] doctor
γίνομαι [**yinomeh**] become; happen

τι γίνεται; [ti **yi**neteh?] what's
happening?

ΓΙΟΡΤΗ ΚΡΑΣΙΟΥ γιορτή
κρασιού (η) [**yorti** krasi**oo** (i)]
wine festival

γιός (ο) [**yos** (o)] son

γιώτ (το) [**yot** (to)] yacht

γκάζι (το) [**gazi** (to)] gas;
accelerator

ΓΚΑΛΕΡΙ γκαλερί (η) [**galeri**
(i)] art gallery

ΓΚΑΡΑΖ γκαράζ (το) [**garaz**
(to)] garage (for parking/repairs)

ΓΚΑΡΝΤΑΡΟΜΠΑ
γκαρνταρόμπα (η) [gardar**oba** (i)]
cloakroom (for coats)

Γ΄ ΚΑΤΗΓΟΡΙΑΣ
Γ΄ κατηγορίας third class

γκολφ (το) [**golf** (to)] golf

γκρίζος [**grizos**] grey

γκρουπ (το) [**groop** (to)] group

γλάρος (ο) [**glaros** (o)] seagull

ΓΛΙΦΙΤΖΟΥΡΙ γλιφιτζούρι (το)
[glifidz**oori** (to)] lollipop

ΓΛΥΚΟ γλυκό (το) [**gliko** (to)]
sweet, candy

γλυκός [**glikos**] sweet (adj)

γλυστερός [**glisteros**] slippery

γλυστράω [**glistrao**] skid (verb)

γλώσσα (η) [**glosa** (i)] language;
tongue

γνωρίζω [**gnorizo**] know

δεν γνωρίζω [then gn**orizo**] I
don't know

γόνατο (το) [**gonato** (to)] knee

γονείς (οι) [**gonis** (i)] parents

γουίντσερφ (το) [goo**indserf** (to)]
sailboard

ΓΟΥΝΑΡΙΚΑ γουναρικά (τα)

[goonari**ka** (ta)] furrier

ΓΟΥΝΕΣ γούνες [**goones**] furs

γουόκμαν (το) [goo-**okman** (to)]
personal stereo

γουρούνι (το) [goor**ooni** (to)] pig

γοφός (ο) [**gofos** (o)] hip

γραβάτα (η) [gra**vata** (i)] tie,
necktie

γράμμα (το) [**grama** (to)] letter

γράμματα (τα) [**gramata** (ta)]
post, mail

γραμματική (η) [gra**matiki** (i)]
grammar

ΓΡΑΜΜΑΤΟΚΙΒΩΤΙΟ
γραμματοκιβώτιο (το)
[gramatoki**votio** (to)] letterbox,
mailbox

γραμματόσημο (το) [grama**tosimo**
(to)] stamp

ΓΡΑΜΜΕΣ ΤΡΑΙΝΟΥ
γραμμές τραίνου railway
crosses road

ΓΡΑΜΜΗ γραμμή (η) [gra**mi**
(i)] route, line

γρασίδι (το) [gras**ithi** (to)] lawn

γραφείο (το) [gr**afio** (to)] office

ΓΡΑΦΕΙΟ ΤΑΞΙΔΙΩΝ γραφείο
ταξιδίων [gr**afio** taxi**thion**] travel
agency

γραφομηχανή (η) [grafomi**khani**
(i)] typewriter

γράφω [**grafo**] write

γρήγορα [**grigora**] quick;
quickly

γρήγορος [**grigoros**] fast

ΓΡΙΠΠΗ γρίππη (η) [**gripi** (i)]
flu

γρύλλος (ο) [**grilos** (o)] jack

γυαλί (το) [**yali** (to)] glass

(material)

ΓΥΑΛΙΑ γυαλιά (τα) [yalia (ta)]
glasses, eyeglasses

ΓΥΑΛΙΑ ΗΛΙΟΥ γυαλιά ηλίου
[yalia ilioo] sunglasses

ΓΥΜΝΑΣΙΟ γυμνάσιο (το)
[yimnasio (to)] secondary
school

γυμνασμένος [yimnasmenos] fit
(healthy)

ΓΥΜΝΑΣΤΗΡΙΟ γυμναστήριο
(το) [yimnastirio (to)] gym

γυμνός [yimnos] naked

γυναίκα (η) [yineka (i)] woman;
wife

ΓΥΝΑΙΚΕΙΑ γυναικεία (τα)
[yinekia (ta)] ladies' wear

ΓΥΝΑΙΚΕΙΑΙ ΚΟΜΜΩΣΕΙΣ
γυναικείαι κομμώσεις (οι)
[yinekieh komosis (i)] ladies'
salon

ΓΥΝΑΙΚΕΙΑ ΦΟΡΕΜΑΤΑ
γυναικεία φορέματα [yinekia
foremata] ladies' dresses

ΓΥΝΑΙΚΕΙΕΣ ΚΑΛΤΣΕΣ -
ΚΑΛΣΟΝ γυναικείες κάλτσες
- καλσόν [yinekies kaltses -
kalson] ladies' socks -
stockings

ΓΥΝΑΙΚΩΝ γυναικών ladies'
(toilet), ladies' room

γυρνώ [yirno] turn (verb)

γυρνώ πίσω [yirno piso] arrive
back, return; take back

γυρνώ σπίτι [yirno spiti] return
home

Δ

δακτυλίδι (το) [thaktilithi (to)]
ring (on finger)

δανείζομαι [thanizomeh] borrow

δανείζω [thanizo] lend

δασκάλα (η) [thaskala (i)]
instructor; teacher

δάσκαλος (ο) [thaskalos (o)]
instructor; teacher

δάσος (το) [thasos (to)] forest

δάχτυλο (το) [thakhtilo (to)]
finger

δάχτυλο του ποδιού [thakhtilo too
pothioo] toe

δε [theh] ξου

Δ.Ε.Η. public electricity
company

δείκτης (ο) [thiktis (o)] gauge;
index finger

ΔΕΙΠΝΟ δείπνο (το) [thipno
(to)] evening meal

δείχνω [thikhno] show (verb)

δέκα [theka] ten

δεκαεννιά [theka-enia] nineteen

δεκαέξι [theka-exi] sixteen

δεκαεπτά [theka-epta]
seventeen

δεκαοχτώ [theka-okhto]
eighteen

δεκαπενθήμερο
[thekapenthimero] fortnight

δεκαπέντε [thekapendeh] fifteen

ΔΕΚΑΡΙΚΟ δεκάρικο (το)
[thekariko (to)] 10-drachma
coin

δεκατέσσερα [thekatesera]
fourteen

δέκατος [thekatos] tenth

δεκατρία [thekatria] thirteen

ΔΕΚΕΜΒΡΙΟΣ Δεκέμβριος (ο)
[thekemvrios (o)] December

δέμα (το) [thema (to)] parcel

ΔΕΜΑΤΑ δέματα parcels,
packages

δεν [then] not

δένδρο (το) [thenthro (to)] tree

ΔΕΝ ΛΕΙΤΟΥΡΓΕΙ δεν
λειτουργεί [then litooryi] out of
order

ΔΕΝ ΣΙΔΕΡΩΝΕΤΑΙ δεν
σιδερώνεται do not iron

δεξιός, δεξιά [thexios, thexia]
right (side)

δεξίωση (η) [thexiosi (i)]
reception (party)

ΔΕΡΜΑ δέρμα (το) [therma (to)]
skin; leather

ΔΕΡΜΑΤΑ δέρματα (τα)
[thermata (ta)] leather goods

ΔΕΣΠΟΙΝΙΔΑ δεσποινίδα (η)
[thespinitha (i)] young woman;
Miss; Ms

ΔΕΣΠΟΙΝΙΣ δεσποινίς
[thespinis] Miss; Ms

ΔΕΥΤΕΡΑ Δευτέρα (η) [theftera
(i)] Monday

ΔΕΥΤΕΡΗ ΘΕΣΗ δεύτερη
θέση second class

δευτερόλεπτο (το) [thefterolepto
(to)] second

δεύτερος [thefteros] second
(adj)

ΔΕΥΤΕΡΟ ΧΕΡΙ δεύτερο χέρι
[theftero kheri] second-hand

δέχομαι [thekhomeh] accept;
receive

δηλητηρίαση (η) [thilitiriasi (i)]
poisoning

δηλητήριο (το) [thilitirio (to)]
poison

ΔΗΜΑΡΧΕΙΟ δημαρχείο (το)
[thimarkhio (to)] town hall

ΔΗΜΟΣΙΑ ΛΟΥΤΡΑ δημόσια
λουτρά (τα) [thimosia lootra (ta)]
public baths

δημόσιος [thimosios] public

δημοσιογράφος (ο/η)
[thimosiografos (o/i)] reporter

δημοτική μουσική (η) [thimotiki
moosiki (i)] folk music

διαβάζω [thiavazo] read

ΔΙΑΒΑΣΗ ΠΕΖΩΝ διάβαση
πεζών (η) pedestrian crossing

ΔΙΑΒΑΤΗΡΙΟ διαβατήριο (το)
[thiavatirio (to)] passport

διαβητικός (ο) [thiavitikos (o)]
diabetic

διαβητική (η) [thiavitiki (i)]
diabetic

ΔΙΑΔΡΟΜΗ ΜΕΤ'
ΕΠΙΣΤΡΟΦΗΣ διαδρομή μετ'
επιστροφής (η) [thiathromi met'
epistrofis (i)] return/round trip
fare

διάδρομος (ο) [thiathromos (o)]
corridor

διάθεση (η) [thiaτHesi (i)] mood

δίαιτα (η) [thieta (i)] diet

διακοπές (οι) [thiakopes (i)]
holiday, vacation

διακοπή (η) [thiakopi (i)]
interruption; power cut

διακόπτης (ο) [thiakoptis (o)]
switch

διακόπτω [thiakopto] interrupt

διακόσια [thiakosia] two hundred

διαλέγω [thialego] choose

ΔΙΑΛΕΙΜΜΑ διάλειμμα (το) [thialima (to)] interval, intermission

διάλεκτος (η) [thialektos (i)] dialect

ΔΙΑΛΥΜΑ διάλυμα (το) [thialima (to)] solution

διαμάντι (το) [thiamandi (to)] diamond

Διαμαρτυρόμενος (ο) [thiamartiromenos (o)] Protestant

ΔΙΑΜΕΡΙΣΜΑ διαμέρισμα (το) [thiamerisma (to)] apartment, flat

διά μέσου [thia mesoo] through

διαμονή (η) [thiamoni (i)] accommodation; stay

ΔΙΑΝΥΚΤΕΡΕΥΟΝ διανυκτερεύον open all night

διάρκεια (η) [thiarkia (i)] duration

ΔΙΑΡΚΕΙΑ ΠΤΗΣΕΩΣ διάρκεια πτήσεως [thiarkia ptiseos] flight time

διαρροή (η) [thiaroi (i)] leak

ΔΙΑΡΡΟΙΑ διάρροια (η) [thiaria (i)] diarrhoea

διάσημος [thiasimos] famous

ΔΙΑΣΤΑΥΡΩΣΗ διασταύρωση (η) [thiastavrosi (i)] junction, crossroads, intersection

διασχίζω [thiaskhizo] go through

ΔΙΑΤΗΡΕΙΤΑΙ ΣΕ ΨΥΓΕΙΟ διατηρείται σε ψυγείο keep refrigerated

διαφημιστικό (το) [thiafimistiko (to)] leaflet; advertisements (on TV); trailer (cinema)

διαφορετικά [thiaforetika] otherwise

διαφορετικός [thiaforetikos] different

διάφραγμα (το) [thiafragma (to)] shutter (in camera)

διαχειριστής (ο) [thiakhiristis (o)] manager

διαχειρίστρια (η) [thiakhiristria (i)] manageress

διδάσκω [thithasko] teach

δίδυμοι (οι) [thithimi (i)] twins

ΔΙΕΥΘΥΝΣΗ διεύθυνση (η) [thiefthinsi (i)] address

δίκαιος [thikeos] fair, just

δικά μας [thika mas] ours

δικά μου [thika moo] mine

δικά σας, δικά σου [thika sas, thika soo] yours

ΔΙΚΑΣΤΗΡΙΟ δικαστήριο (το) [thikastirio (to)] law court

δικά της [thika tis] hers

δικά του [thika too] his, its

δικά τους [thika toos] theirs

δικηγόρος (ο/η) [thikigoros (o/i)] lawyer

δική μας [thiki mas] ours

δική μου [thiki moo] mine

δική σας, δική σου [thiki sas, thiki soo] yours

δική του [thiki too] his

δική τους [thiki toos] theirs

ΔΙΚΛΙΝΟ ΔΩΜΑΤΙΟ δίκλινο δωμάτιο (το) [thiklino thomatio (to)] double room

δικό μας [thiko mas] ours

δικό μου [thiko moo] mine

δικό σας, δικό σου [thiko sas, thiko soo] yours

δικό τους [thiko toos] theirs

δικό της [thiko tis] hers

δικό του [thiko too] his; its

δικός μας [thikos mas] ours

δικός μου [thikos moo] mine

δικός σας, δικός σου [thikos sas, thikos soo] yours

δικός του [thikos too] his

δικός τους [thikos toos] theirs

δίνω [thino] give

ΔΙΟΔΙΑ διόδια (τα) [thiothia (ta)] toll

διορθώνω [thiorthono] mend, correct

ΔΙΠΛΗ ΤΑΡΙΦΑ διπλή ταρίφα (η) double tariff

διπλό [thiplo] double

ΔΙΠΛΟ ΔΩΜΑΤΙΟ διπλό δωμάτιο (το) [thiplo thomatio (to)] double room

διπλό κρεβάτι (το) [thiplo krevati (to)] double bed

ΔΙΣ. δις. Miss

ΔΙΣΚΑΔΙΚΟ δισκάδικο (το) [thiskathiko (to)] record shop

ΔΙΣΚΟΙ - ΚΑΣΕΤΕΣ δίσκοι - κασέτες [thiski - kasetes] records – cassettes

δίσκος (ο) [thiskos (o)] record; tray

Δ΄ΚΑΤΗΓΟΡΙΑΣ Δ΄κατηγορίας fourth class

δοκιμάζω [thokimazo] taste (verb); try (on)

ΔΟΛΛΑΡΙΟ δολλάριο (το) [tholario (to)] dollar

δόντι (το) [thondi (to)] tooth

ΔΟΣΟΛΟΓΙΑ ΕΝΗΛΙΚΩΝ δοσολογία ενηλίκων adult dosage

ΔΟΣΟΛΟΓΙΑ ΠΑΙΔΩΝ δοσολογία παίδων children's dosage

δουλειά (η) [thoolia (i)] job; work

δουλειές (οι) [thoolies (i)] business

δουλεύω [thoolevo] work (verb)

δεν δουλεύει [then thoolevi] it's not working

ΔΡΑΧΜΗ δραχμή (η) [thrakhmi (i)] drachma

ΔΡΟΜΟΛΟΓΙΑ δρομολόγια (τα) [thromoloyia (ta)] timetable, (US) schedule

δρόμος (ο) [thromos (o)] road; street

δροσερός [throseros] cool

ΔΡΧ. δρχ. drachma

δυνατός [thinatos] loud; possible; strong

δύο [thio] two

ΔΥΟ ΠΑΡΑΣΤΑΣΕΙΣ δύο παραστάσεις two shows

δυσάρεστος [thisarestos] unpleasant

δύση του ήλιου (η) [thisi too ilioo (i)] sunset

ΔΥΣΚΟΙΛΙΑ δυσκοίλια (η) [thiskilia (i)] constipation

δύσκολος [thiskolos] difficult

ΔΥΣΠΕΨΙΑ δυσπεψία (η) [thispepsia (i)] indigestion

δυστύχημα (το) [thistikhima (to)] accident

δυστυχώς [thistikh**os**] unfortunately

δώδεκα [**tho**theka] twelve

ΔΩΔΕΚΑΔΑ δωδεκάδα (η) [thothek**a**da (i)] dozen

ΔΩΜΑΤΙΟ δωμάτιο (το) [thom**a**tio (to)] room

ΔΩΡΑ δώρα gifts

ΔΩΡΕΑΝ δωρεάν [thor**e**an] free (of charge)

δώρο (το) [th**o**ro (to)] gift

ΔΩΡΟ ΠΑΣΧΑ Δώρο Πάσχα [**tho**ro **Pas**kha] Easter supplement paid to taxi drivers

ΔΩΡΟ ΧΡΙΣΤΟΥΓΕΝΝΩΝ Δώρο Χριστουγέννων [**tho**ro khristooy**e**non] Christmas supplement paid to taxi drivers

E

E.A.Σ. Athens Public Transport Corporation

εβδομάδα (η) [evthom**a**tha (i)] week

εβδομήντα [evthom**i**nda] seventy

έβδομος [**ev**thomos] seventh

Εβραίος [Evr**e**os] Jewish

έγγραφο (το) [**en**grafo (to)] document

εγγύηση (η) [eg**i**-isi (i)] guarantee

έγινε! [**e**yineh!] OK, coming up!

εγκαίρως [eng**e**ros] on time

έγκαυμα από τον ήλιο (το) [engavma ap**o** ton **i**lio (to)] sunburn

έγκυος [**en**gios] pregnant

έγκυρος [**en**giros] valid

έγχρωμο φιλμ (το) [**en**khromo film (to)] colour film

εγώ [eg**o**] I

εγώ ο ίδιος [eg**o** o **i**thios] myself

εδώ [eth**o**] here

έθιμο (το) [**e**THimo (to)] custom

ΕΘΝΙΚΗ ΟΔΟΣ εθνική οδός (η) [eTHnik**i** oth**o**s (i)] motorway, highway, freeway

ΕΘΝΙΚΗ ΠΙΝΑΚΟΘΗΚΗ Εθνική Πινακοθήκη [ETHnik**i** Pinakoτ**Hi**ki] National Art Gallery

ΕΘΝΙΚΟΤΗΤΑ εθνικότητα (η) [eTHnik**o**tita (i)] nationality

ΕΙΔΗ είδη (τα) [**i**thi (ta)] goods

ΕΙΔΗ ΑΥΤΟΚΙΝΗΤΟΥ είδη αυτοκινήτου auto accessories

ΕΙΔΗ ΔΩΡΩΝ είδη δώρων gifts

ΕΙΔΗ ΜΠΕΜΠΕ είδη μπεμπέ [**i**thi bebeh] babywear

ΕΙΔΗ ΡΟΥΧΙΣΜΟΥ είδη ρουχισμού [**i**thi roukhism**oo**] clothes

ΕΙΔΗ ΣΠΟΡ είδη σπορ [**i**thi spor] sports equipment, sportswear

ΕΙΔΗ ΧΑΡΤΟΠΩΛΕΙΟΥ είδη χαρτοπωλείου [**i**thi khartopol**ioo**] stationery

ΕΙΔΙΚΗ ΠΡΟΣΦΟΡΑ ειδική προσφορά special price, special offer

ειδικώς [ithik**os**] especially

είχες [**i**khes] you had

ΕΙΚΟΣΑΡΙΚΟ εικοσάρικο
[ikosariko] 20-drachma coin

είκοσι [ikosi] twenty

ειλικρινής [ilikrinis] sincere

είμαι [imeh] I am

είμαστε [imasteh] we are

είναι [ineh] he/she/it is; they
are

είστε [isteh] you are

ΕΙΣΑΓΩΓΗΣ εισαγωγής
imported

είσαι [iseh] you are

ΕΙΣΙΤΗΡΙΟ εισιτήριο (το)
[isitirio (to)] ticket

ΕΙΣΙΤΗΡΙΟ ΜΕ ΕΠΙΣΤΡΟΦΗ
εισιτήριο με επιστροφή [isitirio
meh epistrofi] return/round
trip ticket

ΕΙΣΟΔΟΣ είσοδος (η) [isothos
(i)] entrance, way in

ΕΙΣΟΔΟΣ ΕΛΕΥΘΕΡΑ είσοδος
ελευθέρα admission free

ΕΙΣΟΔΟΣ ΠΡΑΤΗΡΙΟΥ
είσοδος πρατηρίου entrance
to petrol/gas station

ΕΙΣΠΡΑΚΤΩΡ εισπράκτωρ (ο)
ticket collector

είχα [ikha] I had

είχαμε [ikhameh] we had

είχαν [ikhan] they had

είχατε [ikhateh] you had

είχε [ikheh] he/she/it had

είχες [ikhes] you had

Ε΄ ΚΑΤΗΓΟΡΙΑΣ
Ε΄ κατηγορίας fifth class

εκατό [ekato] hundred

εκατομμύριο: ένα εκατομμύριο
[ena ekatomirio] one million

ΕΚΔΟΣΗ ΕΙΣΙΤΗΡΙΩΝ

έκδοση εισιτηρίων [ekthosi
isitirion] ticket office

εκεί [eki] there, over there

εκεί κάτω [eki kato] down
there

εκείνα, εκείνες [ekina, ekines]
those

εκείνη, εκείνο [ekini, ekino] that

εκείνοι [ekini] those

εκείνος [ekinos] that

ΕΚΘΕΣΗ έκθεση (η) [ekthesi
(i)] exhibition, showroom

ΕΚΚΛΗΣΙΑ εκκλησία (η)
[eklisia (i)] church

Ε.Κ.Ο. Greek state petrol
company

εκπληκτικός [ekpliktikos]
surprising

έκπληξη (η) [ekplixi (i)] surprise

ΕΚΠΤΩΣΕΙΣ εκπτώσεις (οι)
sales

ΕΚΤΑΚΤΗ ΑΝΑΓΚΗ έκτακτη
ανάγκη (η) [ektakti anangi (i)]
emergency

εκτός [ektos] except

έκτος [ektos] sixth

έλα! [ela!] you don't say!;
come on!, hurry up!

ΕΛ.ΑΣ. Greek police

ΕΛΑΣΤΙΚΑ ελαστικά tyres

ελαστικός [elastikos] elastic

ελατήριο (το) [elatirio (to)]
spring (in seat etc)

ελαττωματικός [elatomatikos]
faulty

ΕΛΑΤΤΩΣΑΤΕ ΤΑΧΥΤΗΤΑ
ελαττώσατε ταχύτητα reduce
speed

ελαφρός [elafros] light (not

heavy)

ελάχιστος [elakhistos] smallest; few

ελεγκτής (ο) [elenktis (o)] inspector (bus)

ΕΛΕΓΧΟΣ έλεγχος (ο) [elenkhos (o)] check, inspection

ΕΛΕΓΧΟΣ ΑΠΟΣΚΕΥΩΝ έλεγχος αποσκευών baggage control

ΕΛΕΓΧΟΣ ΔΙΑΒΑΤΗΡΙΩΝ έλεγχος διαβατηρίων passport control

ΕΛΕΓΧΟΣ ΕΙΣΙΤΗΡΙΩΝ έλεγχος εισιτηρίων ticket inspection

ΕΛΕΓΧΟΣ ΕΠΙΒΑΤΩΝ έλεγχος επιβατών passenger control

ΕΛΕΥΘΕΡΑ ΕΙΣΟΔΟΣ ελευθέρα είσοδος [elefтнera isothos] admission free

ΕΛΕΥΘΕΡΟΝ ελεύθερον [elefтнeron] free; for hire (taxi)

ελεύθερος [elefтнeros] free; single (unmarried)

ελιά (η) [elia (i)] olive; spot (blemish)

ελικόπτερο (το) [elikoptero (to)] helicopter

ελκυστικός [elkistikos] attractive

ΕΛΛΑΔΑ Ελλάδα (η) [Elatha (i)] Greece

Έλληνας (ο) [Elinas (o)] Greek (man)

Ελληνίδα (η) [Elinitha (i)] Greek (woman)

ΕΛΛΗΝΙΚΑ Ελληνικά (τα) [Elinika (ta)] Greek (language)

ΕΛΛΗΝΙΚΗ ΑΣΤΥΝΟΜΙΑ Ελληνική Αστυνομία (η) Greek police

ΕΛΛΗΝΙΚΗ ΡΑΔΙΟΦΩΝΙΑ Ελληνική Ραδιοφωνία Greek radio

ΕΛΛΗΝΙΚΗ ΤΗΛΕΟΡΑΣΗ Ελληνική Τηλεόραση Greek television

ΕΛΛΗΝΙΚΗΣ ΚΑΤΑΣΚΕΥΗΣ Ελληνικής κατασκευής made in Greece

ΕΛΛΗΝΙΚΟ ΠΡΟΙΟΝ Ελληνικό προιόν produce of Greece

ΕΛΛΗΝΙΚΟΣ Ελληνικός [Elinikos] Greek (adj)

Ε.Λ.Π.Α. [E.L.P.A.] Greek motoring organization

ελπίζω [elpizo] hope (verb)

ΕΛ.ΤΑ. Greek Post Office

εμάς [emas] us

εμβολιασμός (ο) [emvoliasmos (o)] vaccination

εμβόλιο (το) [emvolio (to)] vaccine

εμείς [emis] we

εμένα [emena] me

ΕΜΠΟΡΙΚΟ ΚΕΝΤΡΟ εμπορικό κέντρο (το) [emboriko kendro (to)] shopping centre

εμπρός [ebros] come in; hello (response on phone)

ένα(ν) [ena(n)] a; one

εναντίον [enandion] against

ένας [enas] a; one

ένατος [enatos] ninth

ενδιαφέρον [enthiaferon]
interesting

ενενήντα [eneninda] ninety

ένεση (η) [enesi (i)] injection

ενήλικη (η) [eniliki (i)] adult

ΕΝΗΛΙΚΟΣ ενήλικος (ο)
[enilikos (o)] adult

ΕΝΘΥΜΙΟ ενθύμιο (το)
[enThimio (to)] souvenir

εννιά [enia] nine

εννοώ [enoo] mean (verb)

ΕΝΟΙΚΙΑΖΟΝΤΑΙ
ενοικιάζονται [enikiazondeh]
for hire, to rent

ΕΝΟΙΚΙΑΖΟΝΤΑΙ
ΑΥΤΟΚΙΝΗΤΑ ενοικιάζονται
αυτοκίνητα car rental

ΕΝΟΙΚΙΑΖΟΝΤΑΙ ΒΑΡΚΕΣ
ενοικιάζονται βάρκες boats
for hire

ΕΝΟΙΚΙΑΖΟΝΤΑΙ ΔΩΜΑΤΙΑ
ενοικιάζονται δωμάτια rooms
to let

ΕΝΟΙΚΙΑΣΗ
ΑΥΤΟΚΙΝΗΤΩΝ ενοικίαση
αυτοκινήτων car rental

ενοίκιο (το) [enikio (to)] rent

ενός [enos] of a

ενοχλητικός [enokhlitikos]
annoying

ενοχλώ [enokhlo] disturb

εντάξει [endaxi] that's all right;
OK

έντεκα [endeka] eleven

έντομο (το) [endomo (to)]
insect

ΕΝΤΥΠΑ έντυπα printed
matter

ενώ [eno] while

εξαιρετικός [exeretikos] terrific

εξ αιτίας [ex etias] because of

εξαρτάται [exartateh] it
depends

ΕΞΑΤΜΙΣΗ εξάτμιση (η)
[exatmisi (i)] exhaust

εξαφανίζομαι [exafanizomeh]
disappear

ΕΞΕΤΑΣΕΙΣ εξετάσεις (οι)
[exetasis (i)] check-up; exams

εξηγώ [exigo] explain

εξήντα [exinda] sixty

έξι [exi] six

ΕΞΟΔΟΣ έξοδος (η)
[exothos (i)] exit; gate (at
airport); door

ΕΞΟΔΟΣ ΑΥΤ/ΤΩΝ έξοδος
αυτ/των vehicle exit

ΕΞΟΔΟΣ ΚΙΝΔΥΝΟΥ έξοδος
κινδύνου emergency exit

εξοχή (η) [exokhi (i)]
countryside

έξοχος [exokhos] excellent

ΕΞΠΡΕΣ εξπρές [expres]
special delivery; express

εξυπηρετώ [exipireto] serve
(verb), assist

έξυπνος [exipnos] clever,
intelligent

έξω! [exo!] get out!

ΕΞΩΣΤΗΣ εξώστης [exostis]
circle (in cinema etc)

εξωτερικός [exoterikos] external

στο εξωτερικό [sto exoteriko]
abroad

ΕΞΩΤΕΡΙΚΟΥ εξωτερικού
postage abroad

εξωφρενικός [exofrenikos]
shocking

E.O.K. [E.O.K.] EEC, EU

E.O.T. [E.O.T.] National Tourist Agency

επαληθεύω [epaliThevo] check (verb), verify

επαναλαμβάνω [epanalamvano] repeat

επαφή: έρχομαι σε επαφή [erkhomeh seh epafi] contact (verb)

Ε.Π.Ε. Ltd

επείγον [epigon] urgent

επειδή [epithi] because

επέκταση (η) [epektasi (i)] extension lead

επέτειος (η) [epetios (i)] anniversary

ΕΠΙΒΑΤΗΣ επιβάτης (ο/η) [epivatis (o/i)] passenger

επιβεβαιώνω [epineveono] confirm

επίδεσμος (ο) [epithesmos (o)] bandage

επίθεση (η) [epiThesi (i)] attack (noun)

επιθετικός [epiThetikos] aggressive

ΕΠΙΘΕΤΟ επίθετο (το) [epiTheto (to)] surname

επικίνδυνος [epikinthinos] dangerous

ΕΠΙΛΕΞΑΤΕ ΤΟΝ ΑΡΙΘΜΟ επιλέξατε τον αριθμό dial the number

επίπεδος [epipethos] flat (even)

έπιπλα (τα) [epipla (ta)] furniture

ΕΠΙΠΛΩΜΕΝΑ ΔΩΜΑΤΙΑ επιπλωμένα δωμάτια furnished rooms

επίσης [episis] too, also

επισκέπτομαι [episkeptomeh] visit (verb)

ΕΠΙΣΚΕΥΑΖΟΝΤΑΙ ΥΠΟΔΗΜΑΤΑ επισκευάζονται υποδήματα shoe repairs

επισκευή (η) [episkevi (i)] repair

επίσκεψη (η) [episkepsi (i)] visit

επιστήμη (η) [epistimi (i)] science

ΕΠΙΣΤΟΛΕΣ επιστολές letters

επιστρέφω [epistrefo] give back; arrive back

ΕΠΙΣΤΡΕΦΩ ΣΕ 5′ επιστρέφω σε 5′ back in 5 minutes

ΕΠΙΤΑΓΗ επιταγή (η) [epitayi (i)] cheque, (US) check

επιτέλους [epiteloos] at last

επίτηδες [epitithes] deliberately

επιτρέπω [epitrepo] let (allow)

επιτρέπεται [epitrepeteh] it is permitted

επιτυχία (η) [epitikhia (i)] success

επόμενος (ο) [epomenos (o)] next

εποχή (η) [epokhi (i)] season

επτά [epta] seven

Ε.Ρ.Α. Greek radio

ΕΡΓΑ έργα roadworks

ΕΡΓΑ ΕΠΙ ΤΗΣ ΟΔΟΥ ΣΕ ΜΗΚΟΣ ... ΧΙΛ. έργα επί της οδού σε μήκος ... χιλ. roadworks for ... kms

εργάζομαι [ergazomeh] work (verb)

ΕΡΓΑΛΕΙΑ ΠΥΡΑΣΦΑΛΕΙΑΣ εργαλεία πυρασφάλειας fire-fighting equipment εργαλείο (το) [ergalio (to)] tool

ΕΡΓΑΣΤΗΡΙΟ
ΗΛΕΚΤΡΟΝΙΚΩΝ
εργαστήριο ηλεκτρονικών
electronics

εργένης (ο) [eryenis (o)]
bachelor

εργοστάσιο (το) [ergostasio (to)]
factory

ερυθρά (η) [eriTHra (i)] German
measles

έρχομαι [erkhomeh] come

έρωτας (ο) [erotas (o)] love
κάνω έρωτα [kano erota] make
love

ερώτηση (η) [erotisi (i)]
question

εσάς, εσείς, εσένα [esas, esis,
esena] you

ΕΣΤΙΑΤΟΡΙΟ εστιατόριο (το)
[estiatorio (to)] restaurant

εσύ [esi] you

Ε.Σ.Υ. National Health
Service

εσώρουχα (τα) [esorookha (ta)]
underwear

ΕΣΩΡΟΥΧΑ ΓΥΝΑΙΚΕΙΑ
εσώρουχα γυναικεία [esorookha
yinekia] ladies' underwear

ΕΣΩΤΕΡΙΚΟΥ εσωτερικού
inland postage

Ε.Τ. Greek television

εταιρεία (η) [eteria (i)] company

ετικέτα (η) [etiketa (i)] label

ΕΤΟΙΜΑ ΓΥΝΑΙΚΕΙΑ έτοιμα
γυναικεία ladies' clothing

ετοιμάζω [etimazo] prepare

ΕΤΟΙΜΑ ΠΑΙΔΙΚΑ έτοιμα
παιδικά children's clothing

έτοιμος [etimos] ready

έτσι [etsi] so; like this

έτσι κι έτσι [etsi ki etsi] so-so

ευαίσθητος [evesTHitos]
sensitive

ευγενικός [evyenikos] kind;
polite

ευγνώμων [evgnomon] grateful

ΕΥΚΑΙΡΙΑ ευκαιρία (η)
[efkeria (i)] bargain

ΕΥΚΑΙΡΙΕΣ ευκαιρίες
bargains

εύκολος [efkolos] easy

ΕΥΡΩΠΑΪΚΟΣ Ευρωπαϊκός
[Evropa-ikos] European

ΕΥΡΩΠΗ Ευρώπη (η) [Evropi
(i)] Europe

ευτυχισμένος [eftikhismenos]
happy

ευτυχώς [eftikhos]
fortunately

ευχαριστημένος [efkharistimenos]
glad; pleased

ευχάριστος [efkharistos]
pleasant

ευχαριστώ [efkharisto] thank
you

ΕΦΗΜΕΡΙΔΑ εφημερίδα (η)
[efimeritha (i)] newspaper

εφημεριδοπώλης (ο)
[efimerithopolis (o)] newsagent

ΕΦΟΡΙΑ εφορία (η) tax office

έχει [ekhi] he/she/it has

έχεις [ekhis] you have
έχεις ...; [ekhis ...?] do you
have ...?

έχετε [ekheteh] you have
έχετε ...; [ekheteh ...?] do you
have ...?

έχουμε [ekhoomeh] we have
έχουν [ekhoon] they have
έχω [ekho] I have

Z

ζακέτα (η) [zaketa (i)] cardigan
ΖΑΧΑΡΟΠΛΑΣΤΕΙΟ
ζαχαροπλαστείο (το)
  [zakharoplastio (to)] cake shop
  or café selling cakes and soft
  drinks
ζέστη (η) [zesti (i)] heat
  κάνει ζέστη [kani zesti] it's
  warm
ΖΕΣΤΟ ζεστό [zesto] hot
ΖΕΣΤΟ ΝΕΡΟ ζεστό νερό
  [zesto nero] hot water
ζεστός [zestos] hot; warm
ζευγάρι (το) [zevgari (to)] pair
ζηλιάρης [ziliaris] jealous
ζημιά (η) [zimia (i)] damage
ζημιές: κάνω ζημιές [kano
  zimies] break (verb)
ζητάω συγγνώμη [zitao signomi]
  apologize
ζω [zo] live (verb)
ζωγραφίζω [zografizo] paint
  (verb: pictures)
ζωγραφική (η) [zografiki (i)]
  painting
ζωή (η) [zoi (i)] life
ζώνη (η) [zoni (i)] belt
ζώνη ασφαλείας (η) [zoni asfalias
  (i)] seat belt
ζωντανός [zondanos] alive
ζώο (το) [zo-o (to)] animal
ΖΩΟΛΟΓΙΚΟΣ ΚΗΠΟΣ

ζωολογικός κήπος (ο)
  [zo-oloyikos kipos (o)] zoo

Η

η [i] the
ή [i] or
ή ... ή ... [i ... i ...] either ...
  or ...
ήδη [ithi] already
ήθελα: θα ήθελα [THа іTHela] I
  would like
ηθοποιός (ο/η) [iTHopios (o/i)]
  actor, actress
ΗΛ/ΓΕΙΟ ηλ/γειο electrical
  goods
ΗΛΕΚΤΡΙΚΑ ΕΙΔΗ ηλεκτρικά
  είδη [ilektrika ithi] electrical
  goods
ηλεκτρική σκούπα (η) [ilektriki
  skoopa (i)] vacuum cleaner
ηλεκτρικό ρεύμα (το) [ilektriko
  revma (to)] electricity
ΗΛΕΚΤΡΙΚΟΣ ηλεκτρικός (ο)
  [ilektrikos (o)] underground,
  (US) subway
ηλεκτρικό σίδερο (το) [ilektriko
  sithero (to)] iron (for ironing)
ηλεκτρικός [ilektrikos] electric
ΗΛΕΚΤΡΟΛΟΓΟΣ
  ηλεκτρολόγος (ο) [ilektrologos
  (o)] electrician
ηλίαση (η) [iliasi (i)] sunstroke
ηλικία (η) [ilikia (i)] age
ηλιοθεραπεία: κάνω
  ηλιοθεραπεία [kano ilioTHerapia]
  sunbathe
ηλιόλουστος [ilioloostos] sunny

A
B
Γ
Δ
E
Z
H
Θ
I
K
Λ
M
N
Ξ
O
Π
P
Σ
T
Y
Φ
X
Ψ
Ω

ήλιος (ο) [**i**lios (o)] sun

ήμαστε [**i**masteh] we were

ημέρα (η) [**i**mera (i)] day

ημερολόγιο (το) [imerol**o**yio (to)] calendar, diary

ημερομηνία (η) [imerominia (i)] date (time)

ΗΜΕΡΟΜΗΝΙΑ ΛΗΞΗΣ ημερομηνία λήξης best before

ΗΜΕΡΟΜΗΝΙΑ ΠΑΡΑΣΚΕΥΗΣ ημερομηνία παρασκευής date of manufacture

ΗΜΙΔΙΑΤΡΟΦΗ ημιδιατροφή (η) [imithiatrof**i** (i)] half board

ΗΜΙΣΚΛΗΡΟΙ ΦΑΚΟΙ ΕΠΑΦΗΣ ημίσκληροι φακοί επαφής (οι) [im**i**skliri fak**i** ep**a**fis (i)] gas permeable lenses

ήμουν [**i**moon] I was

ΗΝΩΜΕΝΕΣ ΠΟΛΙΤΕΙΕΣ ΑΜΕΡΙΚΗΣ Ηνωμένες Πολιτείες Αμερικής (οι) [In**o**menes Polit**i**es Amerik**i**s (i)] United States of America

Η.Π.Α. (οι) [I.P.A. (i)] USA

ηρεμώ [irem**o**] calm down

ΗΡΩΩΝ ηρώων (το) [ir**o**-on (to)] war memorial

ήσουν, ήστε [**i**soon, **i**steh] you were

ΗΣΥΧΙΑ ησυχία [isikh**i**a] quiet

ήσυχος [**i**sikhos] quiet

ήταν [**i**tan] he/she/it was; they were

Θ

θάλασσα (η) [TH**a**lasa (i)] sea

ΘΑΛΑΣΣΙΑ ΣΠΟΡ θαλάσσια σπορ water sports

ΘΑΛΑΣΣΙΟ ΣΚΙ θαλάσσιο σκι (το) [TH**a**lasio ski (to)] waterskiing

θάνατος (ο) [TH**a**natos (o)] death

θα σε δω! [TH**a** seh tho!] see you!

θαυμάσιος [THavm**a**sios] wonderful

θεά (η) [TH**ea** (i)] goddess

θέα (η) [TH**ea** (i)] view

ΘΕΑΤΡΙΚΟ ΕΡΓΟ θεατρικό έργο (το) [THeh-atrik**o** ergo (to)] play (theatre)

ΘΕΑΤΡΟ θέατρο (το) [TH**eatro** (to)] theatre

θεία (η) [TH**i**a (i)] aunt

θείος (ο) [TH**i**os (o)] uncle

θέλετε ...; [TH**e**leteh ...?] do you want ...?

θέλω [TH**elo**] want (verb)

θεός (ο) [THe**os** (o)] God

ΘΕΡΙΝΟΣ θερινός (ο) open-air cinema/movie theater

θέρμανση (η) [TH**e**rmansi (i)] heating

θερμοκρασία (η) [THermokras**i**a (i)] temperature

θερμόμετρο (το) [THerm**o**metro (to)] thermometer

θερμός (το) [THerm**os** (to)] Thermos® flask

ΘΕΣΕΙΣ θέσεις seats

ΘΕΣΕΙΣ ΚΑΘΗΜΕΝΩΝ θέσεις καθημένων seats

ΘΕΣΕΙΣ ΟΡΘΙΩΝ θέσεις ορθίων standing room

θέση (η) [THesi (i)] seat

κλείνω θέση [klino THesi] book a seat

ΘΕΩΡΕΙΑ θεωρεία [THeoria] boxes (in theatre)

θλιμμένος [THlimenos] depressed; sad

θορυβώδης [THorivothis] noisy

θρησκεία (η) [THriskia (i)] religion

θύελλα (η) [THiela (i)] storm; thunderstorm

θυμάμαι [THimameh] remember

θυμωμένος [THimomenos] angry

θυρωρός (ο) [THiroros (o)] doorman; caretaker

Ι
■

ΙΑΜΑΤΙΚΕΣ ΠΗΓΕΣ ιαματικές πηγές [iamatikes piyes] spa

ΙΑΝΟΥΑΡΙΟΣ Ιανουάριος (ο) [Ianooarios (o)] January

ιδέα (η) [ithea (i)] idea

ιδιοκτήτης (ο) [ithioktitis (o)] owner

ιδιοκτήτρια (η) [ithioktitria (i)] owner

ΙΔΙΟΚΤΗΤΟ ΠΑΡΚΙΝΓΚ ιδιόκτητο πάρκινγκ private parking

ίδιος [ithios] same

ΙΔΙΩΤΙΚΗ/ΚΡΑΤΙΚΗ ΙΔΙΟΚΤΗΣΙΑ ιδιωτική/κρατική ιδιοκτησία private/state property

ΙΔΙΩΤΙΚΗ ΠΙΝΑΚΟΘΗΚΗ ιδιωτική πινακοθήκη private art gallery

ΙΔΙΩΤΙΚΟΣ ιδιωτικός [ithiotikos] private

ΙΔΙΩΤΙΚΟΣ ΔΡΟΜΟΣ ιδιωτικός δρόμος private road

ιδρώνω [ithrono] sweat (verb)

ιλαρά (η) [ilara (i)] measles

ΙΝΣΤΙΤΟΥΤΟ ΑΙΣΘΗΤΙΚΗΣ ινστιτούτο αισθητικής (το) [institooto esTHitikis (to)] beauty salon

ΙΟΥΛΙΟΣ Ιούλιος (ο) [Ioolios (o)] July

ΙΟΥΝΙΟΣ Ιούνιος (ο) [Ioonios (o)] June

ιππασία (η) [ipasia (i)] horse-riding

ΙΠΠΟΔΡΟΜΟΣ ιππόδρομος (ο) [ipothromos (o)] race course (for horses)

Ιρλανδέζα (η) [Irlantheza (i)] Irishwoman

ΙΡΛΑΝΔΙΑ Ιρλανδία (η) [Irlanthia (i)] Ireland

Ιρλανδικός [Irlanthikos] Irish

Ιρλανδός (ο) [Irlanthos (o)] Irishman

ίσια [isia] straight

ΙΣΟΓΕΙΟ ισόγειο (το) [isoyio (to)] ground floor, (US) first floor

ΙΣΟΠΕΔΟΣ ΔΙΑΒΑΣΙΣ ισόπεδος διάβασις level crossing

ΙΣΠΑΝΙΑ Ισπανία (η) [Ispania (i)] Spain

Ισπανικός [**Ispanikos**] Spanish (adj)

ιστιοπλοΐα (η) [**istioploia (i)**] sailing

ιστιοπλοϊκό σκάφος (το) [**istioplo-iko skafos (to)**] sailing boat

ΙΣΤΙΟΦΟΡΟ ιστιοφόρο (το) [**istioforo (to)**] sailing boat

ιστορία (η) [**istoria (i)**] story; history

ίσως [**isos**] maybe, perhaps

ΙΤΑΛΙΑ Ιταλία (η) [**Italia (i)**] Italy

Ιταλικός [**Italikos**] Italian (adj)

ΙΧΘΥΟΠΩΛΕΙΟ ιχθυοπωλείο (το) [**ikhTHiopolio (to)**] fishmonger's

K
▬

K. κ. Mr

ΚΑ. κα. Mrs

ΚΑΖΙΝΟ καζίνο (το) [**kazino (to)**] casino

καθαρίζω [**kaTHarizo**] clean

ΚΑΘΑΡΙΣΤΗΡΙΟ καθαριστήριο (το) [**kaTHaristirio (to)**] laundry and dry cleaner's

ΚΑΘΑΡΙΣΤΙΚΟ ΔΕΡΜΑΤΟΣ καθαριστικό δέρματος (το) [**kaTHaristiko thermatos (to)**] skin cleanser

ΚΑΘΑΡΟ ΒΑΡΟΣ καθαρό βάρος net weight

καθαρός [**kaTHaros**] clean (adj)

ΚΑΘΑΡΤΙΚΟ καθαρτικό (το)

[**kaTHartiko (to)**] laxative

κάθε [**kaTHeh**] every

καθεμία, καθένα, καθένας [**kaTHemia, kaTHena, kaTHenas**] each

κάθε τι [**kaTHeh ti**] everything

καθηγητής (ο) [**kaTHiyitis (o)**] teacher, professor

καθηγήτρια (η) [**kaTHiyitria (i)**] teacher, professor

ΚΑΘΗΜΕΡΙΝΑ καθημερινά [**kaTHimerina**] daily

καθήστε [**kaTHisteh**] please sit down

ΚΑΘΟΔΟΣ κάθοδος [**kaTHothos**] way down, descent

καθολικός [**kaTHolikos**] Catholic (adj)

καθόλου [**kaTHoloo**] not at all; none; any

κάθομαι [**kaTHomeh**] sit down

καθρέφτης (ο) [**kaTHreftis (o)**] mirror

καθρέφτης αυτοκινήτου (ο) [**kaTHreftis aftokinitoo (o)**] rearview mirror

ΚΑΘΥΣΤΕΡΗΣΗ καθυστέρηση (η) [**kaTHisterisi (i)**] delay

καθυστερώ [**kaTHistero**] delay (verb); be late

και [**keh**] and

και εγώ επίσης [**k ego episis**] me too

και οι δύο [**k i thio**] both of them

ΚΑΙ ΛΟΙΠΑ και λοιπά etc

καινούργιο [**kenooryio**] brand-new

ευτυχισμένος ο καινούργιος χρόνος! [eftikhismenos o kenooryios khronos!] happy New Year!

καιρός (ο) [keros (o)] weather

καίω [keo] burn (verb)

κακός [kakos] bad

καλά [kala] well

καλά! [kala!] good!

καλάθι (το) [kalaτHi (to)] basket

καλεί [kali] it's ringing

ΚΑΛΕΣΑΤΕ καλέσατε dial

ΚΑΛΕΣΤΕ ΤΟΝ ΑΡΙΘΜΟ καλέστε τον αριθμό dial number

καλή διασκέδαση [kali thiaskethasi] have fun

καλημέρα [kalimera] good morning

καληνύχτα [kalinikhta] good night

καλησπέρα [kalispera] good afternoon; good evening

καλλιτέχνηδα (η) [kalitekhnitha (i)] artist

καλλιτέχνης (ο) [kalitekhnis (o)] artist

ΚΑΛΛΥΝΤΙΚΑ καλλυντικά (τα) [kalindika (ta)] perfume and cosmetics

ΚΑΛΟΚΑΙΡΙ καλοκαίρι (το) [kalokeri (to)] summer

καλοκαιρινές διακοπές (οι) [kalokerines thiakopes (i)] summer holidays/vacation

καλοριφέρ (το) [kalorifer (to)] radiator (heater)

καλός [kalos] good; kind

καλοψημένος [kalopsimenos] well-done (meat)

καλσόν (το) [kalson (to)] tights, pantyhose

κάλτσες (οι) [kaltses (i)] socks

καλύτερος (ο) [kaliteros (o)] the best

καλύτερος [kaliteros] better

καλύτερος από [kaliteros apo] better than

καλώς ήλθατε! [kalos ilτHateh!] welcome!

ΚΑΛΩΣ ΩΡΙΣΑΤΕ ΣΤΗΝ ... καλώς ωρίσατε στην ... welcome to ...

καμαριέρα (η) [kamariera (i)] chambermaid

καμμία [kamia] no-one

καμμιά φορά [kamia fora] sometimes

καμπάνα (η) [kabana (i)] bell

ΚΑΜΠΙΝΑ καμπίνα (η) [kabina (i)] cabin (on ship)

ΚΑΜΠΙΝΓΚ κάμπινγκ (το) [camping (to)] campsite, caravan site, trailer park

ΚΑΜΠΙΝΕΣ καμπίνες [kabines] changing rooms

ΚΑΝΑΔΑΣ Καναδάς (ο) [Kanathas (o)] Canada

Καναδή (η) [Kanathi (i)] Canadian (woman)

Καναδικός [Kanathikos] Canadian (adj)

Καναδός (ο) [Kanathos (o)] Canadian (man)

κανάτα (η) [kanata (i)] jug

κάνει ... [kani ...] it is ..., it costs ...

κάνεις [kanis] you do

A
B
Γ
Δ
E
Z
H
Θ
I
K
Λ
M
N
Ξ
O
Π
P
Σ
T
Y
Φ
X
Ψ
Ω

τι κάνεις; [ti **kanis**?] how are you?, how do you do?

κανένα [**kanena**] nothing

κανένας [**kanenas**] no-one, nobody

κάνετε [**kaneteh**] you do

τι κάνετε; [ti **kaneteh**?] how are you?, how do you do?

κανό (το) [**kano** (to)] canoe

κάνω [**kano**] do; make

καπάκι (το) [**kapaki** (to)] lid, cap (of bottle)

καπαρντίνα (η) [kapardina (i)] raincoat

καπέλο (το) [**kapelo** (to)] hat, cap

ΚΑΠΕΤΑΝΙΟΣ καπετάνιος (ο) [kapetanios (o)] captain (of ship)

ΚΑΠΝΙΖΟΝΤΕΣ καπνίζοντες [kapnizondes] smoking

καπνίζω [**kapnizo**] smoke (verb)

ΚΑΠΝΙΣΤΕΣ καπνιστές [kapnistes] smokers

ΚΑΠΝΙΣΤΗΡΙΟ καπνιστήριο (το) [kapnistirio (to)] smoking room

ΚΑΠΝΟΠΩΛΕΙΟ καπνοπωλείο (το) [kapnopolio (to)] tobacconist's

ΚΑΠΝΟΣ καπνός (ο) [**kapnos** (o)] smoke; tobacco

καπό (το) [**kapo** (to)] bonnet (car), (US) hood

κάποιος [**kapios**] somebody

κάπου [**kapoo**] somewhere

ΚΑΡΑΜΕΛΑ καραμέλα (η) [karamela (i)] caramel

καρδιά (η) [karthia (i)] heart

καρδιακή προσβολή (η) [karthiaki prosvoli (i)] heart

attack

καρέκλα (η) [karekla (i)] chair

καρμπιρατέρ (το) [karbirater (to)] carburettor

καρνέ επιταγών (το) [karneh epitagon (to)] cheque book, (US) check book

καροτσάκι (το) [karotsaki (to)] pram; pushchair, buggy

καρπός (ο) [karpos (o)] wrist

ΚΑΡΤΑ κάρτα (η) [karta (i)] postcard; business card

κάρτα επιβιβάσεως (η) [karta epivivaseos (i)] boarding pass

κάρτα επιταγών (η) [karta epitagon (i)] cheque card, (US) check card

ΚΑΡΤΠΟΣΤΑΛ καρτποστάλ (η) [kartpostal (i)] postcard

καρφί (το) [karfi (to)] nail (in wall)

καρφίτσα (η) [karfitsa (i)] pin; brooch

κασκόλ (το) [kaskol (to)] scarf (for neck)

ΚΑΣΣΕΤΑ κασσέτα (η) [kaseta (i)] cassette, tape

κασσεττόφωνο (το) [kasetofono (to)] cassette player

καστόρι (το) [kastori (to)] suede

κάστρο (το) [kastro (to)] castle

κατά [kata] against; about

κάταγμα (το) [katagma (to)] fracture

καταδύσεις (οι) [katathisis (i)] skin-diving

ΚΑΤΑΘΕΣΗ κατάθεση (η) [kataтнesi (i)] deposit

καταλαβαίνω [katalaveno]

understand

δεν καταλαβαίνω [then katalaveno] I don't understand

ΚΑΤΑΛΛΗΛΟ κατάλληλο suitable for all ages

κατάλογος (ο) [katalogos (o)] list; menu

ΚΑΤΑΝΑΛΩΣΗ ΠΡΙΝ ... κατανάλωση πριν ... consume before ...

καταπίνω [katapino] swallow (verb)

καταρράκτης (ο) [kataraktis (o)] waterfall

ΚΑΤΑΣΚΕΥΑΖΟΝΤΑΙ ΚΛΕΙΔΙΑ κατασκευάζονται κλειδιά keys cut here

κατασκήνωση (η) [kataskinosi (i)] camping

ΚΑΤΑΣΤΗΜΑ ΑΦΟΡΟΛΟΓΗΤΩΝ κατάστημα αφορολογήτων (το) [katastima aforoloyiton (to)] duty-free shop

καταστροφή (η) [katastrofi (i)] disaster

ΚΑΤΑΣΤΡΩΜΑ κατάστρωμα (το) [katastroma (to)] deck

κατά τη διάρκεια [kata ti thiarkia] while, during

καταψύκτης (ο) [katapsiktis (o)] freezer

κατάψυξη (η) [katapsixi (i)] freezer compartment

κατεβαίνω [kateveno] get off; go down

ΚΑΤΕΙΛΗΜΜΕΝΟΣ κατειλημμένος [katilimenos] engaged, occupied

ΚΑΤΕΠΕΙΓΟΝ κατεπείγον [katepigon] express

κατευθείαν [katefrнian] direct

ΚΑΤΕΨΥΓΜΕΝΑ κατεψυγμένα (τα) [katepsigmena (ta)] frozen food

ΚΑΤΕΨΥΓΜΕΝΟ κατεψυγμένο [katepsigmeno] frozen (food)

κάτι [kati] something

κάτι άλλο [kati alo] something else

ΚΑΤΟΛΙΣΘΗΣΕΙΣ κατολισθήσεις falling rocks

ΚΑΤΟΣΤΑΡΙΚΟ κατοστάρικο (το) [katostariko (to)] 100-drachma note/bill

κατσαβίδι (το) [katsavithi (to)] screwdriver

κατσαρόλα (η) [katsarola (i)] saucepan

κατσίκα (η) [katsika (i)] goat

ΚΑΤΩ κάτω [kato] down; downstairs

κάτω από [kato apo] under

καυτερός [kafteros] spicy, hot

καυτός [kaftos] hot (to taste)

καφέ [kafe] brown

ΚΑΦΕΚΟΠΤΕΙΟ καφεκοπτείο (το) [kafekoptio (to)] coffee shop

ΚΑΦΕΝΕΙΟ καφενείο (το) [kafenio (to)] coffee house, where Greek coffee is served with traditional sweets

ΚΑΦΕΤΕΡΙΑ καφετέρια (η) [kafeteria (i)] café, coffee shop

κάψιμο (το) [kapsimo (to)] burn

ΚΕΛΣΙΟΥ Κελσίου [Kelsioo]
centigrade

κέλυφος (το) [kelifos (to)] shell

ΚΕΝΤΗΜΑΤΑ κεντήματα (τα)
[kendimata (ta)] embroidery

κεντρική θέρμανση (η) [kendriki
THermansi (i)] central heating

ΚΕΝΤΡΟ κέντρο (το) [kendro
(to)] centre

κέντρο της πόλης [kendro tis
polis] city centre

ΚΕΡΑΜΙΚΑ κεραμικά (τα)
[keramika (ta)] ceramics

κερδίζω [kerthizo] earn; win
(verb)

κερί (το) [keri (to)] candle

ΚΕΡΚΥΡΑ Κέρκυρα (η)
[Kerkira (i)] Corfu

ΚΕΡΜΑ κέρμα (το) [kerma (to)]
coin

ΚΕΡΜΑΤΑ κέρματα [kermata]
coins

ΚΕΣ. κες. Mrs

κεφάλι (το) [kefali (to)] head

κηδεία (η) [kithia (i)] funeral

ΚΗΠΟΘΕΑΤΡΟ κηποθέατρο
(το) open-air theatre

ΚΗΠΟΣ κήπος (ο) [kipos (ο)]
garden, park

κιβώτιο ταχυτήτων (το) [kivotio
takhititon (to)] gearbox

κιθάρα (η) [kiThara (i)] guitar

ΚΙΛΟ κιλό (το) [kilo (to)] kilo

ΚΙΝΔΥΝΟΣ κίνδυνος (ο)
[kinthinos (ο)] danger; caution

ΚΙΝΔΥΝΟΣ ΠΥΡΚΑΓΙΑΣ
κίνδυνος πυρκαγιάς fire risk

κινηματογραφική μηχανή (η)
[kinimatografiki mikhani (i)]
camcorder

ΚΙΝΗΜΑΤΟΓΡΑΦΟΣ
κινηματογράφος (ο)
[kinimatografos (ο)] cinema,
movie theater

κίτρινος [kitrinos] yellow

ΚΚ. κκ. Messrs

κλαίω [kleo] cry (verb)

κλάξον (το) [klaxon (to)] horn (in
car)

κλέβω [klevo] steal

κλειδαριά (η) [klitharia (i)] lock

κλειδί (το) [klithi (to)] key;
spanner, wrench

ΚΛΕΙΔΙΑ κλειδιά keys cut
here

κλειδώνω [klithono] lock (verb)

ΚΛΕΙΝΕΤΕ ΤΗΝ ΠΟΡΤΑ
κλείνετε την πόρτα close the
door

κλείνω [klino] close (verb);
switch off

ΚΛΕΙΣΤΑ κλειστά [klista]
closed

ΚΛΕΙΣΤΟ ΑΠΟ ... ΩΣ ...
κλειστό από ... ως ... [klisto apo
... os ...] closed from ...
to ...

ΚΛΕΙΣΤΟΝ κλειστόν [kliston]
closed

κλειστός [klistos] closed; off
(lights)

κλέφτης (ο) [kleftis (ο)] thief

κλέφτρα (η) [kleftra (i)] thief

κλίμα (το) [klima (to)] climate

ΚΛΙΜΑΤΙΖΟΜΕΝΟΣ
κλιματιζόμενος [klimatizomenos]
air-conditioned

ΚΛΙΜΑΤΙΣΜΟΣ κλιματισμός

(ο) 〖klimatismos (o)〗 air-conditioning

κλοπή (η) 〖klopi (i)〗 theft

Κ.Λ.Π. κλπ etc

ΚΛΩΣΤΗ κλωστή (η) 〖klosti (i)〗 thread

κόβω 〖kovo〗 cut (verb)

κοιλάδα (η) 〖kilatha (i)〗 valley

κοιμάμαι 〖kimameh〗 sleep (verb); be asleep

ΚΟΙΜΗΤΗΡΙΟ κοιμητήριο (το) 〖kimitirio (to)〗 cemetery

ΚΟΙΝΟΤΙΚΟ ΓΡΑΦΕΙΟ κοινοτικό γραφείο (το) local government office

κοκκαλιάρης 〖kokaliaris〗 skinny

κόκκαλο (το) 〖kokalo (to)〗 bone

κόκκινος 〖kokinos〗 red

κόλλα (η) 〖kola (i)〗 glue

κολλιέ (το) 〖kolie (to)〗 necklace

κόλπος (ο) 〖kolpos (o)〗 vagina; gulf

ΚΟΛΥΜΒΗΤΗΡΙΟ κολυμβητήριο (το) 〖kolimvitirio (to)〗 swimming pool

κολυμπάω 〖kolibao〗 swim (verb)

κολύμπι (το) 〖kolibi (to)〗 swimming

κολυμπώ 〖kolibo〗 swim (verb)

κολώνια (η) 〖kolonia (i)〗 eau de toilette

κολώνια μετά το ξύρισμα 〖kolonia meta to xirisma〗 aftershave

κομμάτι (το) 〖komati (to)〗 piece

ΚΟΜΜΩΣΕΙΣ κομμώσεις (οι) 〖komosis (i)〗 hairdresser's

ΚΟΜΜΩΤΗΡΙΟ κομμωτήριο (το) 〖komotirio (to)〗 hairdresser's

κομμώτρια (η) 〖komotria (i)〗 hairdresser

κομπιουτεράκι (το) 〖kombi-ooteraki (to)〗 calculator

κομπολόι (το) 〖komboloi (to)〗 worry beads

κοντά 〖konda〗 near, close by

κοντέρ (το) 〖konder (to)〗 speedometer

ΚΟΝΤΙΣΙΟΝΕΡ κοντίσιονερ (το) 〖kondisioner (to)〗 conditioner

κοντός 〖kondos〗 short (person)

ΚΟΡΔΟΝΙΑ ΠΑΠΟΥΤΣΙΩΝ κορδόνια παπουτσιών (τα) 〖korthonia papootsion (ta)〗 shoelaces

κόρη (η) 〖kori (i)〗 daughter

κορίτσι (το) 〖koritsi (to)〗 girl

κόρνα (η) 〖korna (i)〗 horn (in car)

κορυφή (η) 〖korifi (i)〗 top

ΚΟΣΜΗΜΑΤΑ κοσμήματα (τα) 〖kosmimata (ta)〗 jewellery

ΚΟΣΜΗΜΑΤΟΠΩΛΕΙΟ κοσμηματοπωλείο (το) 〖kosmimatopolio (to)〗 jeweller's

κόσμος (ο) 〖kosmos (o)〗 world; people, crowd

κοστίζει 〖kostizi〗 it costs

κόστος (το) 〖kostos (to)〗 cost

κουβάς (ο) 〖koovas (o)〗 bucket

κουβέρτα (η) 〖kooverta (i)〗 blanket

κουδούνι (το) 〖koothooni (to)〗 bell (for door)

ΚΟΥΖΙΝΑ κουζίνα (η) 〖koozina (i)〗 cooker; kitchen

ΚΟΥΚΕΤΑ κουκέτα (η)

[kook**e**ta (i)] couchette

κουκέτες (οι) [kook**e**tes (i)] bunk beds

κούκλα (η) [k**oo**kla (i)] doll

κουμπί (το) [koob**i** (to)] button

κουνέλι (το) [koon**e**li (to)] rabbit

κούνια (η) [k**oo**nia (i)] cot

κουνούπι (το) [koon**oo**pi (to)] mosquito

κουπέ (το) [koop**eh** (to)] compartment

κουρασμένος [koorasm**e**nos] tired

ΚΟΥΡΕΑΣ κουρέας (ο) [koor**e**as (ο)] barber

ΚΟΥΡΕΙΟ κουρείο (το) [koor**io** (to)] barber's shop

κούρεμα (το) [k**oo**rema (to)] haircut

κουρτίνα (η) [koort**i**na (i)] curtain

κουστούμι (το) [koost**oo**mi (to)] suit

κουτάλι (το) [koot**a**li (to)] spoon

ΚΟΥΤΑΛΙΕΣ ΓΛΥΚΟΥ κουταλιές γλυκού teaspoonfuls

ΚΟΥΤΑΛΙΕΣ ΣΟΥΠΑΣ κουταλιές σούπας tablespoonfuls

κουτί (το) [koot**i** (to)] box; can

κουφός [koof**os**] deaf

ΚΡΑΓΙΟΝ κραγιόν (το) [kray**on** (to)] lipstick

κράμπα (η) [kr**a**mba (i)] cramp

κρανίο (το) [kr**a**nio (to)] skull

κρατάω [krat**a**o] hold; keep

ΚΡΑΤΗΣΕΙΣ ΘΕΣΕΩΝ κρατήσεις θέσεων

reservations; seat reservations

κράτηση θέσης (η) [kr**a**tisi тн**e**sis (i)] reservation

κρεβάτι (το) [krev**a**ti (to)] bed

ΚΡΕΜΑ ΠΡΟΣΩΠΟΥ κρέμα προσώπου (η) [kr**e**ma pros**o**poo (i)] moisturizer

κρεμάστρα (η) [krem**a**stra (i)] coathanger; peg

ΚΡΕΟΠΩΛΕΙΟ κρεοπωλείο (το) [kreop**o**lio (to)] butcher's

κρίμα: είναι κρίμα [**i**neh kr**i**ma] it's a pity

κρουαζιέρα (η) [kroo-azi**e**ra (i)] cruise

κρύβομαι [kr**i**vomeh] hide (oneself)

κρύβω [kr**i**vo] hide (something)

κρύο (το) [kr**i**o (to)] cold

κάνει κρύο [k**a**ni kr**i**o] it's cold

ΚΡΥΟ ΝΕΡΟ κρύο νερό [kr**i**o ner**o**] cold water

κρύος [kr**i**os] cold (adj)

κρύωμα (το) [kr**i**oma (to)] cold (illness)

Κ.Τ.Ε.Λ. long-distance bus station

κτηνίατρος (ο/η) [ktini**a**tros (o/i)] vet

κτίριο (το) [kt**i**rio (to)] building

κυβέρνηση (η) [kiv**e**rnisi (i)] government

κυκλοφορία (η) [kiklofor**i**a (i)] traffic

κυκλοφοριακή συμφόρηση (η) [kiklofor**i**aki simf**o**risi (i)] traffic jam

ΚΥΛΙΚΕΙΟ κυλικείο (το) [kilik**i**o (to)] snackbar

ΚΥΛΟΤΕΣ κυλότες (οι) [kilotes (i)] panties; underpants

κύμα (το) [kima (to)] wave

κυνηγώ [kinigo] hunt (verb), chase

ΚΥΠΡΟΣ Κύπρος (η) [Kipros (i)] Cyprus

Κυρία (η) [Kiria (i)] Mrs; Ms

κυρία (η) [kiria (i)] lady; madam

ΚΥΡΙΑΚΕΣ ΚΑΙ ΕΟΡΤΕΣ Κυριακές και Εορτές Sundays and holidays

ΚΥΡΙΑΚΗ Κυριακή (η) [Kiriaki (i)] Sunday

ΚΥΡΙΑΚΗ ΤΟΥ ΠΑΣΧΑ Κυριακή του Πάσχα (η) [Kiriaki too Paskha (i)] Easter Sunday

κύριε [kiri-eh] sir

ΚΥΡΙΕΣ κυρίες [kiries] Mrs

ΚΥΡΙΟΙ κύριοι Messrs

ΚΥΡΙΟΣ Κύριος [Kirios] Mr

κύριος (ο) [kirios (o)] gentleman

κύριος [kirios] main

κύστη (η) [kisti (i)] bladder

κυττάζω [kitazo] look (verb)

ΚΩΔΙΚΟΣ κωδικός (ο) [kothikos (o)] code

ΚΩΔΙΚΟΣ ΑΡΙΘΜΟΣ κωδικός αριθμός [kothikos ariTHmos] dialling code

Λ

ΛΑΔΙ λάδι (το) [lathi (to)] oil

ΛΑΔΙΑ λάδια (τα) [lathia (ta)] engine oil

ΛΑΔΙ ΜΑΥΡΙΣΜΑΤΟΣ λάδι μαυρίσματος [lathi mavrismatos] suntan oil

λάθος (το) [laTHos (to)] mistake

λάθος [laTHos] wrong

λάθος νούμερο [laTHos noomero] wrong number

λαιμός (ο) [lemos (o)] neck; throat

λακ (η) [lak (i)] hairspray

λάμπα (η) [lamba (i)] light bulb; lamp

λαστιχάκι (το) [lastikhaki (to)] rubber band

λάστιχο (το) [lastikho (to)] rubber (material); tyre

λεβιές ταχυτήτων [levies takhititon (o)] gear lever

λείπω [lipo] be missing; be out; be away

λειτουργία (η) [litooryia (i)] mass (church)

λεκές (ο) [lekes (o)] stain

ΛΕΜΒΟΣ λέμβος (η) [lemvos (i)] lifeboat

λένε: λένε ότι [leneh oti] they say that

με λένε ... [meh leneh ...] my name is ...

πως σε λένε; [pos seh leneh?] what's your name?

λέξη (η) [lexi (i)] word

λεξικό (το) [lexiko (to)] dictionary

λεπτό (το) [lepto (to)] minute

λεπτός [leptos] slim

λέσχη (η) [leskhi (i)] club

λευκοπλάστ (το) [lefkoplast (to)] (sticking) plaster, Bandaid®

ΛΕΦΤΑ λεφτά (τα) [lefta (ta)] money

λέω [leo] say

ΛΕΩΦΟΡΕΙΟ λεωφορείο (το) [leoforio (to)] bus

ΛΕΩΦΟΡΕΙΟ ΥΠ᾽ ΑΡΙΘΜ ... λεωφορείο υπ᾽ αριθμ ... bus number ...

ΛΕΩΦΟΡΟΣ λεωφόρος (η) [leoforos (i)] avenue

ΛΗΓΕΙ ΤΗΝ ... λήγει την ... expires on ...

λιακάδα (η) [liakatha (i)] sunshine

λίγα [liga] a few

λίγο [ligo] a little bit

ΣΕ ΛΙΓΟ σε λίγο [seh ligo] in a little while

λίγος [ligos] little, short

λιγότερος [ligoteros] fewer

λιγότερο [ligotero] less

ΛΙΜΑΝΙ λιμάνι (το) [limani (to)] harbour

λίμα νυχιών (η) [lima nikhion (i)] nailfile

ΛΙΜΕΝΑΡΧΕΙΟ λιμεναρχείο (το) port authorities

ΛΙΜΕΝΑΡΧΗΣ λιμενάρχης (ο) harbour master

ΛΙΜΕΝΙΚΗ ΑΣΤΥΝΟΜΙΑ Λιμενική Αστυνομία (η) [limeniki Astinomia (i)] harbour police

ΛΙΜΗΝ λιμήν (ο) [limin (o)] port

λίμνη (η) [limni (i)] lake

λιμνούλα (η) [limnoola (i)] pond

λίμπρα (η) [libra (i)] pound (weight)

λιπαρός [liparos] greasy

λιποθυμώ [lipoτHimo] faint (verb)

ΛΙΡΑ ΑΓΓΛΙΑΣ λίρα Αγγλίας (η) [lira Anglias (i)] pound sterling

ΛΙΤΑΝΕΙΑ λιτανεία (η) litany

ΛΙΤΡΟ λίτρο (το) [litro (to)] litre

ΛΟΓΑΡΙΑΣΜΟΣ λογαριασμός (ο) [logariasmos (o)] bill, (US) check

λογικός [loyikos] sensible

ΛΟΓΙΣΤΗΡΙΟ λογιστήριο (το) [loyistirio (to)] purser's office

ΛΟΝΔΙΝΟ Λονδίνο (το) [Lonthino (to)] London

λόξυγγας (ο) [loxingas (o)] hiccups

λουλούδι (το) [looloothi (to)] flower

λούσιμο (το) [loosimo (to)] wash

ΛΟΥΤΡΟ λουτρό (το) [lootro (to)] bathroom

λόφος (ο) [lofos (o)] hill

λυπάμαι [lipameh] I'm sorry

λυπημένος [lipimenos] sad

ΛΥΡΙΚΗ ΣΚΗΝΗ λυρική σκηνή (η) [liriki skini (i)] opera house

M

μαγαζί (το) [magazi (to)] shop

μαγειρεύω [mayirevo] cook (verb)

μαγειρικά σκεύη (τα) [mayirika skevi (ta)] cooking utensils

μαγείρισσα (η) [mayirisa (i)] cook

μάγειρος (ο) [mayiros (o)] cook

μάγκας (ο) [mangas (o)]

streetwise/smart person

μαγιό (το) [mayo (to)] swimming trunks

μάγουλο (το) [magoolo (to)] chin

μαζί [mazi] together

μαζί με [mazi meh] with, together with

μαθαίνω [maTHeno] learn

μάθημα (το) [maTHima (to)] lesson

κάνω μάθημα [kano maTHima] teach; take a lesson

ΜΑΘΗΜΑΤΑ ΣΚΙ μαθήματα σκι [maTHimata ski] skiing lessons

ΜΑΙΟΣ Μάιος (ο) [Maios (o)] May

μακριά [makria] far, at a distance

μαλάκας (ο) [malakas (o)] arsehole, wanker

μακρύς [makris] long

ΜΑΛΑΚΟΙ ΦΑΚΟΙ μαλακοί φακοί (οι) [malaki faki (i)] soft lenses

μάλιστα [malista] yes, certainly

μάλιστα! [malista!] well!

ΜΑΛΛΙ μαλλί (το) [mali (to)] wool

μαλλιά (τα) [malia (ta)] hair

ΜΑΛΛΙΝΟ μάλλινο [malino] wool

μάλλον [malon] rather; probably

μαλώνω [malono] fight (verb)

μαμά (η) [mama (i)] mum

ΜΑΝΑΒΗΣ μανάβης (ο) [manavis (o)] greengrocer's

ΜΑΝΟ μανό (το) [mano (to)] nail polish

μανταλάκι (το) [mandalaki (to)] clothes peg

μαντήλι (το) [mandili (to)] handkerchief; headscarf

μαξιλάρι (το) [maxilari (to)] pillow

μαραγκός (ο) [marangos (o)] carpenter

ΜΑΡΙΝΑ μαρίνα (η) [marina (i)] marina

μαρκαδόρος (ο) [markathoros (o)] felt-tip pen

ΜΑΡΤΙΟΣ Μάρτιος (ο) [Martios (o)] March

μάρτυρας (ο) [martiras (o)] witness

μασέλα (η) [masela (i)] dentures

μας [mas] us; our

μάτι (το) [mati (to)] eye; ring (on cooker)

ματς (το) [mats (to)] match (sport)

μαυρίζω [mavrizo] tan (verb)

μαύρισμα (το) [mavrisma (to)] tan (colour)

μαύρισμα από τον ήλιο [mavrisma apo ton ilio] suntan

μαύρος [mavros] black

μαχαίρι (το) [makheri (to)] knife

μαχαιροπήρουνα (τα) [makheropiroona (ta)] cutlery

με [meh] with; by; me

με αυτοκίνητο [meh aftokinito] by car

ΜΕΓΑΛΗ ΒΡΕΤΑΝΝΙΑ Μεγάλη Βρεταννία (η) [Megali Vretania (i)] Great Britain

Μεγάλη Παρασκευή (η) [Megali

Paraskevi (i)] Good Friday

μεγάλος [megalos] big

μεγαλύτερος [megaliteros] bigger

ΜΕΓΕΘΟΣ μέγεθος (το) [meyeTHos (to)] size

μεγέθυνση (η) [meyeTHinsi (i)] enlargement

ΜΕΓΙΣΤΟ ΒΑΡΟΣ μέγιστο βάρος maximum permitted weight

μέγιστος (ο) [meyistos (o)] biggest

μεζ (η) [mez (i)] highlights (in hair)

μεθαύριο [meTHavrio] the day after tomorrow

μεθυσμένος [meTHismenos] drunk

μέικ απ (το) [meik ap (to)] make-up

μελανιά (η) [melania (i)] bruise

μέλλον (το) [melon (to)] future

ΜΕ ΜΠΑΝΙΟ με μπάνιο [meh banio] with bathroom

ΜΕ ΝΤΟΥΣ με ντους [meh doos] with shower

μένω [meno] live (in town etc); stay (in hotel etc)

μέρα (η) [mera (i)] day

μερίδα (η) [meritha (i)] portion

μερικά, μερικές, μερικοί [merika, merikes, meriki] some

μέρος (το) [meros (to)] part, place; WC

μέσα [mesa] in; inside

μεσάνυχτα (τα) [mesanikhta (ta)] midnight

μέση (η) [mesi (i)] middle; waist

μεσημέρι (το) [mesimeri (to)] midday

Μεσόγειος (η) [Mesoyios (i)] Mediterranean

μετά [meta] after; afterwards

μετά από σας [meta apo sas] after you

μετά μεσημβρίας [meta mesimvrias] pm

μετακινούμαι [metakinoomeh] move (verb)

μέταλλο (το) [metalo (to)] metal

ΜΕΤΑΞΙ μετάξι (το) [metaxi (to)] silk

μεταξύ [metaxi] between

μεταφέρω [metafero] carry

μεταφράζω [metafrazo] translate

μετεωρολογικό δελτίο (το) [meteoroloyiko theltio (to)] weather forecast

ΜΕΤΡΗΤΑ μετρητά [metrita] cash

ΤΟΙΣ ΜΕΤΡΗΤΟΙΣ τοις μετρητοίς [tis metritis] in cash

μετρητής βενζίνης (ο) [metritis venzinis (o)] fuel gauge

μέτριο μέγεθος [metrio meyeTHos] medium-sized

ΜΕΤΡΙΟΣ μέτριος [metrios] medium; average

ΜΕΤΡΟ μέτρο (το) [metro (to)] metre

μέτωπο (το) [metopo (to)] forehead

μέχρι [mekhri] until

ΜΗ μη do not

ΜΗ ΒΓΑΖΕΤΕ ΤΗΝ ΚΑΡΤΑ μη βγάζετε την κάρτα do not remove the card yet

μηδέν [mithen] zero

ΜΗΝ ΚΑΠΝΙΖΕΤΕ μην
καπνίζετε no smoking

ΜΗ ΚΑΠΝΙΖΟΝΤΕΣ μη
καπνίζοντες [mi kapnizondes]
non-smoking

ΜΗ ΚΑΠΝΙΣΤΕΣ μη
καπνιστές [mi kapnistes] non-
smokers

μήκος (το) [mikos (to)] length

μήνας (ο) [minas (o)] month

μήνας του μέλιτος [minas too
melitos] honeymoon

ΜΗΝ ΕΝΟΧΛΕΙΤΕ μην
ενοχλείτε do not disturb

ΜΗΝ ΟΜΙΛΕΙΤΕ ΣΤΟΝ
ΟΔΗΓΟ μην ομιλείτε στον
οδηγό do not speak to the
driver

ΜΗΝ ΠΑΤΑΤΕ ΤΟ ΧΟΡΤΟ
μην πατάτε το χόρτο keep off
the grass

ΜΗ ΠΟΣΙΜΟ (ΝΕΡΟ) μη
πόσιμο (νερό) not for
drinking (water)

μητέρα (η) [mitera (i)] mother

ΜΗ ΤΟΞΙΚΟ μη τοξικό non-
toxic

μητρόπολη (η) [mitropoli (i)]
cathedral

μηχανάκι (το) [mikhanaki (to)]
moped

μηχανή (η) [mikhani (i)] engine

μηχανικός (ο) [mikhanikos (o)]
mechanic; engineer

μία [mia] a; one

μία φορά [mia fora] once

μιάς [mias] of a

μίζα (η) [miza (i)] ignition

ΜΙΚΡΟ ΟΝΟΜΑ μικρό όνομα
(το) [mikro onoma (to)]
Christian name

ΜΙΚΡΟΣ μικρός [mikros] little,
small

ΜΙΚΤΟ ΒΑΡΟΣ μικτό βάρος
gross weight

μικρότερος [mikroteros]
smaller

ΜΙΛΑΕΙ μιλάει [milai]
engaged, occupied

μιλάω [milao] speak

μιλάτε ...; [milateh ...?] do you
speak ...?

μισός [misos] half

ΜΙΣΟΤΙΜΗΣ μισοτιμής half-
price

μισώ [miso] hate (verb)

μ.μ. [m.m.] pm

μνημείο (το) [mnimio (to)]
monument

μόδα (η) [motha (i)] fashion

της μόδας [tis mothas]
fashionable

ΜΟΔΕΣ μόδες fashions

μοιάζει [miazi] it looks/seems

μοιράζομαι [mirazomeh] share
(verb)

μοκέτα (η) [moketa (i)] carpet

μολύβι (το) [molivi (to)] pencil

μόλυνση (η) [molinsi (i)]
infection

ΜΟΛΥΣΜΕΝΑ ΥΔΑΤΑ
μολυσμένα ύδατα polluted
water

μολυσμένος [molismenos]
polluted

ΜΟΝΑΔΕΣ μονάδες units

ΜΟΝΑΔΙΚΗ ΕΥΚΑΙΡΙΑ

μοναδική ευκαιρία (η) special offer

μονή [moni] monastery

μόνο [mono] only

ΜΟΝΟΔΡΟΜΟΣ μονόδρομος one-way street

ΜΟΝΟ ΔΩΜΑΤΙΟ μονό δωμάτιο (το) [mono thomatio (to)] single room

ΜΟΝΟΚΛΙΝΟ ΔΩΜΑΤΙΟ μονόκλινο δωμάτιο (το) [monoklino thomatio (to)] single room

μονό κρεβάτι [mono krevati] single bed

μονοπάτι (το) [monopati (to)] path

μόνος [monos] alone

μοντέρνος [mondernos] modern

μοτοσυκλέτα (η) [motosikleta (i)] motorbike

μου [moo] my

ΜΟΥΣΕΙΟ μουσείο (το) [moosio (to)] museum

ΜΟΥΣΙΚΑ ΟΡΓΑΝΑ μουσικά όργανα [moosika organa] musical instruments

μουσική (η) [moosiki (i)] music

μουσική ποπ (η) [moosiki pop (i)] pop music

μουστάκι (το) [moostaki (to)] moustache

μπαίνω [beno] go in, enter

ΜΠΑΚΑΛΙΚΟ μπακάλικο (το) [bakaliko (to)] grocer's

μπαλκόνι (το) [balkoni (to)] balcony

μπάλλα (η) [bala (i)] ball (large)

μπαλλάκι (το) [balaki (to)] ball (small)

μπαμπάς (ο) [babas (o)] dad

μπανιέρα (η) [baniera (i)] bathtub

ΜΠΑΝΙΟ μπάνιο (το) [banio (to)] bath

κάνω μπάνιο [kano banio] swim (verb); have a bath

πάω για μπάνιο [pao ya banio] go swimming

ΜΠΑΡ μπαρ (το) [bar (to)] bar

μπάρμαν (ο) [barman (o)] barman

μπάρ γούμαν (η) [bar woman (i)] barmaid

μπαταρία (η) [bataria (i)] battery

μπεζ [bez] beige

μπέιμπι-σίττερ (η) [baby-sitter (i)] babysitter

μπερδεμένος [berthemenos] complicated

μπικίνι (το) [bikini (to)] bikini

μπλε [bleh] blue

μπλούζα (η) [blooza (i)] blouse

μπλουζάκι (το) [bloozaki (to)] T-shirt

μπόρα (η) [bora (i)] shower (rain)

μπορείς [boris] you can
μπορείς να ...; [boris na ...?] can you ...?

μπορείτε [boriteh] you can
μπορείτε να ...; [boriteh na ...?] can you ...?

μπρος [bros] forwards; in front of
βάζω μπρος [vazo bros] switch on (engine)

μπορώ [boro] I can

μπότα (η) [bota (i)] boot (shoe)

μπουγάδα (η) [boogatha (i)] washing

βάζω μπουγάδα [vazo boogatha] do the washing

μπουζί (το) [boozi (to)] spark plug

ΜΠΟΥΖΟΥΚΙΑ μπουζούκια (τα) [boozookia (ta)] club with bouzouki music

μπουκάλι (το) [bookali (to)] bottle

μπουκιά (η) [bookia (i)] bite

μπούτι (το) [booti (to)] thigh

ΜΠΟΥΤΙΚ μπουτίκ (η) [bootik (i)] boutique

μπροστινό μέρος (το) [brostino meros (to)] front (part)

ΜΠΥΡΑ μπύρα [bira] beer, lager

μπωλ (το) [bol (to)] bowl

μύγα (η) [miga (i)] fly

μυθιστόρημα (το) [miTHistorima (to)] novel

μυρίζω [mirizo] smell (verb)

μυρμήγκι (το) [mirmingi (to)] ant

μυρωδιά (η) [mirothia (i)] smell

μυστικός [mistikos] secret

μυς (ο) [mis (o)] muscle

μύτη (η) [miti (i)] nose

μύωπας [miopas] shortsighted

μωβ [mov] purple

μωρό (το) [moro (to)] baby

N

να [na] here is/are

ναι [neh] yes

ναι, ναι! [neh neh!] oh yes I do!

νάιτκλαμπ (το) [nightclub (to)] nightclub

ΝΑ ΛΑΜΒΑΝΕΤΑΙ ΜΟΝΟΝ ΑΠΟ ΤΟ ΣΤΟΜΑ να λαμβάνεται μόνον από το στόμα to be taken orally only

ΝΑ ΛΑΜΒΑΝΕΤΑΙ ... ΦΟΡΕΣ ΗΜΕΡΗΣΙΩΣ να λαμβάνεται ... φορές ημερησίως to be taken ... times daily

ναρκωτικά (τα) [narkotika (ta)] drugs (narcotics)

ΝΑ ΦΥΛΑΣΣΕΤΑΙ ΜΑΚΡΙΑ ΑΠΟ ΠΑΙΔΙΑ να φυλάσσεται μακριά από παιδιά keep out of reach of children

νέα (η) [nea (i)] teenager

νέα (τα) [nea (ta)] news

ΝΕΑ ΖΗΛΑΝΔΙΑ Νέα Ζηλανδία (η) [Nea Zilanthia (i)] New Zealand

ΝΕΚΡΟΤΑΦΕΙΟ νεκροταφείο (το) [nekrotafio (to)] cemetery

Νέο Έτος (το) [Neo Etos (to)] New Year

ΝΕΟΖΗΛΑΝΔΕΖΑ Νεοζηλανδέζα (η) [Neozilantheza (i)] New Zealander

ΝΕΟΖΗΛΑΝΔΟΣ Νεοζηλανδός (ο) [Neozilanthos (o)] New Zealander

νέοι (οι) [nei (i)] young people

νέος (ο) [neos (o)] teenager

νέος [neos] new; young

ΝΕΡΟ νερό (το) [nero (to)] water

νεροχύτης (ο) [nerokhitis (o)] sink

νευρικός [nevrikos] nervous

νεφρά (τα) [nefra (ta)] kidneys

νησί (το) [nisi (to)] island

νιπτήρας (ο) [niptiras (o)] washbasin

νιώθω [nioTHo] feel

ΝΟΕΜΒΡΙΟΣ Νοέμβριος (ο) [Noemvrios (o)] November

νοικιάζω [nikiazo] rent (verb)

ΝΟΜΑΡΧΙΑ νομαρχία (η) local government office

νομίζω [nomizo] think

ΝΟΜΟΣ νομός (ο) county

νόμος (ο) [nomos (o)] law

ΝΟΣΟΚΟΜΕΙΟ νοσοκομείο (το) [nosokomio (to)] hospital

νόστιμο [nostimo] tasty

νοστιμώτατο [nostimotato] delicious

ΝΟΥΜΕΡΟ νούμερο (το) [noomero (to)] number

ΝΤΕΜΙ ΠΑΝΣΙΟΝ ντεμί πανσιόν (η) [demi pansion (i)] half board

ντεπόζιτο (το) [ndepozito (to)] tank

ΝΤΗΖΕΛ ντήζελ (το) [dizel (to)] diesel

ντισκοτέκ (η) [ndiskotek (i)] disco

ντιστριμπυτέρ (το) [ndistribiter (to)] distributor

ντουλάπι (το) [ndoolapi (to)] cupboard

ΝΤΟΥΣ ντους (το) [doos (to)] shower (in bathroom)

ΝΤΡΑΙΒ - ΙΝ ντραιβ - ιν drive-in

ντροπαλός [ndropalos] shy

ντύνομαι [ndinomeh] dress (oneself)

ντύνω [ndino] dress (verb: someone)

νύφη (η) [nifi (i)] daughter-in-law; sister-in-law; bride

νύχι (το) [nikhi (to)] fingernail

νυχοκόπτης (ο) [nikhokoptis (o)] nail clippers

νύχτα (η) [nikhta (i)] night

ΝΥΧΤΕΡΙΝΟ ΚΕΝΤΡΟ νυχτερινό κέντρο [nikhterino kendro] nightclub

νυχτικό (το) [nikhtiko (to)] nightdress

νωρίς [noris] early

Ξ

ξαδέλφη (η) [xathelfi (i)] cousin

ξάδελφος (ο) [xathelfos (o)] cousin

ξανά [xana] again

ξανθός [xanTHos] blond

ξαπλώνω [xaplono] lie down

ξαφνικά [xafnika] suddenly

ξεκουράζομαι [xekoorazomeh] relax

ξεναγός (ο/η) [xenagos (o/i)] guide

ΞΕΝΟΔΟΧΕΙΟ ξενοδοχείο (το) [xenothokhio (to)] hotel

ξένος [xenos] foreign

ΞΕΝΩΝΑΣ ξενώνα (ο) [xenonas (o)] guesthouse

ΞΕΝΩΝΑΣ ΝΕΟΤΗΤΑΣ

ξενώνας νεότητας [xenonas neotitas] youth hostel

ΞΕΝΩΝΑΣ ΝΕΩΝ ξενώνας νέων [xenonas neon] youth hostel

ΞΕΠΟΥΛΗΜΑ ξεπούλημα closing-down sale

ξέρω [xero] know

δεν ξέρω [then xero] I don't know

ξεφωνίζω [xefonizo] scream (verb)

ξεχνώ [xekhno] leave (verb); forget

ξεχωριστά [xekhorista] separately

ξηρός [xiros] dry

ξοδεύω [xothevo] spend

ξύλο (το) [xilo (to)] wood

ξινός [xinos] sour

ξυπνάω [xipnao] wake up

ξυπνητήρι (το) [xipnitiri (to)] alarm clock

ξύπνιος [xipnios] awake

ξυραφάκι (το) [xirafaki (to)] razor

ξυρίζομαι [xirizomeh] shave (verb)

ξύρισμα (το) [xirisma (to)] shave

ξυριστική μηχανή (η) [xiristiki mikhani (i)] electric shaver

Ο

ο [o] the

Ο.Α. Olympic Airways

Ο/Γ ferry

ογδόντα [ogthonda] eighty

όγδοος [ogthoos] eighth

οδηγάω [othigao] drive

οδηγός (ο/η) [othigos (o/i)] driver

ΟΔΙΚΑ ΕΡΓΑ οδικά έργα roadworks

ΟΔΟΝΤΙΑΤΡΟΣ οδοντιατρος (ο/η) [othondiatros (o/i)] dentist

οδοντόβουρτσα (η) [othondovoortsa (η)] toothbrush

ΟΔΟΝΤΟΓΙΑΤΡΟΣ οδοντογιατρός (ο/η) [othondoyatros (o/i)] dentist

ΟΔΟΝΤΙΑΤΡΕΙΟ οδοντιατρείο (το) [othondiatrio (to)] dentist's

ΟΔΟΝΤΟΚΡΕΜΑ οδοντόκρεμα (η) [othondokrema (i)] toothpaste

ΟΔΟΣ οδός (η) [othos (i)] road, street

ΟΔΟΣ ΑΝΕΥ ΣΗΜΑΝΣΕΩΣ ΣΕ ΜΗΚΟΣ ... ΧΙΛ. οδός άνευ σημάνσεως σε μήκος ... χιλ no road markings for ... kms

οδυνηρός [othiniros] painful

όζα (η) [oza (i)] nail polish

Ο.Η.Ε. UN

ΟΧΙ ΕΠΙΤΑΓΕΣ όχι επιταγές no cheques/checks

οι [i] the

οικογένεια (η) [ikoyenia (i)] family

ΟΚΤΩΒΡΙΟΣ Οκτώβριος (ο) [Oktovrios (o)] October

όλα [ola] all

όλα καλά [ola kala] that'll do nicely, everything's fine

όλα πληρωμένα [ola pliromena] all inclusive

όλες, όλη [oles, oli] all

ΟΛΙΣΘΗΡΟ ΟΔΟΣΤΡΩΜΑ
ολισθηρό οδόστρωμα slippery
road surface

όλο [olo] αμμ

όλοι [oli] everyone; all

ολόκληρος [olokliros] whole

όλος [olos] all

Ο.Λ.Π. Piraeus Port
Authorities

ΟΛΥΜΠΙΑΚΗ ΑΕΡΟΠΟΡΙΑ
Ολυμπιακή Αεροπορία
Olympic Airways

ομάδα (η) [omatha (i)] group;
team

ομάδα αίματος (η) [omatha
ematos (i)] blood group

ομίχλη (η) [omikhli (i)] fog

όμοιος [omios] similar

όμορφος [omorfos] fine,
beautiful

ομοφυλόφιλος (ο) [omofilofilos
(o)] gay

ομπρέλλα (η) [ombrella (i)]
umbrella

όνειρο (το) [oniro (to)] dream

ΟΝΟΜΑ όνομα (το) [onoma
(to)] name; first name

οπά! [opa!] watch it!

ΟΠΕΡΑ όπερα (η) [opera (i)]
opera

όπισθεν (η) [opisτHen (i)] reverse
(gear)

όπλο (το) [oplo (to)] gun; rifle

ΟΠΤΙΚΑ οπτικά (τα) [optika
(ta)] optician's

ΟΠΤΙΚΟΣ οπτικός (ο) [optikos
(o)] optician

ΟΠΩΡΟΠΩΛΕΙΟ

οπωροπωλείο (το) [oporopolio
(to)] grocer's

όπως [opos] like; as

όπως και νάναι [opos keh naneh]
anyway

ΟΡΓΑΝΙΣΜΟΣ ΗΝΩΜΕΝΩΝ
ΕΘΝΩΝ Οργανισμός
Ηνωμένων Εθνών United
Nations Organization

οργανωμένη εκδρομή (η)
[organomeni ekthromi (i)]
package tour

οργανώνω [organono] organize

όρεξη (η) [orexi (i)] appetite

καλή όρεξη! [kali orexi!] enjoy
your meal!, bon appetit!

ΟΡΘΙΩΝ ορθίων standing

ΟΡΙΟ ΤΑΧΥΤΗΤΑΣ όριο
ταχύτητας (το) speed limit

ορίστε; [oristeh?] can I help
you?

όροφος (ο) [orofos (o)] floor,
storey

ΟΡΥΚΤΕΛΑΙΟ ορυκτέλαιο
(το) [orikteleo (to)] engine oil

ορχήστρα (η) [orkhistra (i)]
orchestra

Ο.Σ.Ε. Greek Railways

όταν [otan] when

Ο.Τ.Ε. Greek
Telecommunications
Company

ότι [oti] that

οτιδήποτε [otithipoteh] anything

Ο.Υ. water authorities

Ουαλλή (η) [Ooali (i)]
Welshwoman

ΟΥΑΛΛΙΑ Ουαλλία (η) [Ooalia
(i)] Wales

Ουαλλικός [Ooalikos] Welsh (adj)

Ουαλλός (ο) [Ooalos (o)] Welshman

ΟΥΖΕΡΙ ουζερί [oozeri] bar serving ouzo and beer with snacks or full meals

ούλο (το) [oolo (to)] gum (in mouth)

ΟΥΡΑ ουρά (η) [oora (i)] queue; tail; queue here

κάνω ουρά [kano oora] queue (verb)

ουρανός (ο) [ooranos (o)] sky

ούτε ... ούτε ... [oote ... oote ...] neither ... nor ...

ΟΦΘΑΛΜΙΑΤΡΟΣ οφθαλμίατρος (ο/η) eye specialist

όχημα (το) [okhima (to)] vehicle

ΟΧΙ όχι [okhi] no; not

όχι άλλο [okhi allo] no more

ΟΧΙ ΥΠΕΡΑΣΤΙΚΑ όχι υπεραστικά no long-distance calls

οχτώ [okhto] eight

Π

ΠΑΓΟΣ πάγος (ο) [pagos (o)] ice

ΠΑΓΩΤΟ παγωτό (το) [pagoto (to)] ice cream

ΠΑΓΩΤΟ ΞΥΛΑΚΙ παγωτό ξυλάκι (το) [pagoto xilaki (to)] ice lolly

πάει: πώς πάει; [pos pai?] how are things?

ΠΑΖΑΡΙ παζάρι (το) [pazari (to)] bazaar

ΠΑΘΟΛΟΓΟΣ παθολόγος (ο/η) [paτHologos (o/i)] doctor, general practitioner

ΠΑΙΔΙ παιδί (το) [pethi (to)] child

ΠΑΙΔΙΑΤΡΟΣ παιδίατρος (ο/η) paediatrician

ΠΑΙΔΙΚΑ παιδικά (τα) [pethika (ta)] children's wear

ΠΑΙΔΙΚΑ ΕΙΔΗ παιδικά είδη (τα) [pethika ithi (ta)] children's department

ΠΑΙΔΙΚΑ ΕΣΩΡΟΥΧΑ παιδικά εσώρουχα [pethika esorookha] children's underwear

ΠΑΙΔΙΚΑ ΦΟΡΜΑΚΙΑ παιδικά φορμάκια [pethika formakia] babywear, toddlers' clothes

ΠΑΙΔΙΚΟ παιδικό [pethiko] children's (adj)

παίζω [pezo] play (verb)

παίρνω [perno] get; take

παίρνω τηλέφωνο [perno tilefono] phone (verb)

ΠΑΙΧΝΙΔΙ παιχνίδι (το) [pekhnithi (to)] game; toy

ΠΑΚΕΤΟ πακέτο (το) [paketo (to)] package; packet

ΠΑΛΑΙΟΠΩΛΕΙΟ παλαιοπωλείο (το) [paleopolio (to)] antique shop

παλαιός [paleos] old, ancient, antique

παλάτι (το) [palati (to)] palace

παλίρροια (η) [paliria (i)] tide

παλτό (το) [pal**to** (to)] coat

πάνα (η) [p**a**na (i)] nappy, diaper

ΠΑΝΕΠΙΣΤΗΜΙΟ
πανεπιστήμιο (το) [panepist**i**mio (to)] university

ΠΑΝΗΓΥΡΙ πανηγύρι (το) [paniy**i**ri (to)] fair, funfair

πανί (το) [pan**i** (to)] sail

ΠΑΝ/ΜΙΟ παν/μιο university

ΠΑΝΣΙΟΝ πανσιόν (η) [pans**i**on (i)] guesthouse

πάντα [p**a**nda] always; still

πανταλόνι (το) [pandal**o**ni (to)] trousers, (US) pants

παντζούρια (τα) [pandz**oo**ria (ta)] shutters

ΠΑΝΤΟΠΩΛΕΙΟ παντοπωλείο (το) [pandopol**i**o (to)] grocery store

πάντοτε [p**a**ndoteh] always

παντού [pand**oo**] everywhere

παντόφλες (οι) [pand**o**fles (i)] slippers

παντρεμένος [pandrem**e**nos] married

παντρεμένη [pandrem**e**ni] married

πάνω [p**a**no] on; up; upstairs

πάνω από [p**a**no ap**o**] above

παξιμάδι (το) [paxim**a**thi (to)] nut (for bolt)

παπάς (ο) [pap**a**s (o)] priest

πάπια (η) [p**a**pia (i)] duck

πάπλωμα (το) [p**a**ploma (to)] quilt

παπούτσι (το) [pap**oo**tsi (to)] shoe

παππούς (ο) [papp**oo**s (o)] grandfather

παραγγελία (η) [parangel**i**a (i)]

message

παραγγέλνω [parag**e**lno] order (verb: in restaurant)

παράδειγμα (το) [par**a**thigma (to)] example

παραδείγματος χάρι [par**a**th**i**gmatos kh**a**ri] for example

παράδοση (η) [par**a**thosi (i)] tradition

παραδοσιακός [parathosiak**o**s] traditional

παράθυρο (το) [par**a**Thiro (to)] window

παρακαλώ [parakal**o**] please; excuse me; don't mention it

παρακαλώ; [parakal**o**?] can I help you?

ΠΑΡΑΚΑΜΠΤΗΡΙΟΣ
παρακαμπτήριος (η) diversion

ΠΑΡΑΛΑΒΗ ΑΠΟΣΚΕΥΩΝ
παραλαβή αποσκευών (η) [paralav**i** aposkev**o**n (i)] baggage claim

ΠΑΡΑΛΙΑ παραλία (η) [paral**i**a (i)] beach

κοντά στην παραλία [kond**a** stin paral**i**a] at the seaside

παραμάνα (η) [param**a**na (i)] safety pin

παραμένω [param**e**no] stay (verb), remain

παράξενος [par**a**xenos] strange

παραπονούμαι [parapon**oo**meh] complain

ΠΑΡΑΣΚΕΥΗ Παρασκευή (η) [Parask**e**vi (i)] Friday

παρατηρώ [paratir**o**] watch (verb)

παρατσούκλι (το) [paratsookli (to)] nickname

παρεξήγηση (η) [parexiyisi (i)] misunderstanding

παρκάρω [parkaro] park (verb)

ΠΑΡΚΙΝΓΚ πάρκινγκ (το) [parking (to)] car park, parking lot

πάρκο (το) [parko (to)] park

ΠΑΡΟΔΟΣ πάροδος (η) [parothos (i)] side street

παρπρίζ (το) [parpriz (to)] windscreen

πάρτυ (το) [parti (to)] party, celebration

παστίλιες λαιμού (οι) [pastili-es lemoo (i)] throat pastilles

Πάσχα (το) [Paskha (to)] Easter

πατέρας (ο) [pateras (o)] father

πατερίτσες (οι) [pateritses (i)] crutches

πάτωμα (το) [patoma (to)] floor (of room)

ΠΑΥΣΙΠΟΝΟ παυσίπονο (το) [pafsipono (to)] painkiller

πάχος (το) [pakhos (to)] fat (on meat)

παχύς [pakhis] fat; thick

πάω [pao] go (verb)

πεζοδρόμιο (το) [pezothromio (to)] pavement, sidewalk

ΠΕΖΟΔΡΟΜΟΣ πεζόδρομος (ο) [pezothromos (o)] pedestrian precinct

ΠΕΖΟΙ πεζοί pedestrians

πεθαίνω [petHeno] die

πεθαμένος [petHamenos] dead

πεθερά (η) [petHera (i)] mother-in-law

πεθερός (ο) [petHeros (o)] father-in-law

πειράζει [pirazi] it matters

θα σε πείραζε αν ...; [THa seh pirazeh an ...?] do you mind if I ...?

δεν πειράζει [then pirazi] it doesn't matter

ΠΕΙΡΑΙΑΣ Πειραιάς [Pireas] Piraeus

ΠΕΜΠΤΗ Πέμπτη (η) [Pempti (i)] Thursday

πέμπτος [pemptos] fifth

πενήντα [peninda] fifty

ΠΕΝΗΝΤΑΡΙΚΟ πενηντάρικο (το) [penindariko (to)] 50-drachma coin or note/bill

πενικιλλίνη (η) [penikilini (i)] penicillin

πέννα (η) [pena (i)] pen

πένσα (η) [pensa (i)] pliers

ΠΕΝΤΑΚΟΣΑΡΙΚΟ πεντακοσάρικο (το) [pendakosariko (to)] 500-drachma note/bill

πέντε [pendeh] five

πέος (το) [peos (to)] penis

περάστε [perasteh] come in; come back

ΠΕΡΙΕΧΟΜΕΝΟ περιεχόμενο contains

περίμενε [perimeneh] wait

περιμένω [perimeno] wait (for); expect

ΠΕΡΙΟΔΙΚΟ περιοδικό (το) [periothiko (to)] magazine

περίοδος (η) [periothos (i)] period

περιοχή (η) [periokhi (i)] area

περίπατος (ο) [peripatos (o)] walk

πάω περίπατο [pao peripato] go for a walk

περίπου [peripoo] about, approximately

ΠΕΡΙΠΤΕΡΟ περίπτερο [periptero] newspaper kiosk

ΣΕ ΠΕΡΙΠΤΩΣΗ ΑΝΑΓΚΗΣ ΣΠΑΣΤΕ ΤΟ ΤΖΑΜΙ σε περίπτωση ανάγκης σπάστε το τζάμι [seh periptosi anangis spaste to tzami] in emergency break glass

περισσότερο [perisotero] more, most (of)

περισσότερος [perisoteros] more, most (of)

ΠΕΡΜΑΝΑΝΤ περμανάντ (η) [permanand (i)] perm

περνάω [pernao] cross, go through

περπατάω [perpatao] walk (verb)

πέρσυ [persi] last year

πετάλι (το) [petali (to)] pedal

πετάω [petao] throw away (verb)

πέτρα (η) [petra (i)] stone

πετσέτα (η) [petseta (i)] napkin; towel

πετσέτα κουζίνας [petseta koozinas] tea towel

πετώ [peto] fly (verb)

πέφτω [pefto] fall (verb)

πηγή (η) [piyi (i)] fountain

πηγούνι (το) [pigooni (to)] chin

πηδάω [pithao] jump (verb)

πηρούνι (το) [pirooni (to)] fork

πιάνω [piano] catch (verb)

πιατάκι (το) [piataki (to)] saucer

πιατικά (τα) [piatika (ta)] crockery

πιάτο (το) [piato (to)] dish; plate

ΠΙΕΣΗ ΑΙΜΑΤΟΣ πίεση αίματος (η) blood pressure

πιθανώς [piTHanos] probably

πικάντικος [pikandikos] spicy

πικάπ (το) [pikap (to)] record player

πικνίκ (το) [piknik (to)] picnic

πικρός [pikros] bitter

πιλότος (ο) [pilotos (o)] pilot

πινακίδες (οι) [pinakithes (i)] number plates

ΠΙΝΑΚΟΘΗΚΗ πινακοθήκη (η) [pinakoTHiki (i)] art gallery

πινγκ-πονγκ (το) [ping-pong (to)] table tennis

πινέλο (το) [pinelo (to)] paintbrush

πινέλο για ξύρισμα [pinelo ya xirisma] shaving brush

πίνω [pino] drink (verb)

πίπα (η) [pipa (i)] pipe (for smoking)

ΠΙΣΙΝΑ πισίνα (η) [pisina (i)] swimming pool

πιστεύω [pistevo] believe

πιστολάκι (το) [pistolaki (to)] hairdryer

πιστόλι (το) [pistoli (to)] gun, pistol

πιστοποιητικό (το) [pistopi-itiko (to)] certificate

ΠΙΣΤΩΤΙΚΗ ΚΑΡΤΑ πιστωτική κάρτα (η) [pistotiki karta (i)] credit card

πίσω [piso] back; behind

πίσω φώτα (τα) [piso fota (ta)] rear lights

ΠΙΤΣΑΡΙΑ πιτσαρία (η) [pitsaria (i)] pizzeria

πλαστική σακούλα (η) [plastiki sakoola (i)] plastic bag

πλαστικός [plastikos] plastic

ΠΛΑΤΕΙΑ πλατεία (η) [platia (i)] square (in town); stalls (in theatre)

πλάτη (η) [plati (i)] back (of person)

πλατύς [platis] wide

ΠΛΑΤΦΟΡΜΑ πλατφόρμα (η) [platforma (i)] platform, (US) track

πλέκω [pleko] knit

πλένομαι [plenomeh] wash (oneself)

πλένω [pleno] wash (verb: something)

πλευρά (η) [plevra (i)] side

πλευρό (το) [plevro (to)] rib

πληγή (η) [pliyi (i)] wound

πλήθος (το) [plithos (to)] crowd

ΠΛΗΡΕΣ πλήρες no vacancies, full

ΠΛΗΡΟΦΟΡΙΕΣ πληροφορίες (οι) [plirofories (i)] information; directory enquiries

ΠΛΗΡΩΜΑ πλήρωμα (το) crew

πληρώνω [plirono] pay (verb)

πλοίο (το) [plio (to)] boat, ship

πλούσιος [ploosios] rich

πλυντήριο (το) [plindirio (to)] washing machine

ΠΛΥΝΤΗΡΙΟ ΑΥΤΟΚΙΝΗΤΩΝ πλυντήριο αυτοκινήτων car wash

ΠΛΥΝΤΗΡΙΟ ΡΟΥΧΩΝ πλυντήριο ρούχων [plindirio rookhon] launderette, laundromat

ΠΛΥΣΙΜΟ ΜΕ ΤΟ ΧΕΡΙ πλύσιμο με το χέρι handwash only

πλύσιμο των πιάτων (το) [plisimo ton piaton (to)] washing up

πνεύμονες (οι) [pnevmones (i)] lungs

ποδηλασία (η) [pothilasia (i)] cycling

ποδηλάτης (ο/η) [pothilatis (o/i)] cyclist

ΠΟΔΗΛΑΤΟ ποδήλατο (το) [pothilato (to)] bicycle

πόδι (το) [pothi (to)] foot; leg

με τα πόδια [meh ta pothia] on foot

ποδόσφαιρο (το) [pothosfero (to)] football

ποιά; [pia?] who?

ποιανού; [pianoo?] whose?

ποιό; [pio?] which?

ποιός; [pios?] who?

ποιός είναι; [pios ineh?] who is it?

πόλεμος (ο) [polemos (o)] war

πόλη (η) [poli (i)] city, town

πολιτεία (η) [politia (i)] state

πολιτικά (τα) [politika (ta)] politics

πολιτικός [politikos] political; politician

πολλά, πολλές, πολλή, πολλοί [pola, poles, poli, poli] many, a lot (of) πολύ [poli] a lot of; very; too much

πάρα πολύ [para poli] too much; very much

πολυσύχναστος [polisikhnastos] busy (place)

πολύς [polis] a lot (of)

ΠΟΛΥΤΕΛΕΙΑΣ πολυτελείας luxury class, four-star (hotel)

πονάει [ponai] hurt

πονόδοντος (ο) [ponothondos (o)] toothache

πονοκέφαλος (ο) [ponokefalos (o)] headache

πόνος (ο) [ponos (o)] ache, pain

ποντίκι (το) [pondiki (to)] mouse

πόνυ (το) [poni (to)] pony

πορεία (η) [poria (i)] route

πόρτα (η) [porta (i)] door

πορτ-μπαγκάζ (το) [port-bangaz (to)] boot (car), (US) trunk

πορτ-μπε-μπέ (το) [port-be-be (to)] carrycot

πορτοκαλί [portokali] orange (colour)

πορτοφολάς (ο) [portofolas (o)] pickpocket

πορτοφόλι (το) [portofoli (to)] wallet

πόσα;, πόσες; [posa?, poses?] how many?

ΠΟΣΙΜΟ ΝΕΡΟ πόσιμο νερό (το) [posimo nero (to)] drinking water

πόσο; [poso?] how much?

πόσοι; [posi?] how many?

πόστερ (το) [poster (to)] poster

ΠΟΣΤ ΡΕΣΤΑΝΤ ποστ ρεστάντ [post restant] poste restante

ποτάμι (το) [potami (to)] river

ποτέ [poteh] never

πότε; [poteh?] when?

έχετε ποτέ ...; [ekheteh poteh ...?] have you ever ...?

ποτήρι (το) [potiri (to)] glass

ΠΟΤΟΠΩΛΕΙΟ ποτοπωλείο (το) [potopolio (to)] off-licence, liquor store

που [poo] who, which, that

πού; [poo?] where?

πούδρα ταλκ (η) [poothra talk (i)] talcum powder

πουθενά [pooтнena] nowhere

πουκάμισο (το) [pookamiso (to)] shirt

πουλί (το) [pooli (to)] bird

ΠΟΥΛΜΑΝ πούλμαν (το) [poolman (to)] bus, coach

πουλόβερ (το) [poolover (to)] jumper

πουλώ [poolo] sell

πούρο (το) [pooro (to)] cigar

πράγμα (το) [pragma (to)] thing

πραγματικά [pragmatika] really

πρακτικός [praktikos] practical

πρακτορείο (το) [praktorio (to)] agency

ΠΡΑΚΤΟΡΕΙΟ ΕΦΗΜΕΡΙΔΩΝ πρακτορείο εφημερίδων newsagent, news vendor

ΠΡΑΚΤΟΡΕΙΟ ΛΕΩΦΟΡΕΙΩΝ πρακτορείο λεωφορείων [praktorio leoforion] bus station

πράσινος [prasinos] green

ΠΡΑΤΗΡΙΟ ΒΕΝΖΙΝΗΣ πρατήριο βενζίνης (το) [pratirio venzinis (to)] petrol station, gas station πρέπει να ... [prepi na ...] I must ...

ΠΡΕΣΒΕΙΑ πρεσβεία (η) [presvia (i)] embassy

πρησμένος [prismenos] swollen

πρίγκηπας (ο) [pringipas (o)] prince

πριγκίπισσα (η) [pringipisa (i)] princess

πρίζα (η) [priza (i)] socket; plug

πρίζα ταυ (η) [priza taf (i)] adaptor

πριν [prin] before; ago

πριν τρεις μέρες [prin tris meres] three days ago

προάστια (τα) [proastia (ta)] suburbs

πρόβατο (το) [provato (to)] sheep

πρόβλημα (το) [provlima (to)] problem

ΠΡΟΒΛΗΤΑ προβλήτα (η) [provlita (i)] quay

προβολείς (οι) [provolis (i)] headlights

ΠΡΟΓΕΥΜΑ πρόγευμα (το) [proyevma (to)] breakfast

πρόγονος (ο/η) [progonos (o/i)] ancestor

ΠΡΟΓΡΑΜΜΑ πρόγραμμα (το) [programa (to)] timetable, (US) schedule; programme

προκαταβάλλω [prokatavalo] advance (verb)

προκαταβολικά [prokatavolika] in advance

ΠΡΟΞΕΝΕΙΟ προξενείο (το) [proxenio (to)] consulate

ΠΡΟΟΡΙΣΜΟΣ προορισμός [pro-orismos] destination

προσβάλλω [prosvalo] offend

ΠΡΟΣ ΓΚΑΡΑΖ προς γκαράζ to car deck

ΠΡΟΣΔΕΘΗΤΕ προσδεθήτε fasten your seat belt

προσεκτικός [prosektikos] careful

πρόσεξε! [prosexeh!] look out!

ΠΡΟΣΕΧΕ! πρόσεχε! [prosekheh!] look out!

προσέχω [prosekho] take care of

ΠΡΟΣΕΧΩΣ προσεχώς coming soon

πρόσθετο (το) [prosτHeto (to)] supplementary

προσκαλώ [proskalo] invite

πρόσκληση (η) [prosklisi (i)] invitation

ΠΡΟΣ ΟΡΟΦΟΥΣ προς ορόφους to all floors

ΠΡΟΣΟΧΗ! προσοχή! caution!

ΠΡΟΣΟΧΗ ΑΡΓΑ προσοχή αργά caution: slow

ΠΡΟΣΟΧΗ ΕΞΟΔΟΣ ΟΧΗΜΑΤΩΝ προσοχή έξοδος οχημάτων caution: vehicle exit

ΠΡΟΣΟΧΗ ΕΥΦΛΕΚΤΟΝ προσοχή εύφλεκτον caution: highly inflammable

ΠΡΟΣΟΧΗ ΚΙΝΔΥΝΟΣ προσοχή κίνδυνος caution: danger

προσοχή παρακαλώ [prosokhi parakalo] attention please

ΠΡΟΣΟΧΗ ΣΚΥΛΟΣ προσοχή σκύλος beware of the dog

ΠΡΟΣ ΠΑΡΑΣΚΗΝΙΑ προς παρασκήνια to dressing rooms

προσπέκτους (το) [prospektoos (to)] brochure

προσπερνώ [prosperno] overtake

προστατεύω [prostatevo] protect

ΠΡΟΣΤΙΜΟ πρόστιμο (το) [prostimo (to)] fine

προσφέρω [prosfero] offer (verb); give

ΠΡΟΣΦΟΡΑ προσφορά special bargain

πρόσωπο (το) [prosopo (to)] face

προς [pros] towards

προτείνω [protino] recommend

ΠΡΟΤΕΡΑΙΟΤΗΤΑ προτεραιότητα (η) right of way

προτιμώ [protimo] prefer

προφανής [profanis] obvious

προφέρω [profero] pronounce

προφορά (η) [profora (i)] accent

προφυλακτήρας (ο) [profilaktiras (o)] bumper, fender

ΠΡΟΦΥΛΑΚΤΙΚΑ προφυλακτικά contraceptives

ΠΡΟΦΥΛΑΚΤΙΚΟ προφυλακτικό (το) [profilaktiko (to)] condom

προχτές [prokhtes] the day before yesterday

πρωί (το) [proi (to)] morning

το πρωί [to proi] in the morning

ΠΡΩΙΝΟ πρωινό (το) [pro-ino (to)] breakfast

πρώτα [prota] first, firstly

ΠΡΩΤΕΣ ΒΟΗΘΕΙΕΣ πρώτες βοήθειες (οι) [protes voiTHI-es (i)] first aid

ΠΡΩΤΗ ΘΕΣΗ πρώτη θέση first class

πρώτο! [proto!] great!

ΠΡΩΤΟ ΠΑΤΩΜΑ πρώτο πάτωμα (το) [proto patoma (to)] first floor, (US) second floor

πρώτος [protos] first

ΠΡΩΤΟΣ ΟΡΟΦΟΣ πρώτος όροφος [protos orofos] first floor, (US) second floor

Πρωτοχρονιά (η) [Protokhronia (i)] New Year's Day

ΠΤΗΣΕΙΣ ΕΞΩΤΕΡΙΚΟΥ πτήσεις εξωτερικού international flights

ΠΤΗΣΕΙΣ ΕΣΩΤΕΡΙΚΟΥ πτήσεις εσωτερικού domestic flights

ΠΤΗΣΗ πτήση (η) [ptisi (i)] flight

ΠΤΗΣΗ ΤΣΑΡΤΕΡ πτήση τσάρτερ charter flight

πυζάμες (οι) [pizames (i)] pyjamas

πυξίδα (η) [pixitha (i)] compass

πύργος (ο) [pirgos (o)] tower

πυρετός (ο) [piretos (o)] fever

πυρκαγιά (η) [pirkaya (i)] fire

ΠΥΡΟΣΒΕΣΤΗΡ πυροσβεστήρ (ο) fire extinguisher

ΠΥΡΟΣΒΕΣΤΗΡΑΣ πυροσβεστήρας (ο) fire extinguisher

ΠΥΡΟΣΒΕΣΤΙΚΗ ΣΩΛΗΝΑ πυροσβεστική σωλήνα (η) fire hose

ΠΥΡΟΣΒΕΣΤΙΚΗ
(ΥΠΗΡΕΣΙΑ) πυροσβεστική
(υπηρεσία) (η) [pirosvestiki
ipiresia (i)] fire brigade

πυροτεχνήματα (τα)
[pirotekhnimata (ta)] fireworks

πυτζάμες (οι) [pitzames (i)]
pyjamas

ΠΩΛΕΙΤΑΙ πωλείται for sale

ΠΩΛΗΣΗ πώληση (η) sale

πώς; [pos?] how?; what?

Ρ

ράβω [ravo] sew

ραδιόφωνο (το) [rathiofono (to)]
radio

ραντεβού (το) [randevoo (to)]
appointment

ράντζο (το) [randzo (to)]
campbed

ΡΑΦΕΙΟ ραφείο (το) [rafio (to)]
tailor's

ρεζέρβα (η) [rezerva (i)] spare
tyre

ΡΕΣΕΨΙΟΝ ρεσεψιόν (η)
[resepsion (i)] reception

ρεσεψιονίστ (ο/η) [resepsionist
(o/i)] receptionist

ρε συ! [reh si!] you there!, oy
you!

ρεύμα (το) [revma (to)] current;
draught

ρευματισμοί (οι) [revmatismi (i)]
rheumatism

ρίχνω [rikhno] throw (verb)

ρόδα (η) [rotha (i)] wheel

ροζ [roz] pink

ρόκ (η) [rok (i)] rock music

ρολόι (το) [roloi (to)] clock;
watch

ρόμπα (η) [roba (i)] dressing
gown

ΡΟΥΦ - ΓΚΑΡΝΤΕΝ Ρουφ -
Γκάρντεν [Roof - garden] roof
garden

ρούχα (τα) [rookha (ta)] clothes

ροχαλίζω [rokhalizo] snore

ρυμούλκα (η) [rimoolka (i)]
trailer (for car)

ρυμουλκό [rimoolko] trailer (for
car etc)

ρωτώ [roto] ask

Σ

ΣΑΒΒΑΤΟ Σάββατο (το)
[Savato (to)] Saturday

σαββατοκύριακο (το)
[savatokiriako (to)] weekend

ΣΑΓΙΟΝΑΡΕΣ σαγιονάρες
[sayonares] beach sandals,
flip-flops

σαγόνι (το) [sagoni (to)] jaw

σακάκι (το) [sakaki (to)] jacket

σακβουαγιάζ (το) [sakvooayaz
(to)] hand luggage, hand
baggage

σακίδιο (το) [sakithio (to)]
rucksack

σάκος (ο) [sakos (o)] backpack,
rucksack

ΣΑΛΟΝΙ σαλόνι (το) [saloni
(to)] lounge

ΣΑΜΠΟΥΑΝ σαμπουάν (το)
[sampooan (to)] shampoo

σαμπρέλα (η) ⟦sabrela (i)⟧ inner
tube

σαν ⟦san⟧ like, as

σανδάλια (τα) ⟦santhalia (ta)⟧
sandals

σάουνα (η) ⟦saoona (i)⟧ sauna

σάπιος ⟦sapios⟧ rotten

ΣΑΠΟΥΝΙ ΠΙΑΤΩΝ σαπούνι
πιάτων (το) ⟦sapooni piaton (to)⟧
washing-up liquid

ΣΑΠΟΥΝΙ σαπούνι (το)
⟦sapooni (to)⟧ soap

σαράντα ⟦saranda⟧ forty

σας ⟦sas⟧ you; your

σβήνω ⟦svino⟧ switch off
(engine); put out (fire)

ΣΒΗΣΤΕ ΤΗΝ ΜΗΧΑΝΗ
σβήστε την μηχανή switch off
engine

σβήστρα (η) ⟦svistra (i)⟧ rubber,
eraser

σγουρά ⟦sgoora⟧ curly

σε ⟦seh⟧ you; to; at; in

σεζ λόνγκ (η) ⟦sez long (i)⟧
deckchair

ΣΕΙΡΑ σειρά (η) ⟦sira (i)⟧ row
(of seats)

σελίδα (η) ⟦selitha (i)⟧ page

ΣΕΛΛΟΤΕΗΠ σέλλοτέηπ (το)
⟦selloteip (to)⟧ Sellotape®,
Scotch tape®

ΣΕΛΦ ΣΕΡΒΙΣ σελφ σέρβις
⟦self servis⟧ self-service

σεντόνι (το) ⟦sendoni (to)⟧ sheet

σέξυ ⟦sexi⟧ sexy

ΣΕ ΠΕΡΙΠΤΩΣΗ ΑΝΑΓΚΗΣ
ΣΠΑΣΤΕ ΤΟ ΤΖΑΜΙ σε
περίπτωση ανάγκης σπάστε το
τζάμι in emergency break

glass

ΣΕΠΤΕΜΒΡΙΟΣ Σεπτέμβριος
(ο) ⟦Septemvrios (o)⟧ September

ΣΕΡΒΙΕΤΕΣ σερβιέτες (οι)
⟦servietes (i)⟧ sanitary
towels/napkins

σερβιτόρα (η) ⟦servitora (i)⟧
barmaid; waitress

σερβιτόρος (ο) ⟦servitoros (o)⟧
waiter

ΣΗΚΩΣΤΕ ΤΟ ΑΚΟΥΣΤΙΚΟ
σηκώστε το ακουστικό lift
receiver

σημαδούρα (η) ⟦simathoora (i)⟧
buoy

σημαία (η) ⟦simea (i)⟧ flag

σημειωματάριο (το) ⟦simiomatario
(to)⟧ notebook

ΣΗΜΕΡΑ σήμερα ⟦simera⟧
today

ΣΗΜΕΡΟΝ σήμερον showing
today

σήραγγα (η) ⟦siranga (i)⟧ tunnel

σιγά-σιγά ⟦siga-siga⟧ slowly;
slow down

σίγουρος ⟦sigooros⟧ sure

σίδερο (το) ⟦sithero (to)⟧ iron

σιδερώνω ⟦sitherono⟧ iron (verb)

ΣΙΔΗΡΟΔΡΟΜΙΚΟΣ
ΣΤΑΘΜΟΣ σιδηροδρομικός
σταθμός (ο) ⟦sithirothromikos
staᴛʜmos (o)⟧ railway station

σιδηρόδρομος (ο) ⟦sithirothromos
(o)⟧ railway

ΣΙΔΗΡΟΥΡΓΕΙΟ σιδηρουργείο
(το) ⟦sithirooryio (to)⟧ hardware
store

ΣΙΝΕΜΑ σινεμά (το) ⟦sinema
(to)⟧ cinema, movie theater

σιωπή (η) [siopi (i)] silence

σκάλα (η) [skala (i)] ladder

ΣΚΑΛΕΣ σκάλες (οι) [skales (i)] stairs

σκέπτομαι [skeptomeh] think

ΣΚΗΝΗ σκηνή (η) [skini (i)] tent

σκιά (η) [skia (i)] shade, shadow
στη σκιά [sti skia] in the shade

ΣΚΙΑ ΜΑΤΙΩΝ σκιά ματιών (η) [skia mation (i)] eye shadow

ΣΚΛΗΡΟΙ ΦΑΚΟΙ σκληροί φακοί (οι) [skliri faki (i)] hard lenses

σκληρός [skliros] hard

ΣΚΟΝΗ ΠΛΥΝΤΗΡΙΟΥ σκόνη πλυντηρίου (η) [skoni plindirioo (i)] washing powder

σκοτεινός [skotinos] dark

σκοτώνω [skotono] kill (verb)

σκουλαρίκια (τα) [skoolarikia (ta)] earrings

σκούπα [skoopa] broom

σκουπίδια (τα) [skoopithia (ta)] rubbish, garbage

σκουπιδοντενεκές (ο) [skoopithondenekes (o)] dustbin, trashcan

σκύλος (ο) [skilos (o)] dog

σκωληκοειδίτις (η) [skoliko-ithitis (i)] appendicitis

ΣΚΩΤΙΑ Σκωτία (η) [Skotia (i)] Scotland

Σκωτσέζικος [Skotsezikos] Scottish

σλάιντ (το) [slaid (to)] slide

σλίπ (το) [slip (to)] underpants; panties

ΣΛΙΠΙΝΓΚ ΜΠΑΓΚ σλίπινγκ μπαγκ (το) [sliping bag (to)] sleeping bag

σοβαρός [sovaros] serious

σοκ (το) [sok (to)] shock

ΣΟΚΟΛΑΤΑ σοκολάτα (η) [sokolata (i)] chocolate

ΣΟΚΟΛΑΤΑ ΓΑΛΑΚΤΟΣ σοκολάτα γάλακτος (η) [sokolata galaktos (i)] milk chocolate

ΣΟΚΟΛΑΤΑΚΙΑ σοκολατάκια (τα) [sokolatakia (ta)] chocolates

σόλα (η) [sola (i)] sole (of shoe)

σόμπα (η) [soba (i)] oil heater

σορτς (το) [sorts (to)] shorts

σου [soo] you; your

σουγιάς (ο) [sooyas (o)] penknife

ΣΟΥΠΕΡ ΒΕΝΖΙΝΗ σούπερ βενζίνη (η) [sooper venzini (i)] four-star petrol, premium

ΣΟΥΠΕΡΜΑΡΚΕΤ σούπερμάρκετ (το) [soopermarket (to)] supermarket

σουτιέν (το) [sootien (to)] bra

ΣΠΑΓΓΟΣ σπάγγος (ο) [spangos (o)] string

σπασμένος [spasmenos] broken

σπάω [spao] break (verb)

σπηλιά (το) [spilia (to)] cave

σπιράλ (το) [spiral (to)] spiral; IUD; incense coil (mosquito repellent)

σπίρτα (τα) [spirta (ta)] matches

σπίτι (το) [spiti (to)] house
στο σπίτι [sto spiti] at home

σπορ (το) [spor (to)] sport

σπουδαίος [spootheos] important

σπρώχνω [sprokhno] push (verb)

σταγόνα (η) [stagona (i)] drop

ΣΤΑΓΟΝΕΣ σταγόνες drops

ΣΤΑΔΙΟ στάδιο (το) [stathio (to)] stadium

ΣΤΑΘΜΟΣ σταθμός (ο) [staTHmos (o)] station

ΣΤΑΘΜΟΣ ΑΝΕΦΟΔΙΑΣΜΟΥ ΘΑΛΑΜΗΓΩΝ σταθμός ανεφοδιασμού θαλαμηγών yacht refuelling station

ΣΤΑΘΜΟΣ ΛΕΩΦΟΡΕΙΩΝ σταθμός λεωφορείων [staTHmos leoforion] bus station

ΣΤΑΘΜΟΣ ΠΡΩΤΩΝ ΒΟΗΘΕΙΩΝ σταθμός πρώτων βοηθειών [staTHmos proton voiTHion] first aid post

ΣΤΑΘΜΟΣ ΤΑΞΙ σταθμός ταξί [staTHmos taxi] taxi stand

ΣΤΑΘΜΟΣ ΥΠΕΡΑΣΤΙΚΩΝ ΛΕΩΦΟΡΕΙΩΝ σταθμός υπεραστικών λεωφορείων [staTHmos iperastikon leoforion] bus station (long distance)

ΣΤΑΘΜΟΣ ΧΩΡΟΦΥΛΑΚΗΣ σταθμός χωροφυλακής [staTHmos khorofilakis] police station

σταματάω [stamatao] stop (verb)

ΣΤΑΣΗ στάση (η) [stasi (i)] stop (for bus, train)

ΣΤΑΣΗ ΑΣΤΙΚΩΝ ΣΥΓΚΟΙΝΩΝΙΩΝ στάση αστικών συγκοινωνιών city bus stop

ΣΤΑΣΗ ΛΕΩΦΟΡΕΙΟΥ στάση λεωφορείου bus stop

ΣΤΑΣΗ ΤΑΞΙ στάση ταξί [stasi

taxi] taxi stand

ΣΤΑΣΙΣ στάσις (η) [stasis (i)] bus stop

στέγη (η) [steyi (i)] roof

ΣΤΕΓΝΟ ΚΑΘΑΡΙΣΜΑ ΜΟΝΟΝ στεγνό καθάρισμα μόνον dryclean only

ΣΤΕΓΝΟΚΑΘΑΡΙΣΤΗΡΙΟ στεγνοκαθαριστήριο (το) [stegnokaTHaristirio (to)] dry cleaner's

στεγνός [stegnos] dry

στεγνώνω [stegnono] dry (verb)

στέλνω [stelno] send

στενός [stenos] narrow; tight

στενοχώρια (η) [stenokhoria (i)] worry (verb)

στήθος (το) [stiTHos (to)] breast; chest

στην [stin] at; in; to; on

ΣΤΙΒΟΣ στίβος (ο) [stivos (o)] athletics stadium

στο [sto] at; in; to

στόμα (το) [stoma (to)] mouth

στομάχι (το) [stomakhi (to)] stomach

στον [ston] at; in; to;

ΣΤΟΠ! στοπ! stop!

στριφτό (το) [strifto (to)] hand-rolled cigarette

στρογγυλός [strongilos] round

στρόφαλος (ο) [strofalos (o)] crankshaft

στροφή (η) [strofi (i)] bend

στρώμα (το) [stroma (to)] mattress

στυλό (το) [stilo (to)] biro®

συγγενείς (οι) [singenis (i)] relatives

συγγνώμη [signomi] sorry; excuse me

συγγνώμη; [signomi?] pardon (me)?, sorry?

σύγκρουση (η) [singroosi (i)] crash

συγχαρητήρια! [sinkharitiria!] congratulations!

συγχωρείτε: με συγχωρείτε [meh sinkhoriteh] excuse me

σύζυγος (ο) [sizigos (o)] husband

συκότι (το) [sikoti (to)] liver

συλλαμβάνω [silamvano] arrest

συλλογή (η) [siloyi (i)] collection

συμβαίνω [simveno] happen

συμβουλεύω [simvoolevo] advise

ΣΥΜΠΕΡΙΛΑΜΒΑΝΕΤΑΙ συμπεριλαμβάνεται included

συμπλέκτης (ο) [siblektis (o)] clutch

συμφωνώ [simfono] agree

ΣΥΝΑΓΕΡΜΟΣ συναγερμός (ο) [sinayermos (o)] alarm

συναίσθημα (το) [sinesthima (to)] feeling

ΣΥΝΑΛΛΑΓΜΑ συνάλλαγμα (το) [sinalagma (to)] foreign exchange

ΣΥΝΑΛΛΑΓΜΑΤΙΚΗ ΙΣΟΤΙΜΙΑ συναλλαγματική ισοτιμία (η) [sinalagmatiki isotimia (i)] exchange rate

συνάντηση (η) [sinandisi (i)] meeting

συναντώ [sinando] meet

συναρπαστικός [sinarpastikos] exciting

συναυλία (η) [sinavlia (i)] concert

ΣΥΝ/ΓΕΙΟ συν/γειο auto repairs

σύνδεση (η) [sinthesi (i)] connection (electrical)

ΣΥΝΕΡΓΕΙΟ (ΑΥΤΟΚΙΝΗΤΩΝ) συνεργείο (αυτοκινήτων) (το) auto repairs

συνήθεια (η) [sinithia (i)] habit

συνηθισμένος [sinithismenos] usual

συνήθως [sinithos] usually

ΣΥΝΘΕΤΙΚΟ συνθετικό synthetic

συννεφιασμένος [sinefiasmenos] cloudy

σύννεφο (το) [sinefo (to)] cloud

συνοδεύω [sinothevo] accompany

ΣΥΝΟΙΚΙΑ συνοικία (η) [sinikia (i)] district

συνολικά [sinolika] altogether

σύνορα (τα) [sinora (ta)] border

συνταγή (η) [sindayi (i)] prescription; recipe

συνταξιούχος (ο/η) [sindaxiookhos (o/i)] old-age pensioner

ΣΥΝΤΗΡΗΤΙΚΟ ΔΙΑΛΥΜΑ συντηρητικό διάλυμα (το) [sindiritiko thialima (to)] soaking solution

σύντομα [sindoma] soon

ΣΥΡΑΤΕ σύρατε pull

σύρμα (το) [sirma (to)] wire

ΣΥΣΤΑΤΙΚΑ συστατικά ingredients

ΣΥΣΤΗΜΕΝΑ συστημένα

[sistimena] registered mail
συστήνω [sistino] introduce; recommend
συχνά [sikhna] often
σφήγγα (η) [sfinga (i)] wasp
σφράγισμα (το) [sfrayisma (to)] filling (in tooth)
σφυρί (το) [sfiri (to)] hammer
σχάρα αυτοκινήτου (η) [skhara aftokinitoo (i)] roof rack
σχέδιο (το) [skhethio (to)] plan
σχεδόν [skhethon] almost
σχοινί (το) [skhini (to)] rope
ΣΧΟΛΕΙΟ σχολείο (το) [skholio (to)] school
σωλήνας (ο) [solinas (o)] pipe (water)
σώμα (το) [soma (to)] body
ΣΩΣΙΒΙΑ σωσίβια lifejackets
σωστός [sostos] correct

T

τα [ta] the; them
ταβάνι (το) [tavani (to)] ceiling
ΤΑΒΕΡΝΑ ταβέρνα (η) [taverna (i)] restaurant
τακούνι (το) [takooni (to)] heel (of shoe)
ΤΑΛΗΡΟ τάληρο (το) [taliro (to)] 5-drachma coin
ΤΑΜΕΙΟ ταμείο (το) [tamio (to)] box office; cash desk, till, cashier
ΤΑΜΙΕΥΤΗΡΙΟ ταμιευτήριο (το) [tami-eftirio (to)] savings bank
ΤΑΜΠΛΕΤΑ ταμπλέτα (η)

[tableta (i)] tablet
ΤΑΜΠΟΝ ταμπόν (τα) [tampon (ta)] tampons
τάξη (η) [taxi (i)] class
ΤΑΞΙ ταξί (το) [taxi (to)] taxi
ταξιδεύω [taxithevo] travel (verb)
ταξίδι (το) [taxithi (to)] journey, trip
καλό ταξίδι! [kalo taxithi!] have a good journey!, bon voyage!
ταξίδι για δουλειές [taxithi ya thoolies] business trip
ΤΑΞΙΔΙΩΤΙΚΗ ΕΠΙΤΑΓΗ ταξιδιωτική επιταγή (η) [taxithiotiki epitayi (i)] traveller's cheque/traveler's check
ΤΑΞΙΔΙΩΤΙΚΟ ΓΡΑΦΕΙΟ ταξιδιωτικό γραφείο (το) [taxithiotiko grafio (to)] travel agent's
τάπα (η) [tapa (i)] plug (in sink)
ΤΑ ΡΕΣΤΑ ΣΑΣ τα ρέστα σας your change
ΤΑΡΙΦΑ ταρίφα [tarifa] taxi tariff
τασάκι (το) [tasaki (to)] ashtray
ταύρος (ο) [tavros (o)] bull
ΤΑΥΤΟΤΗΤΑ ταυτότητα (η) [taftotita (i)] pass, identity card
ΤΑΧΥΔΡΟΜΕΙΟ ταχυδρομείο (το) [takhithromio (to)] post office
ΤΑΧΥΔΡΟΜΙΚΟΣ ΤΟΜΕΥΣ ταχυδρομικός τομεύς (ο) [takhithromikos tomefs (o)] postcode, zipcode
ταχυδρόμος (ο) [takhithromos (o)] postman

ταχυδρομώ [takithromo] post, mail (verb)

ταχύτητα (η) [takhitita (i)] gear (in car)

ταχύτητα (η) [takhitita (i)] speed

τέλειος [telios] perfect

τελειώνω [teliono] finish (verb)

ΤΕΛΕΥΤΑΙΑ ΠΑΡΑΣΤΑΣΗ τελευταία παράσταση last performance

τελευταίος [telefteos] last

τελεφερίκ (το) [teleferik (to)] cable car

ΤΕΛΟΣ τέλος (το) [telos (to)] end

ΤΕΛΩΝΕΙΟ Τελωνείο (το) [Telonio (to)] Customs

τεμπέλης [tebelis] lazy

τέννις (το) [tenis (to)] tennis

τέντα (η) [tenda (i)] tent, marquee

τέσσερα [tesera] four

ΤΕΤΑΡΤΗ Τετάρτη (η) [Tetarti (i)] Wednesday

τέταρτο (το) [tetarto (to)] quarter

τέταρτος [tetartos] fourth

τέχνη (η) [tekhni (i)] art

τεχνητός [tekhnitos] artificial

ΤΕΧΝΗΤΟ ΧΡΩΜΑ τεχνητό χρώμα artificial colouring

τζαζ (η) [tzaz (i)] jazz

τζηνς (τα) [tzins (ta)] jeans

τζόγγιγκ (το) [tzoging (to)] jogging

τη [ti] the

τηγάνι (το) [tigani (to)] frying pan

τηγανίζω [tiganizo] fry

ΤΗΛΕΓΡΑΦΗΜΑ τηλεγράφημα (το) [tilegrafima (to)] telegram

ΤΗΛΕΓΡΑΦΗΜΑΤΑ τηλεγραφήματα telegrams

ΤΗΛΕΓΡΑΦΙΚΗ ΕΝΤΟΛΗ τηλεγραφική εντολή [tilegrafiki endoli] telegram

ΤΗΛΕΚΑΡΤΑ τηλεκάρτα (η) [tilekarta (i)] phonecard

ΤΗΛΕΟΡΑΣΗ τηλεόραση (η) [tileorasi (i)] television

ΤΗΛΕΦΩΝΗΜΑ τηλεφώνημα [tilefonima] call

ΤΗΛΕΦΩΝΗΜΑ ΚΟΛΛΕΚΤ τηλεφώνημα κολλέκτ (το) [tilefonima kollekt (to)] reverse charge call

ΤΗΛΕΦΩΝΙΚΗ ΕΝΤΟΛΗ τηλεφωνική εντολή operator-controlled phone call

ΤΗΛΕΦΩΝΙΚΟΣ ΘΑΛΑΜΟΣ τηλεφωνικός θάλαμος (ο) [tilefonikos THalamos (o)] phone box

ΤΗΛΕΦΩΝΙΚΟΣ ΚΑΤΑΛΟΓΟΣ τηλεφωνικός κατάλογος (ο) [tilefonikos katalogos (o)] phone book

ΤΗΛΕΦΩΝΟ τηλέφωνο (το) [tilefono (to)] phone

ΤΗΛΕΦΩΝΩ τηλεφωνώ [tilefono] ring, phone (verb)

την [tin] her; on; per; the

την εβδομάδα [tin evthomatha] per week

της [tis] her; to her; of her

τι; [ti?] what?

ΤΙΜΗ τιμή (η) [timi (i)] price

ΤΙΜΗ ΑΓΟΡΑΣ τιμή αγοράς buying rate

ΤΙΜΗ ΑΝΕΥ ΠΟΣΟΣΤΩΝ τιμή άνευ ποσοστών price exclusive of extras

ΤΙΜΗ ΔΩΜΑΤΙΟΥ τιμή δωματίου room price

ΤΙΜΗ ΚΑΤ᾽ ΑΤΟΜΟ τιμή κατ᾽ άτομο price per person

ΤΙΜΗ ΚΛΙΝΗΣ τιμή κλίνης price per bed

ΤΙΜΗ ΜΕΤΑ ΠΟΣΟΣΤΩΝ τιμή μετά ποσοστών price inclusive of extras

ΤΙΜΗ ΠΩΛΗΣΗΣ τιμή πώλησης selling rate

τίμιος [timios] honest

τιμόνι (το) [timoni (to)] steering wheel

τίνος; [tinos?] whose

τίποτε [tipoteh] nothing

ΤΙΠΟΤΕ ΠΡΟΣ ΔΗΛΩΣΗ τίποτε προς δήλωση nothing to declare

τις [tis] them

ΤΜΗΜΑ τμήμα (το) [tmima (to)] department

το [to] in; it; the; per

τοις εκατό [tis ekato] per cent

ΤΟΙΣ ΜΕΤΡΗΤΟΙΣ τοις μετρητοίς cash only, no credit cards

τοίχος (ο) [tikhos (o)] wall

ΤΟ ΚΑΤΑΣΤΗΜΑ ΜΕΤΑΦΕΡΘΗΚΕ ΕΙΣ ... το κατάστημα μεταφέρθηκε εις ... we have moved to ...

ΤΟ ΚΟΜΜΑΤΙ το κομμάτι per item

ΤΟΚΟΣ τόκος (ο) [tokos (o)] interest

τολμάω [tolmao] dare (verb)

τον [ton] him; the

ΤΟΞΙΚΟ τοξικό toxic

ΤΟΠΙΚΗ ΩΡΑ τοπική ώρα local time

ΤΟΠΙΚΟ (ΤΗΛΕΦΩΝΗΜΑ) τοπικό (τηλεφώνημα) (το) [topiko tilefonima (to)] local call

τοπίο (το) [topio (to)] landscape

τόσο [toso] so (much); that much

τότε [toteh] then

του [too] his; its; to him

ΤΟΥΑΛΕΤΑ τουαλέτα (η) [tooaleta (i)] toilet, rest room

ΤΟΥΑΛΕΤΑ ΤΩΝ ΓΥΝΑΙΚΩΝ τουαλέτα των γυναικών (η) [tooaleta ton yinekon (i)] ladies' toilet, ladies' room

ΤΟΥΑΛΕΤΕΣ τουαλέτες [tooaletes] toilets, rest room

τουλάχιστον [toolakhiston] at least

του οποίου [too opioo] whose

τουρίστας (ο) [tooristas (o)] tourist

ΤΟΥΡΙΣΤΙΚΗ ΑΣΤΥΝΟΜΙΑ Τουριστική Αστυνομία (η) [Tooristiki Astinomia (i)] Tourist Police

τουριστικός οδηγός (ο) [tooristikos othigos (o)] guidebook

τουρίστρια (η) [tooristria (i)] tourist

ΤΟΥΡΚΑΛΑ τουρκάλα (η)

[toorkala (i)] Turk

ΤΟΥΡΚΙΑ Τουρκία (η) [Toorkia (i)] Turkey

Τούρκος (ο) [Toorkos (o)] Turk

ΤΟΥΡΚΙΚΟΣ Τουρκικός [Toorkikos] Turkish (adj)

τους [toos] them; to them

τραβάω [travao] pull (verb)

τραγούδι (το) [tragoothi (to)] song

τραγουδώ [tragotho] sing

ΤΡΑΠΕΖΑΡΙΑ τραπεζαρία (η) [trapezaria (i)] dining room

ΤΡΑΠΕΖΑ τράπεζα (η) [trapeza (i)] bank

τραπέζι (το) [trapezi (to)] table

τραπεζομάντηλο (το) [trapezomandilo (to)] tablecloth

τραυματίζομαι [travmatizomeh] hurt, injure

τραυματισμένος [travmatismenos] injured

τρελλός [trelos] mad

ΤΡΕΝΟ τρένο (το) [treno (to)] train

τρέχω [trekho] run (verb)

τρία [tria] three

τριακόσια [triakosia] three hundred

τριάντα [trianda] thirty

τριαντάφυλλο (το) [triandafilo (to)] rose

ΤΡΙΚΛΙΝΟ ΔΩΜΑΤΙΟ τρίκλινο δωμάτιο (το) [triklino thomatio (to)] triple room

ΤΡΙΤΗ Τρίτη (η) [Triti (i)] Tuesday

ΤΡΙΤΗ ΘΕΣΗ τρίτη θέση third class

τρίτος [tritos] third

τρόλλεϋ (το) [troleh-i (to)] trolley, trolleybus

τρομερός [tromeros] tremendous

ΤΡΟΦΗ ΓΙΑ ΔΙΑΒΗΤΙΚΟΥΣ τροφή γιά διαβητικούς [trofi ya thiavitikoos] diabetic foods

τροφική δηλητηρίαση (η) [trofiki thilitiriasi (i)] food poisoning

ΤΡΟΧΑΙΑ τροχαία (η) traffic police

τροχονόμος (ο) [trokhonomos (o)] traffic warden

τροχόσπιτο (το) [trokhospito (to)] caravan, (US) trailer

ΤΡΟΧΟΣΠΙΤΑ τροχόσπιτα (το) caravans, (US) trailers

τρύπα (η) [tripa (i)] hole

τρώω [troo] eat; have dinner

τσαγιέρα (η) [tsayera (i)] teapot

ΤΣΑΓΚΑΡΗΣ τσαγκάρης (ο) [tsangaris (o)] shoe repairer's

τσάντα (η) [tsanda (i)] bag; handbag, (US) purse

ΤΣΑΝΤΕΣ ΜΠΑΝΙΟΥ τσάντες μπάνιου beach bags

τσέπη (η) [tsepi (i)] pocket

ΤΣΙΓΑΡΟ τσιγάρο (το) [tsigaro (to)] cigarette

τσίμπημα (το) [tsibima (to)] bite (insect)

τσιμπιδάκι (το) [tsibithaki (to)] tweezers

τσιμπώ [tsibo] sting (verb)

ΤΣΙΠΣ τσιπς (τα) [tsips (ta)] crisps, (US) potato chips

ΤΣΙΧΛΑ τσίχλα (η) [tsikhla (i)] chewing gum

τσόκ (το) [tsok (to)] choke (on car)

τσούχτρα (η) [tsookhtra (i)] jellyfish

τυλίγω [tiligo] wrap (verb)

τυφλός [tiflos] blind

τύχη (η) [tikhi (i)] luck

καλή τύχη! [kali tikhi!] good luck!

των [ton] of them

τώρα [tora] now

Υ

υαλοκαθαριστήρας (ο) [ialokaтharistiras (o)] windscreen wiper

υγεία: στην υγειά σας/σου! [stin iya sas/soo!] your health!, cheers!

υγιής [iyi-is] healthy

ΥΓΡΑΕΡΙΟ υγραέριο (το) [igraerio (to)] camping gas

υγρός [igros] damp, wet

ΥΔΡΑΥΛΙΚΑ υδραυλικά (τα) [ithravlika (ta)] plumber

ΥΔΡΑΥΛΙΚΟΣ υδραυλικός (ο) [ithravlikos (o)] plumber

υπάρχει [iparkhi] there is

υπάρχουν [iparkhoon] there are

ΥΠΕΡΑΣΤΙΚΟ (ΤΗΛΕΦΩΝΗΜΑ) υπεραστικό (τηλεφώνημα) (το) [iperastiko tilefonima (to)] long-distance call, international call

υπερβάλλω [ipervallo] exaggerate

υπέρβαρο (το) [ipervaro (to)] excess baggage

υπερβολικά [ipervolika] too

υπερήφανος [iperifanos] proud

ΥΠΕΡΠΟΛΥΤΕΛΕΙΑΣ υπερπολυτελειας five-star (hotel)

υπεύθυνος [ipefтHinos] responsible

ΥΠΗΡΕΣΙΑ υπηρεσία (η) [ipiresia (i)] service

ύπνο: πάω για ύπνο [pao ya ipno] go to bed

υπνοδωμάτιο (το) [ipnothomatio (to)] bedroom

ύπνος (ο) [ipnos (o)] sleep

ΥΠΝΩΤΙΚΟ ΧΑΠΙ υπνωτικό χάπι (το) [ipnotiko khapi (to)] sleeping pill

ΥΠΟΓΕΙΑ ΔΙΑΒΑΣΗ ΠΕΖΩΝ υπόγεια διάβαση πεζών (η) pedestrian subway

ΥΠΟΓΕΙΟ υπόγειο (το) [ipoyio (to)] basement

ΥΠΟΓΕΙΟΣ υπόγειος (ο) [ipoyios (o)] underground, (US) subway

υπογράφω [ipografo] sign (verb)

ΥΠΟΔΗΜΑΤΑ υποδήματα (τα) [ipothimata (ta)] shoes

ΥΠΟΔΗΜΑΤΑ ΓΥΝΑΙΚΕΙΑ υποδήματα γυναικεία [ipothimata yinekia] ladies' shoes

ΥΠΟΔΗΜΑΤΟΠΟΙΕΙΟ υποδηματοποιείο (το) [ipothimatopi-io (to)] shoe shop

υπολογιστής (ο) [ipoloyistis (o)] computer

υπόλοιπο (το) [ipolipo (to)] rest,

remainder

υπόσχομαι [iposkhomeh] promise (verb)

ΥΠΟΥΡΓΕΙΟ υπουργείο (το) ministry

ύφασμα (το) [ifasma (to)] material

ΥΦΑΣΜΑΤΑ υφάσματα [ifasmata] clothing; cloth, material

Φ

ΦΑΓΗΤΟ φαγητό (το) [fayito (to)] food; meal; lunch

φαγούρα (η) [fagoora (i)] itch

φάκελος (ο) [fakelos (o)] envelope

ΦΑΚΟΙ ΕΠΑΦΗΣ φακοί επαφής (οι) [faki epafis (i)] contact lenses

φακός (ο) [fakos (o)] lens; torch

φαλακρός [falakros] bald

φαλλοκράτης (ο) [falokratis (o)] male chauvinist

φανάρια τροχαίας (τα) [fanaria trokheas (ta)] traffic lights

φανταστικός [fandastikos] fantastic

ΦΑΡΜΑΚΕΙΟ φαρμακείο (το) [farmakio (to)] chemist's, pharmacy

φάρμακο (το) [farmako (to)] medicine

φαρμακοποιός (ο) [farmakopios (o)] chemist, pharmacist

φασαρία (η) [fasaria (i)] noise

ΦΕΒΡΟΥΑΡΙΟΣ Φεβρουάριος (ο) [Fevrooarios (o)] February

φεγγάρι (το) [fengari (to)] moon

φεμινίστρια (η) [feministria (i)] feminist

φερμουάρ (το) [fermooar (to)] zip

φέρνω [ferno] bring

ΦΕΡΡΥ ΜΠΩΤ φέρρυ μπωτ (το) [feri bot (to)] ferry

φέτα (η) [feta (i)] slice

φεύγω [fevgo] go away

φθινόπωρο (το) [fΤΗinoporo (to)] autumn, (US) fall

φίδι (το) [fithi (to)] snake

φιλενάδα (η) [filenatha (i)] girlfriend; friend

φιλί (το) [fili (to)] kiss

ΦΙΛΜ φιλμ (το) [film (to)] film, movie

ΦΙΛΟΔΩΡΗΜΑ φιλοδώρημα (το) [filothorima (to)] service charge; tip

φιλοξενία (η) [filoxenia (i)] hospitality

φιλοξενούμενη (η) [filoxenoomeni (i)] guest

φιλοξενούμενος (ο) [filoxenoomenos (o)] guest

φίλος (ο) [filos (o)] boyfriend; friend

φιλοφρόνηση (η) [filofronisi (i)] compliment

φίλτρο (το) [filtro (to)] filter

φιλώ [filo] kiss (verb)

φλας (το) [flas (to)] flash; indicator

φλέβα (η) [fleva (i)] vein

φλυτζάνι (το) [flitzani (to)] cup

φοβάμαι [fovameh] be afraid

φοβερός [foveros] terrible

φόβος (ο) [**fovos** (o)] fear

φοιτητής (ο) [**fititis** (o)] student

ΦΟΙΤΗΤΙΚΑ ΕΙΣΙΤΗΡΙΑ φοιτητικά εισιτήρια [**fititika** isitiria] student tickets

φοιτήτρια (η) [**fititria** (i)] student

φορά (η) [**fora** (i)] time, occasion

φόρεμα (το) [**forema** (to)] dress

φορτηγό (το) [**fortigo** (to)] lorry

ΦΟΥΑΓΙΕ φουαγιέ (το) [**fooaye** (to)] foyer

ΦΟΥΛ ΠΑΝΣΙΟΝ φουλ πανσιόν (η) [**fool pansion** (i)] full board

ΦΟΥΛ-ΣΑΙΖΟΝ φουλ-σαιζόν high season

ΦΟΥΡΝΟΣ φούρνος (ο) [**foornos** (o)] baker's; oven

φουσκάλα (η) [**fooskala** (i)] blister

φούστα (η) [**foosta** (i)] skirt

φρακαρισμένος [**frakarismenos**] blocked; stuck

φράκτης (ο) [**fraktis** (o)] fence

φρενάρω [**frenaro**] brake (verb)

φρένο (το) [**freno** (to)] brake

ΦΡΕΣΚΟΣ φρέσκος [**freskos**] fresh

φρικτός [**friktos**] horrible

φρύδι (το) [**frithi** (to)] eyebrow

φτάνει [**ftani**] that's enough

φτάνω [**ftano**] arrive

φτέρνα (η) [**fterna** (i)] heel (of foot)

φτερνίζομαι [**fternizomeh**] sneeze (verb)

φτερό (το) [**ftero** (to)] wing

ΦΤΗΝΟΣ φτηνός [**ftinos**] cheap, inexpensive

φτιάχνω τις βαλίτσες [**ftiakhno tis valitses**] pack (verb)

φτυάρι (το) [**ftiari** (to)] spade

φτωχός [**ftokhos**] poor

φύγε! [**fiyeh!**] go away!

φύκια (τα) [**fikia** (ta)] seaweed

ΦΥΛΑΚΗ φυλακή (η) [**filaki** (i)] prison

ΦΥΛΑΞΗ ΑΠΟΣΚΕΥΩΝ φύλαξη αποσκευών [**filaxi aposkevon**] left luggage, baggage check

φύλλο (το) [**filo** (to)] leaf

φύλο (το) [**filo** (to)] gender

φύση (η) [**fisi** (i)] nature

ΦΥΣΙΚΟ ΠΡΟΪΟΝ φυσικό προϊόν natural product

ΦΥΣΙΚΟΣ φυσικός [**fisikos**] natural

ΦΥΣΙΚΟ ΧΡΩΜΑ φυσικό χρώμα natural colouring

φυσιολογικός [**fisioloyikos**] normal

ΦΥΤΟ φυτό (το) [**fito** (to)] plant

φωνάζω [**fonazo**] call; shout (verb)

φωνή (η) [**foni** (i)] voice

ΦΩΣ φως (το) [**fos** (to)] light

φώτα (τα) [**fota** (ta)] lights (on car)

ΦΩΤΙΑ φωτιά (η) [**fotia** (i)] fire έχεις φωτιά; [**ekhis fotia?**] have you got a light?

φωτογραφία (η) [**fotografia** (i)] photograph

ΦΩΤΟΓΡΑΦΙΚΑ φωτογραφικά cameras

φωτογραφική μηχανή (η)

[fotografiki mikhani (i)] camera
φωτόμετρο (το) [fotometro (to)]
light meter

X

χαίρετε [khereteh] hello
χαλάκι (το) [khalaki (to)] rug
χαλί (το) [khali (to)] carpet
χάλια [khalia] awful
χαμηλά φώτα (τα) [khamila fota (ta)] sidelights
χαμηλός [khamilos] low
χαμόγελο (το) [khamoyelo (to)] smile
χαμογελώ [khamoyelo] smile (verb)
χάνω [khano] lose; miss
ΧΑΠΙ χάπι (το) [khapi (to)] pill
χάρηκα! [kharika!] pleased to meet you!
ΧΑΡΠΙΚ χάρπικ (το) [kharpik (to)] bleach (for toilet)
ΧΑΡΤΗΣ χάρτης (ο) [khartis (o)] map
ΧΑΡΤΙ χαρτί (το) [kharti (to)] paper
χαρτιά (τα) [khartia (ta)] playing cards
ΧΑΡΤΙ ΑΛΛΗΛΟΓΡΑΦΙΑΣ χαρτί αλληλογραφίας (το) [kharti alilografias (to)] writing paper
ΧΑΡΤΙΚΑ χαρτικά (τα) [khartika (ta)] stationery
ΧΑΡΤΙ ΠΕΡΙΤΥΛΙΓΜΑΤΟΣ χαρτί περιτυλίγματος [kharti peritiligmatos] wrapping paper

ΧΑΡΤΙ ΥΓΕΙΑΣ χαρτί υγείας [kharti iyias] toilet paper
ΧΑΡΤΟΜΑΝΤΗΛΑ χαρτομάντηλα (τα) [khartomandila (ta)] tissues, Kleenex®
χαρτόνι (το) [khartoni (to)] cardboard
χαρτονόμισμα [khartonomisma] banknote, (US) bill
ΧΑΡΤΟΠΩΛΕΙΟ χαρτοπωλείο (το) [khartopolio (to)] stationer's
χαρτοφύλακας (ο) [khartofilakas (o)] briefcase
ΧΑΣΑΠΗΣ χασάπης (ο) [khasapis (o)] butcher's
χείλι (το) [khili (to)] lip
ΧΕΙΜΕΡΙΝΟΣ χειμερινός [khimerinos] (winter) cinema/movie theater
χειμώνας (ο) [khimonas (o)] winter
ΧΕΙΡΟΠΟΙΗΤΟ χειροποίητο [khiropi-ito] handmade
χειρότερος [khiroteros] worse
χειρότερος (ο) [khiroteros (o)] worst
ΧΕΙΡΟΤΕΧΝΙΑ χειροτεχνία (η) crafts
χειρόφρενο (το) [khirofreno (to)] handbrake
χέρι (το) [kheri (to)] arm; hand
χερούλι (το) [kherooli (to)] handle
χήρα (η) [khira (i)] widow
χήρος (ο) [khiros (o)] widower
χθες [khthes] yesterday
ΧΙΛ. χιλ. thousand, thousands

ΧΙΛΙΑ χίλια [khilia] thousand,
thousands

ΧΙΛΙΑΔΕΣ χιλιάδες [khiliathes]
thousand, thousands

ΧΙΛΙΑΡΙΚΟ χιλιάρικο (το)
[khiliariko (to)] 1,000-drachma
note/bill

χιλιόμετρο (το) [khiliometro (to)]
kilometre

χιούμορ (το) [khioomor (to)]
humour

χλιαρός [khliaros] lukewarm;
cool

ΧΛΩΡΙΝΗ χλωρίνη (η) [khlorini
(i)] bleach

χόμπυ (το) [khobi (to)] hobby

ΧΟΝΔΡΙΚΗΣ χονδρικής
wholesale

χορεύω [khorevo] dance (verb)

χορός (ο) [khoros (o)] dance

χορτάρι (το) [khortari (to)] grass

χορτοφαγικός [khortofayikos]
vegetarian

χορτοφάγος (ο/η) [khortofagos
(o/i)] vegetarian

χρειάζομαι [khriazomeh] need
(verb)

ΧΡΗΜΑΤΙΣΤΗΡΙΟ
χρηματιστήριο (το)
[khrimatistirio (to)] currency
exchange; stock exchange

χρήση (η) [khrisi (i)] use

χρησιμοποιώ [khrisimopio] use
(verb)

χρήσιμος [khrisimos] useful

Χριστούγεννα (τα) [KHristooyena
(ta)] Christmas

Καλά Χριστούγεννα! [Kala
KHristooyena!] Happy

Christmas!

χρονιά (η) [khronia (i)] year

Χρόνια Πολλά! [khronia pola!]
Happy Birthday!

του χρόνου [too khronoo] next
year

πόσο χρονών είσαι; [poso
khronon iseh?] how old are
you?

χρόνος (ο) [khronos (o)] time;
year

ΧΡΥΣΟΣ χρυσός (ο) [khrisos (o)]
gold

ΧΡΥΣΟΣ ΟΔΗΓΟΣ χρυσός
οδηγός (ο) [khrisos othigos (o)]
yellow pages

ΧΡΥΣΟΧΟΕΙΟ χρυσοχοείο
(το) [khrisokhoio (to)] jeweller's

χρώμα (το) [khroma (to)] colour

ΧΡΩΜΑΤΑ - ΣΙΔΕΡΙΚΑ
χρώματα - σιδερικά paint and
hardware store

χτένα (η) [khtena (i)] comb

χτυπώ [khtipo] hit (verb)

χώμα (το) [khoma (to)] earth

χώρα (η) [khora (i)] country

χωράφι (το) [khorafi (to)] field

ΧΩΡΗΤΙΚΟΤΗΤΟΣ ...
ΑΤΟΜΩΝ χωρητικότητος ...
ατόμων max load ... persons

χωριό (το) [khorio (to)] village

χωρίς [khoris] without

ΧΩΡΙΣ ΕΙΣΠΡΑΚΤΟΡΑ χωρίς
εισπράκτορα no ticket
collector

χωρισμένος [khorismenos]
divorced

ΧΩΡΙΣ ΜΠΑΝΙΟ χωρίς μπάνιο
[khoris banio] without

bathroom

ΧΩΡΙΣ ΝΤΟΥΣ χωρίς ντους
[khoris doos] without shower

ΧΩΡΙΣ ΣΥΝΤΗΡΗΤΙΚΑ
χωρίς συντηρητικά no
preservatives

χωριστός [khoristos] separate

ΧΩΡΟΣ ΔΙΑ ΠΟΔΗΛΑΤΕΣ
χώρος διά ποδήλατες cycle
path

χώρος φύλαξης αποσκευών (ο)
[khoros filaxis aposkevon (o)] left
luggage, baggage check

Ψ

ψαλίδι (το) [psalithi (to)] scissors

ΨΑΡΑΔΙΚΟ ψαράδικο (το)
[psarathiko (to)] fishmonger's

ψάρεμα (το) [psarema (to)]
fishing

ΨΑΡΟΤΑΒΕΡΝΑ
ψαροταβέρνα (η) [psarotaverna
(i)] restaurant specializing in
seafood

ψάχνω [psakhno] look for

ψέματα: λέω ψέματα [leo
psemata] lie (say untruth)

ψεύτικος [pseftikos] false

ψήνω [psino] bake

ΨΗΣΤΑΡΙΑ ψησταριά (η)
[psistaria (i)] restaurant
specializing in charcoal-
grilled food

ψιλά (τα) [psila (ta)] small
change

ΨΙΛΙΚΑ ψιλικά (τα) [psilika (ta)]
small shop

ψυγείο (το) [psiyio (to)] fridge

ψυγείο αυτοκινήτου (το) [psiyio
aftokinitoo (to)] radiator (car)

ΨΩΜΑΔΙΚΟ ψωμάδικο
[psomathiko] baker's

ψωμάς (ο) [psomas (o)] baker

ψηλός [psilos] high; tall

ψώνια (τα) [psonia (ta)]
shopping

πάω για ψώνια [pao ya psonia]
go shopping

Ω

ΩΘΗΣΑΤΕ ωθήσατε push

ώμος (ο) [omos (o)] shoulder

ώρα (η) [ora (i)] hour

τι ώρα είναι; [ti ora ineh?] what
time is it?

σε λίγη ώρα [seh liyi ora] soon

στην ώρα του [stin ora too] on
time

ωραίος [oreos] beautiful;
handsome; lovely

ΩΡΕΣ ΕΠΙΣΚΕΨΕΩΣ ώρες
επισκέψεως visiting hours

ΩΡΕΣ ΛΕΙΤΟΥΡΓΕΙΑΣ ώρες
λειτουργείας opening hours

ως [os] as, since

ΩΤΟΡΙΝΟΛΑΡΥΓΓΟΛΟΓΟΣ
ωτορινολαρυγγολόγος (ο/η)
ear, nose and throat specialist

ωτοστόπ (το) [otostop (to)]
hitchhiking

ωτοστόπ: κάνω ωτοστόπ [kano
otostop] hitchhike

Menu Reader: Food

Essential Terms

bread to psomi
butter to vootiro
cup to flidzani
dessert to glikisma
fish to psari
fork to pirooni
glass to potiri
knife to makheri
main course to kirio piato
meat to kreas
menu to menoo
pepper to piperi
plate to piato
salad i salata
salt to alati
set menu to tabl-dot
soup i soopa
spoon to kootali
starter to proto piato
table to trapezi

another ..., please ali mia ..., parakalo
excuse me! parakalo
could I have the bill, please? boro na ekho ton logariasmo,
  parakalo?

ΑΓΓΙΝΑΡΕΣ ΑΥΓΟΛΕΜΟΝΟ
αγγινάρες αυγολέμονο
[aginares avgolemono]
artichokes in egg and
lemon sauce

ΑΓΓΟΥΡΑΚΙΑ αγγουράκια
[agoorakia] cucumbers

ΑΓΓΟΥΡΙ αγγούρι [agoori]
cucumber

ΑΓΓΟΥΡΙΑ ΚΑΙ ΝΤΟΜΑΤΕΣ
ΣΑΛΑΤΑ αγγούρια και
ντομάτες σαλάτα [agooria keh
domates salata] cucumber and
tomato salad

ΑΚΤΙΝΙΔΙΟ ακτινίδιο
[aktinithio] kiwi fruit

ΑΛΑΤΙ αλάτι [alati] salt

ΑΛΕΥΡΙ αλεύρι [alevri] flour

ΑΛΕΥΡΙ ΚΑΛΑΜΠΟΚΙΟΥ
αλεύρι καλαμποκιού [alevri
kalabokioo] cornflour

ΑΛΕΥΡΙ ΣΤΑΡΙΟΥ αλεύρι
σταριού [alevri starioo] wheat
flour

ΑΛΛΑΝΤΙΚΑ αλλαντικά
[alandika] sausages, salami,
ham etc

ΑΜΥΓΔΑΛΑ αμύγδαλα
[amigthala] almonds

ΑΜΥΓΔΑΛΩΤΑ αμυγδαλωτά
[amigthalota] macaroons;
almond pastries

ΑΝΑΝΑΣ ανανάς [ananas]
pineapple

ΑΝΘΟΤΥΡΟ ανθότυρο
[anTHotiro] type of cottage
cheese

ΑΝΤΖΟΥΓΙΑ ΣΤΟ ΛΑΔΙ
αντζούγια στο λάδι [andsoo-yia
sto lathi] anchovies in oil

ΑΡΑΚΑΣ αρακάς [arakas] peas

ΑΡΑΚΑΣ ΛΑΔΕΡΟΣ αρακάς
λαδερός [arakas latheros] peas
cooked with tomato and
oil

ΑΡΑΚΑΣ ΣΩΤΕ αρακάς σωτέ
[arakas soteh] peas fried in
butter

ΑΡΝΑΚΙ αρνάκι [arnaki] lamb

ΑΡΝΑΚΙ ΕΞΟΧΙΚΟ αρνάκι
εξοχικό [arnaki exohiko] leg
of lamb baked in
greaseproof paper

ΑΡΝΑΚΙ ΜΕ ΜΠΑΜΙΕΣ
αρνάκι με μπάμιες [arnaki meh
bami-es] lamb and okra stew

ΑΡΝΑΚΙ ΜΕ ΠΑΤΑΤΕΣ ΣΤΟ
ΦΟΥΡΝΟ αρνάκι με πατάτες
στο φούρνο [arnaki meh patates
sto foorno] roast lamb and
potatoes

ΑΡΝΑΚΙ ΤΑΣ ΚΕΜΠΑΠ
αρνάκι τας κεμπάπ [arnaki tas
kebap] lamb in tomato sauce

ΑΡΝΑΚΙ ΤΗΣ ΣΟΥΒΛΑΣ
αρνάκι της σούβλας [arnaki tis
soovlas] spit-roast lamb

ΑΡΝΑΚΙ ΦΡΙΚΑΣΕ αρνάκι
φρικασέ με μαρούλια [arnaki
frikaseh meh maroolia] lamb
and lettuce in egg and
lemon sauce

ΑΡΝΙ αρνί [arni] mutton,
lamb

ΑΡΝΙ ΓΕΜΙΣΤΟ ΣΤΟ
ΦΟΥΡΝΟ αρνί γεμιστό στο
φούρνο [arni yemisto sto foorno]
oven-cooked stuffed lamb

ΑΡΝΙ ΕΞΟΧΙΚΟ αρνί εξοχικό [arni exokhiko] lamb cooked in greased foil with cheese and spices

ΑΡΝΙ ΚΟΚΚΙΝΙΣΤΟ αρνί κοκκινιστό [arni kokinisto] lamb in tomato sauce

ΑΡΝΙ ΛΑΔΟΡΙΓΑΝΗ ΣΤΟ ΦΟΥΡΝΟ αρνί λαδορίγανη στο φούρνο [arni lathorigani sto foorno] oven-cooked lamb with oil and oregano

ΑΡΝΙ ΜΕ ΑΡΑΚΑ αρνί με αρακά [arni meh araka] lamb with peas

ΑΡΝΙ ΜΕ ΚΟΛΟΚΥΘΑΚΙΑ ΑΥΓΟΛΕΜΟΝΟ αρνί με κολοκυθάκια αυγολέμονο [arni meh kolokiTHakia avgolemono] lamb with courgettes/zucchini in egg and lemon sauce

ΑΡΝΙ ΜΕ ΚΡΙΘΑΡΑΚΙ αρνί με κριθαράκι [arni meh kriTHaraki] lamb with pasta

ΑΡΝΙ ΜΕ ΜΑΚΑΡΟΝΙΑ αρνί με μακαρόνια [arni meh makaronia] lamb with spaghetti

ΑΡΝΙ ΜΕ ΜΕΛΙΤΖΑΝΕΣ αρνί με μελιτζάνες [arni meh melitzanes] lamb with aubergines/eggplants

ΑΡΝΙ ΜΕ ΜΠΑΜΙΕΣ αρνί με μπάμιες [arni meh bami-es] lamb with okra

ΑΡΝΙ ΜΕ ΠΑΤΑΤΕΣ ΡΑΓΟΥ αρνί με πατάτες ραγού [arni meh patates ragoo] lamb with potatoes cooked in tomato sauce

ΑΡΝΙ ΜΕ ΦΑΣΟΛΑΚΙΑ ΦΡΕΣΚΑ αρνί με φασολάκια φρέσκα [arni meh fasolakia freska] lamb with runner beans

ΑΡΝΙ ΜΕ ΧΥΛΟΠΙΤΕΣ αρνί με χυλοπίτες [arni meh khilopites] lamb with a type of lasagne

ΑΡΝΙ ΜΠΟΥΤΙ ΣΤΟ ΦΟΥΡΝΟ αρνί μπούτι στο φούρνο [arni booti sto foorno] oven-cooked leg of lamb

ΑΡΝΙ ΜΠΡΙΖΟΛΕΣ αρνί μπριζόλες [arni brizoles] lamb chops

ΑΡΝΙ ΠΑΪΔΑΚΙΑ αρνί παϊδάκια [arni paithakia] grilled lamb chops

ΑΡΝΙ ΤΑΣ ΚΕΜΠΑΠ αρνί τας κεμπάπ [arni tas kebab] chopped lamb kebab with tomato sauce

ΑΡΝΙ ΤΗΣ ΚΑΤΣΑΡΟΛΑΣ ΜΕ ΠΑΤΑΤΕΣ αρνί της κατσαρόλας με πατάτες [arni tis katsarolas meh patates] casseroled lamb cooked with potatoes

ΑΡΝΙ ΤΗΣ ΣΟΥΒΛΑΣ αρνί της σούβλας [arni tis soovlas] spit-roast lamb

ΑΡΝΙ ΦΡΙΚΑΣΕ αρνί φρικασέ [arni frikaseh] lamb fricassee

ΑΣΤΑΚΟΣ αστακός [astakos] lobster

ΑΣΤΑΚΟΣ ΜΕ ΛΑΔΟΛΕΜΟΝΟ αστακός με λαδολέμονο [astakos meh latholemono] lobster cooked in lemon and oil sauce

ΑΣΤΑΚΟΣ ΜΕ ΜΑΓΙΟΝΕΖΑ αστακός με μαγιονέζα [astakos meh mayoneza] lobster with mayonnaise

ΑΤΖΕΜ ΠΙΛΑΦΙ ατζέμ πιλάφι [atzem pilafi] rice pilaf

ΑΥΓΑ αυγά [avga] eggs

ΑΥΓΑ ΒΡΑΣΤΑ αυγά βραστά [avga vrasta] boiled eggs

ΑΥΓΑ ΒΡΑΣΤΑ ΣΦΙΧΤΑ αυγά βραστά σφιχτά [avga vrasta sfikhta] hard-boiled eggs

ΑΥΓΑ ΓΕΜΙΣΤΑ αυγά γεμιστά [avga yemista] stuffed eggs

ΑΥΓΑ ΓΕΜΙΣΤΑ ΜΕ ΜΑΓΙΟΝΕΖΑ αυγά γεμιστά με μαγιονέζα [avga yemista meh mayoneza] stuffed eggs with mayonnaise

ΑΥΓΑ ΜΑΤΙΑ αυγά μάτια [avga matia] fried eggs

ΑΥΓΑ ΜΕΛΑΤΑ αυγά μελάτα [avga melata] soft-boiled eggs

ΑΥΓΑ ΜΕ ΜΑΝΙΤΑΡΙΑ αυγά με μανιτάρια [avga meh manitaria] mushroom omelette

ΑΥΓΑ ΜΕ ΜΠΕΙΚΟΝ αυγά με μπέικον [avga meh bacon] bacon and eggs

ΑΥΓΑ ΜΕ ΝΤΟΜΑΤΕΣ αυγά με ντομάτες [avga meh domates] eggs cooked in tomato sauce

ΑΥΓΑ ΜΕ ΤΥΡΙ αυγά με τυρί [avga meh tiri] cheese omelette

ΑΥΓΑ ΟΜΕΛΕΤΑ αυγά ομελέτα [avga omeleta] plain omelette

ΑΥΓΑ ΟΜΕΛΕΤΑ ΜΕ ΠΑΤΑΤΕΣ αυγά ομελέτα με πατάτες [avga omeleta meh patates] omelette with chips/fries

ΑΥΓΑ ΠΟΣΕ αυγά ποσέ [avga poseh] poached eggs

ΑΥΓΑ ΣΦΙΧΤΑ αυγά σφιχτά [avga sfikhta] hard-boiled eggs

ΑΥΓΑ ΤΗΓΑΝΗΤΑ αυγά τηγανητά [avga tiganita] fried eggs

ΑΥΓΑ Ω ΓΚΡΑΤΕΝ αυγά ω γκρατέν [avga o graten] eggs au gratin

ΑΥΓΟ αυγό [avgo] egg

ΑΥΓΟΛΕΜΟΝΟ αυγολέμονο [avgolemono] egg and lemon sauce

ΑΥΓΟΛΕΜΟΝΟ ΣΟΥΠΑ αυγολέμονο σούπα [avgolemono soopa] chicken broth with egg and lemon

ΑΥΓΟΤΑΡΑΧΟ αυγοτάραχο [avgotarakho] roe

ΑΧΛΑΔΙ αχλάδι [akhlathi] pear

ΒΑΝΙΛΙΑ βανίλια [vanilia]

A
B
Γ
Δ
E
Z
H
Θ
I
K
Λ
M
N
Ξ
O
Π
P
Σ
T
Y
Φ
X
Ψ
Ω

vanilla

ΒΑΤΟΜΟΥΡΟ βατόμουρο
[vatomooro] blackberry

ΒΕΡΙΚΟΚΟ βερίκοκο
[verikoko] apricot

ΒΟΔΙΝΟ βοδινό [vothino] beef

ΒΟΔΙΝΟ ΒΡΑΣΤΟ βοδινό
βραστό [vothino vrasto] boiled
beef

ΒΟΔΙΝΟ ΡΟΣΜΠΙΦ βοδινό
ροσμπίφ [vothino rosbif] roast
beef

ΒΟΤΑΝΑ βότανα [votana]
herbs

ΒΟΥΤΥΡΟ βούτυρο [vootiro]
butter

ΒΡΑΣΤΟ βραστό [vrasto]
boiled

ΒΥΣΣΙΝΟ βύσσινο [visino]
sour cherries

ΓΑΛΑΚΤΟΜΠΟΥΡΕΚΟ
γαλακτομπούρεκο
[galaktobooreko] cream-filled
sweet filo pastry with
honey

ΓΑΛΟΠΟΥΛΑ γαλοπούλα
[galopoola] turkey

ΓΑΛΟΠΟΥΛΑ ΓΕΜΙΣΤΗ
γαλοπούλα γεμιστή [galopoola
yemisti] stuffed turkey

ΓΑΛΟΠΟΥΛΑ
ΚΟΚΚΙΝΙΣΤΗ γαλοπούλα
κοκκινιστή [galopoola kokinisti]
turkey cooked with
tomatoes

ΓΑΛΟΠΟΥΛΑ ΨΗΤΗ ΣΤΟ
ΦΟΥΡΝΟ γαλοπούλα ψητή
στο φούρνο [galopoola psiti sto
foorno] roast turkey

ΓΑΡΔΟΥΜΠΑ γαρδούμπα
[garthoomba] spit-roast rolled
lamb offal

ΓΑΡΙΔΕΣ γαρίδες [garithes]
prawns

ΓΑΡΙΔΕΣ ΒΡΑΣΤΕΣ γαρίδες
βραστές [garithes vrastes]
boiled shrimps

ΓΑΡΙΔΕΣ ΚΟΚΤΑΙΗΛ
γαρίδες κοκταίηλ [garithes
cocktail] shrimp cocktail

ΓΑΡΙΔΕΣ ΠΙΛΑΦΙ γαρίδες
πιλάφι [garithes pilafi] shrimp
pilaf

ΓΑΡΙΔΟΠΙΛΑΦΟ
γαριδοπίλαφο [garithopilafo]
prawns with rice cooked in
butter

ΓΑΡΝΙΤΟΥΡΑ γαρνιτούρα
[garnitoora] vegetables

ΓΑΡΝΙΤΟΥΡΑ ΚΑΡΟΤΑ
ΣΩΤΕ γαρνιτούρα καρότα
σωτέ [garnitoora karota soteh]
sautéed carrots

ΓΑΡΝΙΤΟΥΡΑ
ΚΟΥΝΟΥΠΙΔΙ ΣΩΤΕ
γαρνιτούρα κουνουπίδι σωτέ
[garnitoora koonoopithi soteh]
sautéed cauliflower

ΓΑΡΝΙΤΟΥΡΑ ΠΑΤΑΤΕΣ
γαρνιτούρα πατάτες [garnitoora
patates] potatoes

ΓΑΡΝΙΤΟΥΡΑ ΣΠΑΝΑΚΙ
ΣΩΤΕ γαρνιτούρα σπανάκι
σωτέ [garnitoora spanaki soteh]
sautéed spinach

ΓΑΡΝΙΤΟΥΡΑ ΦΑΣΟΛΙΑ
ΠΡΑΣΙΝΑ ΣΩΤΕ γαρνιτούρα

φασόλια πράσινα σωτέ
[garnitoora fasolia prasina soteh]
sautéed runner beans

ΓΕΜΙΣΤΑ γεμιστά [yemista]
stuffed, usually with rice
and/or minced meat

ΓΕΜΙΣΤΕΣ γεμιστές [yemistes]
stuffed vegetables

ΓΙΑΛΑΝΤΖΗ ΝΤΟΛΜΑΔΕΣ
γιαλαντζή ντολμάδες [yalantzi
dolmathes] vine leaves stuffed
with rice

ΓΙΑΟΥΡΤΙ γιαούρτι [ya-oorti]
yoghurt

ΓΙΓΑΝΤΕΣ γίγαντες [yigandes]
white haricot beans; butter
beans

ΓΙΟΥΒΑΡΛΑΚΙΑ
γιουβαρλάκια [yoovarlakia]
meatballs, rice and
seasoning in a sauce

ΓΙΟΥΒΑΡΛΑΚΙΑ
ΑΥΓΟΛΕΜΟΝΟ
γιουβαρλάκια αυγολέμονο
[yoovarlakia avgolemono]
meatballs with egg and
lemon sauce

ΓΙΟΥΒΑΡΛΑΚΙΑ ΜΕ
ΣΑΛΤΣΑ ΝΤΟΜΑΤΑΣ
γιουβαρλάκια με σάλτσα
ντομάτας [yoovarlakia meh saltsa
domatas] meatballs with rice
cooked with tomatoes

ΓΙΟΥΒΕΤΣΙ γιουβέτσι
[yoovetsi] oven-roasted lamb
with pasta

ΓΚΡΕΙΠΦΡΟΥΤ γκρέιπφρουτ
[grapefruit] grapefruit

ΓΛΥΚΑ γλυκά [glika] cakes,

desserts

ΓΛΥΚΙΣΜΑ γλύκισμα
[glikisma] dessert

ΓΛΥΚΟ γλυκό [gliko] sweet,
dessert

ΓΛΥΚΟ ΒΥΣΣΙΝΟ γλυκό
βύσσινο [gliko visino] candied
cherries in syrup

ΓΛΥΚΟ ΚΑΡΥΔΑΚΙ
ΦΡΕΣΚΟ γλυκό καρυδάκι
φρέσκο [gliko karithaki fresko]
dried fresh green walnuts
in syrup

ΓΛΥΚΟ ΜΑΣΤΙΧΑ γλυκό
μαστίχα [gliko mastikha]
vanilla-flavoured fudge

ΓΛΥΚΟ ΜΕΛΙΤΖΑΝΑΚΙ
γλυκό μελιτζανάκι [gliko
melitzanaki] dried small
aubergine/eggplant in
syrup

ΓΛΥΚΟ ΝΕΡΑΝΤΖΑΚΙ
γλυκό νεραντζάκι [gliko
nerantzaki] dried bitter
orange in syrup

ΓΛΥΚΟ ΣΥΚΟ γλυκό σύκο
[gliko siko] candied figs in
syrup

ΓΛΥΚΟ ΣΥΚΟ ΦΡΕΣΚΟ
γλυκό σύκο φρέσκο [gliko siko
fresko] dried fig in syrup

ΓΛΥΚΟ ΤΡΙΑΝΤΑΦΥΛΛΟ
γλυκό τριαντάφυλλο [gliko
triandafilo] dried rose petals
in syrup

ΓΛΩΣΣΑ γλώσσα [glosa] sole;
tongue

ΓΛΩΣΣΕΣ ΤΗΓΑΝΗΤΕΣ
γλώσσες τηγανητές [gloses

tiganites] fried sole

ΓΟΥΡΟΥΝΟΠΟΥΛΟ ΣΤΟ
ΦΟΥΡΝΟ ΜΕ ΠΑΤΑΤΕΣ
γουρουνόπουλο στο φούρνο με
πατάτες [gooroonopoolo sto
foorno meh patates] oven-
cooked pork with potatoes

ΓΡΑΒΙΕΡΑ γραβιέρα [gravi-
era] hard cheese like
gruyère

ΓΡΑΝΙΤΑ γρανίτα [granita]
sorbet

ΓΡΑΝΙΤΑ ΛΕΜΟΝΙ γρανίτα
λεμόνι [granita lemoni] lemon
sorbet

ΓΡΑΝΙΤΑ ΜΠΑΝΑΝΑ
γρανίτα μπανάνα [granita
banana] banana sorbet

ΓΡΑΝΙΤΑ ΠΟΡΤΟΚΑΛΙ
γρανίτα πορτοκάλι [granita
portokali] orange sorbet

ΓΡΑΝΙΤΑ ΦΡΑΟΥΛΕΣ
γρανίτα φράουλες [granita
fraooles] strawberry sorbet

ΔΑΜΑΣΚΗΝΑ δαμάσκηνα
[thamaskina] prunes
ΔΑΜΑΣΚΗΝΟ δαμάσκηνο
[thamaskino] plum
ΔΙΠΛΕΣ δίπλες [thiples]
pancakes

ΕΛΑΙΟΛΑΔΟ ελαιόλαδο
[eleolatho] olive oil
ΕΛΙΕΣ ελιές [eli-es] olives
ΕΝΤΟΣΘΙΑ ΑΡΝΙΟΥ
ΛΑΔΟΡΙΓΑΝΗ εντόσθια
αρνιού λαδορίγανη [endosthia
arnioo lathorigani] lambs'

intestines cooked in lemon
and oil

ΕΠΙΔΟΡΠΙΟ επιδόρπιο
[epithorpio] dessert

ΕΣΚΑΛΟΠ ΜΕ ΖΑΜΠΟΝ
ΚΑΙ ΣΑΛΤΣΑ ΝΤΟΜΑΤΑΣ
εσκαλόπ με ζαμπόν και
σάλτσα ντομάτας [eskalop meh
zabon keh saltsa domatas]
escalope of veal with ham
and tomato sauce

ΖΑΜΠΟΝ ζαμπόν [zabon] ham
ΖΑΧΑΡΗ ζάχαρη [zakhari]
sugar
ΖΕΛΕ ζελέ [zeleh] jelly
ΖΥΜΑΡΙΚΑ ζυμαρικά
[zimarika] pasta and rice

ΘΑΛΑΣΣΙΝΑ θαλασσινά
[THalasina] seafood

ΚΑΒΟΥΡΙΑ καβούρια
[kavooria] crab
ΚΑΚΑΒΙΑ κακαβιά [kakavia]
mixed fish soup
ΚΑΚΑΒΙΑ ΨΑΡΟΣΟΥΠΑ
κακαβιά ψαρόσουπα [kakavia
psarosoopa] fish soup
ΚΑΛΑΜΑΡΑΚΙΑ
καλαμαράκια [kalamarakia]
baby squid
ΚΑΛΑΜΑΡΑΚΙΑ ΓΕΜΙΣΤΑ
καλαμαράκια γεμιστά
[kalamarakia yemista] stuffed
baby squid
ΚΑΛΑΜΑΡΑΚΙΑ
ΤΗΓΑΝΗΤΑ καλαμαράκια
τηγανητά [kalamarakia tiganita]

fried baby squid

ΚΑΛΑΜΑΡΙΑ καλαμάρια [kalamaria] squid

ΚΑΝΑΠΕ καναπέ [kanapeh] canapés

ΚΑΝΑΠΕ ΜΕ ΖΑΜΠΟΝ καναπέ με ζαμπόν [kanapeh meh zabon] ham canapés

ΚΑΝΑΠΕ ΜΕ ΚΡΕΑΣ ΨΗΤΟ καναπέ με κρέας ψητό [kanapeh meh kreas psito] meat canapés

ΚΑΝΑΠΕ ΜΕ ΜΑΥΡΟ ΧΑΒΙΑΡΙ καναπέ με μαύρο χαβιάρι [kanapeh meh mavro haviari] black caviar canapés

ΚΑΝΑΠΕ ΜΕ ΤΑΡΑΜΟΣΑΛΑΤΑ καναπέ με ταραμοσαλάτα [kanapeh meh taramosalata] taramosalata canapés

ΚΑΝΕΛΛΑ κανέλλα [kanela] cinnamon

ΚΑΝΕΛΛΟΝΙΑ ΓΕΜΙΣΤΑ κανελλόνια γεμιστά [kanelonia yemista] stuffed canelloni

ΚΑΝΤΑΪΦΙ κανταΐφι [kanda-ifi] shredded and rolled filo pastry in syrup

ΚΑΠΑΜΑΣ ΑΡΝΙ καπαμάς αρνί [kapamas arni] lamb cooked in spices and tomato sauce

ΚΑΠΝΙΣΤΟ καπνιστό [kapnisto] smoked

ΚΑΠΠΑΡΗ κάππαρη [kapari] caper

ΚΑΡΑΒΙΔΕΣ καραβίδες [karavithes] king prawns;

crayfish

ΚΑΡΟΤΑ καρότα [karota] carrots

ΚΑΡΠΟΥΖΙ καρπούζι [karpoozi] watermelon

ΚΑΡΥΔΙ καρύδι [karithi] nut

ΚΑΡΥΔΟΠΙΤΤΑ καρυδόπιττα [karithopita] walnut cake; cake with nuts and syrup

ΚΑΡΧΑΡΙΑΣ καρχαρίας [karkharias] shark

ΚΑΣΕΡΙ κασέρι [kaseri] Cheddar-type cheese

ΚΑΣΤΑΝΑ κάστανα [kastana] chestnuts

ΚΑΣΤΑΝΑ ΓΛΑΣΕ κάστανα γλασέ [kastana glaseh] glazed chestnuts, marrons glacés

ΚΑΤΑΪΦΙ καταΐφι [kata-ifi] shredded filo pastry with honey and nuts

ΚΑΤΑΛΟΓΟΣ κατάλογος [katalogos] menu

ΚΕΙΚ κέικ [cake] cake

ΚΕΙΚ ΚΑΝΕΛΛΑΣ κέικ κανέλλας [cake kanelas] cinnamon cake

ΚΕΙΚ ΜΕ ΑΜΥΓΔΑΛΑ κέικ με αμύγδαλα [cake meh amigthala] almond cake

ΚΕΙΚ ΜΕ ΚΑΡΥΔΙΑ ΚΑΙ ΣΤΑΦΙΔΕΣ κέικ με καρύδια και σταφίδες [cake meh karithia keh stafithes] nut and sultana cake

ΚΕΙΚ ΣΟΚΟΛΑΤΑΣ κέικ σοκολάτας [cake sokolatas] chocolate cake

ΚΕΪΚ ΦΡΟΥΤΩΝ κέικ
φρούτων [cake frooton] fruit
cake

ΚΕΡΑΣΙΑ κεράσια [kerasia]
cherries

ΚΕΦΑΛΟΤΥΡΙ κεφαλοτύρι
[kefalotiri] very salty, hard
cheese

ΚΕΦΤΕΔΕΣ κεφτέδες
[keftethes] meatballs

ΚΕΦΤΕΔΕΣ ΜΕ ΣΑΛΤΣΑ
κεφτέδες με σάλτσα [keftethes
meh saltsa] meatballs in
tomato sauce

ΚΕΦΤΕΔΕΣ ΣΤΟ ΦΟΥΡΝΟ
κεφτέδες στο φούρνο [keftethes
sto foorno] oven-cooked
meatballs

ΚΕΦΤΕΔΕΣ ΤΗΓΑΝΗΤΟΙ
κεφτέδες τηγανητοί [keftethes
tiganiti] fried meatballs

ΚΙΜΑΣ κιμάς [kimas] minced
meat

ΚΛΕΦΤΙΚΟ κλέφτικο [kleftiko]
meat, potatoes and
vegetables cooked together
in a pot or foil

ΚΟΚΚΙΝΙΣΤΟ κοκκινιστό
[kokinisto] in tomato sauce

ΚΟΚΟΡΕΤΣΙ κοκορέτσι
[kokoretsi] spit-roast rolled
lamb offal

ΚΟΛΙΟΙ κολιοί [koli-i]
mackerel

ΚΟΛΙΟΙ ΨΗΤΟΙ κολιοί ψητοί
[koli-i psiti] fried mackerel

ΚΟΛΟΚΥΘΑΚΙΑ
κολοκυθάκια [kolokiΤΗakia]
courgettes/zucchini

ΚΟΛΟΚΥΘΑΚΙΑ ΓΕΜΙΣΤΑ
ΜΕ ΚΙΜΑ κολοκυθάκια
γεμιστά με κιμά [kolokiΤΗakia
yemista meh kima] courgettes/
zucchini stuffed with
minced meat

ΚΟΛΟΚΥΘΑΚΙΑ ΓΕΜΙΣΤΑ
ΜΕ ΡΥΖΙ κολοκυθάκια
γεμιστά με ρύζι [kolokiΤΗakia
yemista meh rizi] courgettes/
zucchini stuffed with rice

ΚΟΛΟΚΥΘΑΚΙΑ ΓΙΑΧΝΙ
κολοκυθάκια γιαχνί
[kolokiΤΗakia yakhni]
courgettes/zucchini and
onions in a tomato sauce

ΚΟΛΟΚΥΘΑΚΙΑ ΛΑΔΕΡΑ
κολοκυθάκια λαδερά
[kolokiΤΗakia lathera]
courgettes/zucchini
cooked in oil

ΚΟΛΟΚΥΘΑΚΙΑ ΜΕ
ΚΡΕΑΣ κολοκυθάκια με
κρέας [kolokiΤΗakia meh kreas]
courgette/zucchini and
beef stew

ΚΟΛΟΚΥΘΑΚΙΑ ΜΕ
ΠΑΤΑΤΕΣ κολοκυθάκια με
πατάτες [kolokiΤΗakia meh
patates] courgettes/zucchini
with potatoes

ΚΟΛΟΚΥΘΑΚΙΑ
ΜΟΥΣΑΚΑΣ κολοκυθάκια
μουσακάς [kolokiΤΗakia
moosakas] courgettes/
zucchini with minced meat
and béchamel

ΚΟΛΟΚΥΘΑΚΙΑ
ΠΑΠΟΥΤΣΑΚΙΑ

κολοκυθάκια παπουτσάκια
⟦kolokiTHakia papootsakia⟧
courgettes/zucchini with
minced meat and onions

ΚΟΛΟΚΥΘΑΚΙΑ
ΤΗΓΑΝΗΤΑ κολοκυθάκια
τηγανητά ⟦kolokiTHakia tiganita⟧
fried courgettes/zucchini

ΚΟΛΟΚΥΘΟΚΕΦΤΕΔΕΣ
κολοκυθοκεφτέδες
⟦kolokiTHokeftethes⟧ fried
courgette/zucchini balls

ΚΟΛΟΚΥΘΟΤΥΡΟΠΙΤΤΑ
κολοκυθοτυρόπιττα
⟦kolokiTHotiropita⟧ courgette/
zucchini and cheese pie

ΚΟΜΠΟΣΤΑ κομπόστα
⟦kobosta⟧ fruit compote

ΚΟΤΑ κότα ⟦kota⟧ chicken

ΚΟΤΑ ΒΡΑΣΤΗ κότα βραστή
⟦kota vrasti⟧ boiled chicken

ΚΟΤΑ ΨΗΤΗ ΣΤΟ ΦΟΥΡΝΟ
κότα ψητή στο φούρνο ⟦kota
psiti sto foorno⟧ roast chicken

ΚΟΤΑ ΨΗΤΗ ΤΗΣ
ΚΑΤΣΑΡΟΛΑΣ κότα ψητή
της κατσαρόλας ⟦kota psiti tis
katsarolas⟧ chicken casserole

ΚΟΤΑ ΨΗΤΗ ΤΗΣ
ΣΟΥΒΛΑΣ κότα ψητή της
σούβλας ⟦kota psiti tis soovlas⟧
spit-roast chicken

ΚΟΤΟΛΕΤΕΣ ΑΡΝΙΣΙΕΣ
ΠΑΝΕ κοτολέτες αρνίσιες
πανέ ⟦kotoletes arnisi-es paneh⟧
lamb cutlets

ΚΟΤΟΛΕΤΕΣ
ΜΟΣΧΑΡΙΣΙΕΣ ΠΑΝΕ
κοτολέτες μοσχαρίσιες πανέ

⟦kotoletes moskharisi-es paneh⟧
veal cutlets

ΚΟΤΟΠΙΤΤΑ κοτόπιττα
⟦kotopita⟧ chicken pie

ΚΟΤΟΠΟΥΛΟ κοτόπουλο
⟦kotopoolo⟧ chicken

ΚΟΤΟΠΟΥΛΟ ΓΙΟΥΒΕΤΣΙ
ΜΕ ΧΥΛΟΠΙΤΤΕΣ
κοτόπουλο γιουβέτσι με
χυλοπίττες ⟦kotopoolo yioovetsi
meh hilopites⟧ chicken with
pasta

ΚΟΤΟΠΟΥΛΟ
ΚΟΚΚΙΝΙΣΤΟ κοτόπουλο
κοκκινιστό ⟦kotopoolo kokinisto⟧
chicken in tomato sauce

ΚΟΤΟΠΟΥΛΟ ΜΕ
ΜΠΑΜΙΕΣ κοτόπουλο με
μπάμιες ⟦kotopoolo meh bami-es⟧
chicken with okra

ΚΟΤΟΠΟΥΛΟ ΜΕ
ΜΠΙΖΕΛΙΑ κοτόπουλο με
μπιζέλια ⟦kotopoolo meh bizelia⟧
chicken with peas

ΚΟΤΟΠΟΥΛΟ ΠΑΝΕ
κοτόπουλο πανέ ⟦kotopoolo
paneh⟧ breaded chicken

ΚΟΤΟΠΟΥΛΟ ΠΙΛΑΦΙ
κοτόπουλο πιλάφι ⟦kotopoolo
pilafi⟧ chicken pilaf

ΚΟΤΟΠΟΥΛΟ ΤΗΣ
ΣΟΥΒΛΑΣ κοτόπουλο της
σούβλας ⟦kotopoolo tis soovlas⟧
spit-roast chicken

ΚΟΤΟΣΟΥΠΑ κοτόσουπα
⟦kotosoopa⟧ chicken soup

ΚΟΥΚΙΑ ΛΑΔΕΡΑ κουκιά
λαδερά ⟦kookia lathera⟧ broad
beans in tomato sauce

ΚΟΥΝΕΛΙ κουνέλι [kooneli] rabbit

ΚΟΥΝΕΛΙ ΜΕ ΣΑΛΤΣΑ κουνέλι με σάλτσα [kooneli meh saltsa] rabbit with tomato sauce

ΚΟΥΝΕΛΙ ΣΤΙΦΑΔΟ κουνέλι στιφάδο [kooneli stifatho] rabbit with onions

ΚΟΥΝΟΥΠΙΔΙ κουνουπίδι [koonoopithi] cauliflower

ΚΟΥΝΟΥΠΙΔΙ ΒΡΑΣΤΟ ΣΑΛΑΤΑ κουνουπίδι βραστό σαλάτα [koonopithi vrasto salata] boiled cauliflower salad

ΚΟΥΡΑΜΠΙΕΔΕΣ κουραμπιέδες [koorabi-ethes] Greek shortbread

ΚΟΥΡΑΜΠΙΕΔΕΣ ΜΕ ΑΜΥΓΔΑΛΟ κουραμπιέδες με αμύγδαλο [koorabi-ethes meh amigthalo] shortbread-type biscuits with sesame seeds and icing sugar

ΚΡΑΚΕΡΣ ΑΛΜΥΡΑ κράκερς αλμυρά [krakers almira] salted crackers

ΚΡΑΣΑΤΟ κρασάτο [krasato] cooked in wine sauce

ΚΡΕΑΣ κρέας [kreas] meat, usually beef

ΚΡΕΑΣ ΜΕ ΑΝΤΙΔΙΑ ΑΥΓΟΛΕΜΟΝΟ κρέας με αντίδια αυγολέμονο [kreas meh antithia avgolemono] beef with endives in egg and lemon sauce

ΚΡΕΑΣ ΜΕ ΦΑΣΟΛΙΑ ΞΕΡΑ κρέας με φασόλια ξερά [kreas meh fasolia xera] beef with butter beans

ΚΡΕΑΤΙΚΑ κρεατικά [kreh-atika] meat dishes

ΚΡΕΑΤΟΠΙΤΤΑ κρεατόπιττα [kreh-atopita] minced meat in filo pastry

ΚΡΕΜΑ κρέμα [krema] cream

ΚΡΕΜΑ ΚΑΡΑΜΕΛΕ κρέμα καραμελέ [krema karameleh] crème caramel

ΚΡΕΜΑ ΜΕ ΜΗΛΑ κρέμα με μήλα [krema meh mila] apples with cream

ΚΡΕΜΑ ΜΕ ΜΠΑΝΑΝΕΣ κρέμα με μπανάνες [krema meh bananes] bananas with cream

ΚΡΕΜΜΥΔΑΚΙΑ ΦΡΕΣΚΑ κρεμμυδάκια φρέσκα [kremithakia freska] spring onions

ΚΡΕΜΜΥΔΙΑ κρεμμύδια [kremithia] onions

ΚΡΕΜΜΥΔΟΣΟΥΠΑ κρεμμυδόσουπα [kremithosoopa] onion soup

ΚΡΕΠΑ κρέπα [krepa] pancake

ΚΡΟΚΕΤΕΣ κροκέτες [kroketes] croquettes

ΚΡΟΚΕΤΕΣ ΑΠΟ ΚΡΕΑΣ κροκέτες από κρέας [kroketes apo kreas] meat croquettes

ΚΡΟΚΕΤΕΣ ΜΕ ΑΥΓΑ ΚΑΙ ΤΥΡΙ κροκέτες με αυγά και τυρί [kroketes meh avga keh tiri] egg and cheese croquettes

ΚΡΟΚΕΤΕΣ ΜΠΑΚΑΛΙΑΡΟΥ κροκέτες

μπακαλιάρου [krok/etes bakaliaroo] cod croquettes

ΚΡΟΚΕΤΕΣ ΠΑΤΑΤΕΣ κροκέτες πατάτες [kroketes patates] potato croquettes

ΚΡΟΥΑΣΑΝ κρουασάν [croissants] croissants

ΚΥΔΩΝΙΑ κυδώνια [kithonia] quinces

ΚΥΔΩΝΟΠΑΣΤΟ κυδωνόπαστο [kithonopasto] thick jelly made from quince

ΚΥΝΗΓΙ κυνήγι [kiniyi] game

ΚΥΡΙΟ ΠΙΑΤΟ κύριο πιάτο [kirio piato] main course

ΚΩΚ κωκ [kok] cake with cream and chocolate topping

ΛΑΓΟΣ λαγός [lagos] hare

ΛΑΓΟΣ ΜΕ ΣΑΛΤΣΑ λαγός με σάλτσα [lagos meh saltsa] hare in tomato sauce

ΛΑΓΟΣ ΣΤΙΦΑΔΟ λαγός στιφάδο [lagos stifatho] hare and shallot stew

ΛΑΔΕΡΑ λαδερά [lathera] in olive oil and tomato sauce

ΛΑΔΙ λάδι [lathi] oil

ΛΑΔΟΛΕΜΟΝΟ λαδολέμονο [latholemono] olive oil and lemon dressing

ΛΑΔΟΞΥΔΟ λαδόξυδο [lathoxitho] oil and vinegar salad dressing

ΛΑΖΑΝΙΑ λαζάνια [lazania] lasagne

ΛΑΧΑΝΙΚΑ λαχανικά [lakhanika] vegetables

ΛΑΧΑΝΙΚΑ ΜΙΚΤΑ λαχανικά μικτά [lakhanika mikta] vegetables

ΛΑΧΑΝΑΚΙΑ ΒΡΥΞΕΛΛΩΝ λαχανάκια Βρυξελλών [lakhanakia vrixelon] Brussels sprouts

ΛΑΧΑΝΟ λάχανο [lakhano] cabbage

ΛΑΧΑΝΟ ΚΟΚΚΙΝΟ λάχανο κόκκινο [lakhano kokino] red cabbage

ΛΑΧΑΝΟ ΝΤΟΛΜΑΔΕΣ ΑΥΓΟΛΕΜΟΝΟ λάχανο ντολμάδες αυγολέμονο [lakhano dolmathes avgolemono] cabbage leaves stuffed with rice in egg and lemon sauce

ΛΑΧΑΝΟ ΝΤΟΛΜΑΔΕΣ λάχανο ντολμάδες [lakhano dolmathes] cabbage leaves stuffed with minced meat and rice

ΛΑΧΑΝΟ ΝΤΟΛΜΑΔΕΣ ΜΕ ΣΑΛΤΣΑ ΝΤΟΜΑΤΑΣ λάχανο ντολμάδες με σάλτσα ντομάτας [lakhano dolmathes meh saltsa domatas] vine leaves stuffed with rice in tomato sauce

ΛΑΧΑΝΟΣΑΛΑΤΑ λαχανοσαλάτα [lakhanosalata] cabbage salad

ΛΕΜΟΝΙ λεμόνι [lemoni] lemon

ΛΙΘΡΙΝΙ λιθρίνι [liTHrini] red snapper

ΛΙΘΡΙΝΙ ΨΗΤΟ λιθρίνι ψητό [líTHrini psito] grilled red snapper

ΛΟΥΚΑΝΙΚΑ λουκάνικα [lookanika] sausages

ΛΟΥΚΑΝΙΚΑ ΒΡΑΣΤΑ λουκάνικα βραστά [lookanika vrasta] boiled sausages

ΛΟΥΚΑΝΙΚΑ ΚΑΠΝΙΣΤΑ ΣΤΗ ΣΧΑΡΑ λουκάνικα καπνιστά στη σχάρα [lookanika kapnista sti skhara] grilled smoked sausages

ΛΟΥΚΑΝΙΚΑ ΤΗΓΑΝΗΤΑ λουκάνικα τηγανητά [lookanika tiganita] fried sausages

ΛΟΥΚΟΥΜΑΔΕΣ λουκουμάδες [lookoomathes] doughnuts

ΛΟΥΚΟΥΜΙΑ λουκούμια [lookoomia] Turkish delight

ΜΑΓΕΙΡΙΤΣΑ μαγειρίτσα [mayiritsa] traditional Easter soup made from lambs' intestines

ΜΑΓΙΑ μαγιά [maya] yeast

ΜΑΓΙΟΝΕΖΑ μαγιονέζα [mayoneza] mayonnaise

ΜΑΪΝΤΑΝΟΣ μαϊντανός [maindanos] parsley

ΜΑΚΑΡΟΝΑΚΙ ΚΟΦΤΟ μακαρονάκι κοφτό [makaronaki kofto] macaroni

ΜΑΚΑΡΟΝΙΑ μακαρόνια [makaronia] pasta

ΜΑΚΑΡΟΝΙΑ ΜΕ ΚΙΜΑ μακαρόνια με κιμά [makaronia meh kima] spaghetti bolognaise

ΜΑΚΑΡΟΝΙΑ ΜΕ ΦΡΕΣΚΟ ΒΟΥΤΥΡΟ ΚΑΙ ΠΑΡΜΕΖΑΝΑ μακαρόνια με φρέσκο βούτυρο και παρμεζάνα [makaronia meh fresko vootiro keh parmezana] spaghetti with butter and parmesan cheese

ΜΑΚΑΡΟΝΙΑ ΠΑΣΤΙΤΣΙΟ ΜΕ ΚΙΜΑ μακαρόνια παστίτσιο με κιμά [makaronia pastitsio meh kima] baked pasta dish with minced meat and béchamel

ΜΑΝΙΤΑΡΙΑ μανιτάρια [manitaria] mushrooms

ΜΑΝΙΤΑΡΙΑ ΤΗΓΑΝΗΤΑ μανιτάρια τηγανητά [manitaria tiganita] fried mushrooms

ΜΑΝΟΥΡΙ μανούρι [manoori] hard cheese

ΜΑΝΤΑΡΙΝΙ μανταρίνι [mandarini] satsuma, tangerine

ΜΑΡΓΑΡΙΝΗ μαργαρίνη [margarini] margarine

ΜΑΡΙΔΕΣ ΤΗΓΑΝΗΤΕΣ μαρίδες τηγανητές [marithes tiganites] small fried fish

ΜΑΡΜΕΛΑΔΑ μαρμελάδα [marmelatha] jam, marmalade

ΜΑΡΜΕΛΑΔΑ ΒΕΡΥΚΟΚΚΑ μαρμελάδα βερύκοκκα [marmelatha verikoka] apricot jam

ΜΑΡΜΕΛΑΔΑ ΠΟΡΤΟΚΑΛΙ μαρμελάδα πορτοκάλι

[marmelatha portokali] orange jam

ΜΑΡΜΕΛΑΔΑ ΡΟΔΑΚΙΝΑ μαρμελάδα ροδάκινα [marmelatha pothakina] peach jam

ΜΑΡΜΕΛΑΔΑ ΦΡΑΟΥΛΕΣ μαρμελάδα φράουλες [marmelatha fraooles] strawberry jam

ΜΑΡΟΥΛΙ μαρούλι [marooli] lettuce

ΜΑΡΟΥΛΙΑ ΣΑΛΑΤΑ μαρούλια σαλάτα [maroolia salata] green salad

ΜΕ ΛΑΔΟΛΕΜΟΝΟ με λαδολέμονο [meh latholemono] with olive oil and lemon dressing

ΜΕΛΙ μέλι [meli] honey

ΜΕΛΙΤΖΑΝΕΣ μελιτζάνες [melidzanes] aubergines/ eggplants

ΜΕΛΙΤΖΑΝΕΣ ΓΕΜΙΣΤΕΣ ΜΕ ΚΙΜΑ μελιτζάνες γεμιστές με κιμά [melitzanes yemistes meh kima] aubergines/eggplants stuffed with minced meat

ΜΕΛΙΤΖΑΝΕΣ ΓΙΑΧΝΙ μελιτζάνες γιαχνί [melitzanes yakhni] aubergines/eggplants with tomato and onions

ΜΕΛΙΤΖΑΝΕΣ ΙΜΑΜ ΜΠΑΪΛΝΤΙ μελιτζάνες ιμάμ μπαϊλντί [melitzanes imam baildi] aubergines/eggplants with garlic and tomato

ΜΕΛΙΤΖΑΝΕΣ ΜΟΥΣΑΚΑ μελιτζάνες μουσακά [melidzanes moosaka] layers of aubergine/eggplant and minced meat topped with béchamel

ΜΕΛΙΤΖΑΝΕΣ ΠΑΠΟΥΤΣΑΚΙΑ μελιτζάνες παπουτσάκια [melidzaness papootsakia] stuffed aubergines/eggplants

ΜΕΛΙΤΖΑΝΕΣ ΤΗΓΑΝΗΤΕΣ μελιτζάνες τηγανητές [melitzanes tiganites] fried aubergines/eggplants

ΜΕΛΙΤΖΑΝΟΣΑΛΑΤΑ μελιτζανοσαλάτα [melidzanosalata] puréed aubergine/eggplant dip

ΜΕΛΟΜΑΚΑΡΟΝΑ μελομακάρονα [melomakarona] sweet cakes with cinammon, nuts and syrup

ΜΕΝΟΥ μενού [menoo] menu

ΜΕ ΣΑΛΤΣΑ με σάλτσα [meh saltsa] with sauce, usually tomato sauce

ΜΗΛΑ ΓΕΜΙΣΤΑ μήλα γεμιστά [mila yemista] stuffed apples with cinammon

ΜΗΛΟ μήλο [milo] apple

ΜΗΛΟΠΙΤΤΑ μηλόπιττα [milopita] apple pie

μισοψημένο [misopsimeno] medium (steak)

ΜΟΣΧΑΡΙ μοσχάρι [moskhari] veal; tender beef

ΜΟΣΧΑΡΙ ΒΡΑΣΤΟ μοσχάρι βραστό [moskhari vrasto] veal stew

ΜΟΣΧΑΡΙ ΚΟΚΚΙΝΙΣΤΟ
μοσχάρι κοκκινιστό [moskhari
kokinisto] veal in tomato
sauce

ΜΟΣΧΑΡΙ ΜΕ ΑΡΑΚΑ
μοσχάρι με αρακά [moskhari
meh araka] veal with peas

ΜΟΣΧΑΡΙ ΜΕ ΚΡΙΘΑΡΑΚΙ
μοσχάρι με κριθαράκι
[moskhari meh kriτΗaraki] veal
with pasta

ΜΟΣΧΑΡΙ ΜΕ
ΜΕΛΙΤΖΑΝΕΣ μοσχάρι με
μελιτζάνες [moskhari meh
melitzanes] veal with
aubergines/eggplants

ΜΟΣΧΑΡΙ ΜΕ ΜΠΑΜΙΕΣ
μοσχάρι με μπάμιες [moskhari
meh bami-es] veal with
okra

ΜΟΣΧΑΡΙ ΜΕ ΠΑΤΑΤΕΣ
μοσχάρι με πατάτες [moskhari
meh patates] veal with
potatoes

ΜΟΣΧΑΡΙ ΜΕ ΠΑΤΑΤΕΣ
ΣΤΟ ΦΟΥΡΝΟ μοσχάρι με
πατάτες στο φούρνο [moskhari
meh patates sto foorno] veal
with potatoes cooked in
the oven

ΜΟΣΧΑΡΙ ΜΕ ΠΟΥΡΕ
μοσχάρι με πουρέ [moskhari
meh pooreh] veal with
mashed potatoes

ΜΟΣΧΑΡΙ ΜΕ ΦΑΣΟΛΑΚΙΑ
μοσχάρι με φασολάκια
[moskhari meh fasolakia] veal
and green beans

ΜΟΣΧΑΡΙ ΡΟΣΜΠΙΦ

μοσχάρι ροσμπίφ [moskhari
rosbif] roast beef

ΜΟΣΧΑΡΙΣΙΟΣ ΚΙΜΑΣ
μοσχαρίσιος κιμάς [mos-
kharisios kimas] minced meat

ΜΟΣΧΑΡΙ ΣΝΙΤΖΕΛ ΜΕ
ΠΑΤΑΤΕΣ ΤΗΓΑΝΗΤΕΣ
μοσχάρι σνίτζελ με πατάτες
τηγανητές [moskhari schnitzel
meh patates tiganites] steak and
chips/fries

ΜΟΣΧΑΡΙ ΣΝΙΤΖΕΛ ΜΕ
ΠΟΥΡΕ μοσχάρι σνίτζελ με
πουρέ [moskhari schnitzel meh
patates pooreh] steak with
mashed potatoes

ΜΟΣΧΑΡΙ ΨΗΤΟ μοσχάρι
ψητό [moskhari psito] veal pot
roast

ΜΟΥΣΑΚΑΣ μουσακάς
[moosakas] moussaka – layers
of vegetables and minced
meat topped with
béchamel sauce

ΜΟΥΣΑΚΑΣ ΠΑΤΑΤΕΣ
μουσακάς πατάτες [moosakas
patates] potatoes with
minced meat and béchamel

ΜΟΥΣΤΑΡΔΑ μουστάρδα
[moostartha] mustard

ΜΟΥΣΤΟΚΟΥΛΟΥΡΑ
μουστοκούλουρα
[moostokooloora] Greek
biscuits

ΜΠΑΚΑΛΙΑΡΟΣ
μπακαλιάρος [bakaliaros] cod;
salt cod; haddock

ΜΠΑΚΑΛΙΑΡΟΣ
ΚΡΟΚΕΤΕΣ μπακαλιάρος

κροκέτες [bakaliaros kroketes] haddock croquettes

ΜΠΑΚΑΛΙΑΡΟΣ ΠΛΑΚΙ μπακαλιάρος πλακί [bakaliaros plaki] salted cod cooked in tomato sauce

ΜΠΑΚΑΛΙΑΡΟΣ ΤΗΓΑΝΗΤΟΣ μπακαλιάρος τηγανητός [bakaliaros tiganitos] fried salted cod

ΜΠΑΚΛΑΒΑΔΕΣ μπακλαβάδες [baklavathes] baklava – layers of thin pastry with nuts and syrup

ΜΠΑΚΛΑΒΑΔΕΣ ΜΕ ΚΑΡΥΔΙΑ μπακλαβάδες με καρύδια [baklavathes meh karithia] baklava – layers of thin pastry with walnuts and syrup

ΜΠΑΚΛΑΒΑΣ μπακλαβάς [baklavas] baklava – filo pastry with nuts and syrup

ΜΠΑΜΙΕΣ μπάμιες [bami-es] okra

ΜΠΑΜΙΕΣ ΛΑΔΕΡΕΣ μπάμιες λαδερές [bami-es latheres] okra in olive oil and tomato sauce

ΜΠΑΝΑΝΑ μπανάνα [banana] banana

ΜΠΑΡΜΠΟΥΝΙΑ μπαρμπούνια [barboonia] red mullet

ΜΠΑΡΜΠΟΥΝΙΑ ΠΑΝΕ μπαρμπούνια πανέ [barboonia paneh] breaded red mullet

ΜΠΑΧΑΡΙΚΟ μπαχαρικό [bakhariko] spice

ΜΠΕΖΕΔΕΣ μπεζέδες [bezethes] meringues with cream

ΜΠΕΙΚΟΝ μπέικον [bacon] bacon

ΜΠΕΙΚΟΝ ΚΑΠΝΙΣΤΟ μπέικον καπνιστό [bacon kapnisto] smoked bacon

ΜΠΕΣΑΜΕΛ ΣΑΛΤΣΑ μπεσαμέλ σάλτσα [besamel saltsa] béchamel sauce

ΜΠΙΖΕΛΙΑ μπιζέλια [bizelia] peas

ΜΠΙΣΚΟΤΑ μπισκότα [biskota] biscuits

ΜΠΙΣΚΟΤΑΚΙΑ ΑΛΜΥΡΑ μπισκοτάκια αλμυρά [biskotakia almira] savoury crackers

ΜΠΙΣΚΟΤΑ ΣΟΚΟΛΑΤΑΣ μπισκότα σοκολάτας [biskota sokolatas] chocolate biscuits

ΜΠΙΦΤΕΚΙ μπιφτέκι [bifteki] hamburger; grilled meatballs

ΜΠΟΝ ΦΙΛΕ μπον φιλέ [bon fileh] fillet steak

ΜΠΟΥΓΑΤΣΑ μπουγάτσα [boogatsa] puff pastry with various fillings

ΜΠΟΥΓΑΤΣΑ ΓΛΥΚΙΑ μπουγάτσα γλυκιά [boogatsa glikia] puff pastry with cream and icing sugar

ΜΠΟΥΡΕΚΑΚΙΑ μπουρεκάκια [boorekakia] cheese or minced meat pies

ΜΠΟΥΡΕΚΙ μπουρέκι [booreki] courgette, potato and cheese pie

ΜΠΡΙΑΜΙ μπριάμι [briami]
ratatouille

ΜΠΡΙΑΜΙ ΜΕ
ΚΟΛΟΚΥΘΑΚΙΑ μπριάμι με
κολοκυθάκια [briami meh
kolokithakia] courgettes/
zucchini cooked with
potatoes in the oven

ΜΠΡΙΖΟΛΑ μπριζόλα [brizola]
chop; steak

ΜΠΡΙΖΟΛΑ ΜΟΣΧΑΡΙΣΙΑ
μπριζόλα μοσχαρίσια [brizola
moskharisia] beef steak

ΜΠΡΙΖΟΛΕΣ μπριζόλες
[brizoles] chops; steaks

ΜΠΡΙΖΟΛΕΣ ΒΟΔΙΝΕΣ ΣΤΗ
ΣΧΑΡΑ μπριζόλες βοδινές
στη σχάρα [brizoles vothines sti
skhara] grilled T-bone
steak

ΜΠΡΙΖΟΛΕΣ ΣΤΟ ΤΗΓΑΝΙ
μπριζόλες στο τηγάνι [brizoles
sto tigani] fried T-bone steak

ΜΠΡΙΖΟΛΕΣ ΧΟΙΡΙΝΕΣ
μπριζόλες χοιρινές [brizoles
khirines] pork chops

ΜΠΡΙΖΟΛΕΣ ΧΟΙΡΙΝΕΣ
ΣΤΗ ΣΧΑΡΑ μπριζόλες
χοιρινές στη σχάρα [brizoles
khirines sti skhara] charcoal-
grilled pork chops

ΜΠΡΟΚΟΛΟ μπρόκολο
[brokolo] broccoli

ΜΥΑΛΑ μυαλά [miala] brains

ΜΥΑΛΑ ΠΑΝΕ μυαλά πανέ
[miala paneh] breaded cows'
brains

ΜΥΔΙΑ μύδια [mithia] mussels

ΜΥΔΙΑ ΤΗΓΑΝΗΤΑ μύδια

τηγανητά [mithia tiganita] fried
mussels

ΝΕΦΡΑ νεφρά [nefra] kidneys

ΝΕΦΡΑ ΨΗΤΑ/ΤΗΓΑΝΗΤΑ
νεφρά ψητά/τηγανητά [nefra
psita/tiganita] grilled/fried
kidneys

ΝΤΟΛΜΑΔΑΚΙΑ
ντολμαδάκια [dolmathakia]
vine leaves stuffed with
minced meat, rice and
herbs

ΝΤΟΛΜΑΔΕΣ ντολμάδες
[dolmathes] vine or cabbage
leaves stuffed with minced
meat and/or rice

ΝΤΟΛΜΑΔΕΣ
ΑΥΓΟΛΕΜΟΝΟ ΜΕ ΚΙΜΑ
ντολμάδες αυγολέμονο με κιμά
[dolmathes avgolemono meh kima]
vine leaves with rice and
minced meat in egg and
lemon sauce

ΝΤΟΛΜΑΔΕΣ ΓΙΑΛΑΝΤΖΙ
ντολμάδες γιαλαντζί [dolmathes
yialantzi] vine leaves stuffed
with rice

ΝΤΟΜΑΤΕΣ ντομάτες
[domates] tomatoes

ΝΤΟΜΑΤΕΣ ΓΕΜΙΣΤΕΣ ΜΕ
ΚΙΜΑ ντομάτες γεμιστές με
κιμά [domates yemistes meh
kima] stuffed tomatoes with
minced meat

ΝΤΟΜΑΤΕΣ ΓΕΜΙΣΤΕΣ ΜΕ
ΡΥΖΙ ντομάτες γεμιστές με
ρύζι [domates yemistes meh rizi]
tomatoes stuffed with rice

ΝΤΟΜΑΤΕΣ ΓΕΜΙΣΤΕΣ
ντομάτες γεμιστές [domates
yemistes] stuffed tomatoes
ΝΤΟΜΑΤΟΣΑΛΑΤΑ
ντοματοσαλάτα [domatosalata]
tomato salad
ΝΤΟΜΑΤΟΣΟΥΠΑ
ντοματόσουπα [domatosoopa]
tomato soup
ΝΤΟΝΑΤΣ ντόνατς [doughnuts]
doughnuts

ΞΗΡΟΙ ΚΑΡΠΟΙ ξηροί καρποί
[xiri karpi] nuts, dried fruit
ΞΙΦΙΑΣ ξιφίας [xifias]
swordfish
ΞΥΔΙ ξύδι [xithi] vinegar

ΟΜΕΛΕΤΑ ομελέτα [omeleta]
omelette
ΟΜΕΛΕΤΑ ΛΟΥΚΑΝΙΚΑ
ομελέτα λουκάνικα [omeleta
lookanika] omelette with
sausages
ΟΡΕΚΤΙΚΑ ορεκτικά
[orektika] hors d'oeuvres,
starters
ΟΣΤΡΑΚΟΕΙΔΗ οστρακοειδή
[ostrako-ithi] shellfish

ΠΑΓΩΤΟ παγωτό [pagoto] ice
cream
ΠΑΓΩΤΟ ΒΕΡΥΚΟΚΚΟ
παγωτό βερύκοκκο [pagoto
verikoko] apricot ice cream
ΠΑΓΩΤΟ ΚΟΚΤΑΙΗΛ
παγωτό κοκταίηλ [pagoto
cocktail] ice cream cocktail
ΠΑΓΩΤΟ ΚΡΕΜΑ παγωτό

κρέμα [pagoto krema] vanilla
ice cream
ΠΑΓΩΤΟ ΜΕ ΣΑΝΤΙΓΥ
παγωτό με σαντιγύ [pagoto meh
sandiyi] ice cream with
whipped cream
ΠΑΓΩΤΟ ΜΟΚΚΑ παγωτό
μόκκα [pagoto moka] coffee-
flavoured ice cream
ΠΑΓΩΤΟ ΜΠΑΝΑΝΑ
παγωτό μπανάνα [pagoto
banana] banana ice cream
ΠΑΓΩΤΟ ΠΑΡΦΑΙ παγωτό
παρφαί [pagoto parfeh] ice
cream parfait
ΠΑΓΩΤΟ ΠΡΑΛΙΝΑ παγωτό
πραλίνα [pagoto pralina]
praline ice cream
ΠΑΓΩΤΟ ΣΟΚΟΛΑΤΑ
παγωτό σοκολάτα [pagoto
sokolata] chocolate ice cream
ΠΑΓΩΤΟ ΦΡΑΟΥΛΑ παγωτό
φράουλα [pagoto fraoola]
strawberry ice cream
ΠΑΓΩΤΟ ΦΥΣΤΙΚΙ παγωτό
φυστίκι [pagoto fistiki]
pistachio ice cream
ΠΑΞΙΜΑΔΙ παξιμάδι
[paximathi] dried, hard bread
ΠΑΝΤΖΑΡΙ παντζάρι
[pandzari] beetroot
ΠΑΠΙΑ πάπια [papia] duck
ΠΑΠΡΙΚΑ πάπρικα [paprika]
paprika
ΠΑΡΜΕΖΑΝΑ παρμεζάνα
[parmezana] parmesan
ΠΑΣΤΑ πάστα [pasta] cake
ΠΑΣΤΑ ΑΜΥΓΔΑΛΟΥ
πάστα αμυγδάλου [pasta

amigthaloo] almond gâteau

ΠΑΣΤΑ ΚΟΡΜΟΣ πάστα κορμός [pasta kormos] chocolate log

ΠΑΣΤΑ ΝΟΥΓΚΑΤΙΝΑ πάστα νουγκατίνα [pasta noogatin] cream gâteau

ΠΑΣΤΑ ΣΟΚΟΛΑΤΙΝΑ πάστα σοκολατίνα [pasta sokolatina] chocolate gâteau

ΠΑΣΤΑ ΦΡΑΟΥΛΑ πάστα φράουλα [pasta fraoola] strawberry gâteau

ΠΑΣΤΙΤΣΙΟ παστίτσιο [pastitsio] macaroni cheese or lasagne-type dish, with minced meat and white sauce

ΠΑΣΤΙΤΣΙΟ ΛΑΖΑΝΙΑ παστίτσιο λαζάνια [pastitsio lazania] lasagne

ΠΑΣΤΙΤΣΙΟ ΜΑΚΑΡΟΝΙΑ ΜΕ ΚΙΜΑ παστίτσιο μακαρόνια με κιμά [pastitsio makaronia meh kima] baked pasta dish with minced meat and béchamel

ΠΑΣΤΟ παστό [pasto] salted

ΠΑΤΑΤΕΣ πατάτες [patates] potatoes

ΠΑΤΑΤΕΣ ΓΑΡΝΙΤΟΥΡΑ πατάτες γαρνιτούρα [patates garnitoora] potatoes

ΠΑΤΑΤΕΣ ΓΙΑΧΝΙ πατάτες γιαχνί [patates yakhni] potatoes cooked with onion and tomato

ΠΑΤΑΤΕΣ ΚΑΙ ΚΟΛΟΚΥΘΑΚΙΑ ΣΤΟ ΦΟΥΡΝΟ πατάτες και κολοκυθάκια στο φούρνο [patates keh kolokiThakia sto foorno] potatoes, courgettes/ zucchini and tomatoes baked in the oven

ΠΑΤΑΤΕΣ ΚΟΛΟΚΥΘΙΑ ΜΟΥΣΑΚΑΣ πατάτες κολοκύθια μουσακάς [patates kolokiThia moosakas] potatoes with courgettes/zucchini, minced meat and cheese sauce

ΠΑΤΑΤΕΣ ΠΟΥΡΕ πατάτες πουρέ [patates pooreh] mashed potatoes

ΠΑΤΑΤΕΣ ΡΙΓΑΝΑΤΕΣ πατάτες ριγανάτες στο φούρνο [patates riganates sto foorno] oven-cooked potatoes with oregano

ΠΑΤΑΤΕΣ ΣΟΥΦΛΕ πατάτες σουφλέ [patates soofleh] potato soufflé

ΠΑΤΑΤΕΣ ΣΤΟ ΦΟΥΡΝΟ ΡΙΓΑΝΑΤΕΣ πατάτες στο φούρνο ριγανάτες [patates sto foorno riganates] potatoes baked in the oven with oregano, lemon and olive oil

ΠΑΤΑΤΕΣ ΤΗΓΑΝΙΤΕΣ πατάτες τηγανιτές [patates tiganites] chips, French fries

ΠΑΤΑΤΕΣ ΤΣΙΠΣ πατάτες τσιπς [patates tsips] chips, French fries

ΠΑΤΑΤΟΣΑΛΑΤΑ πατατοσαλάτα [patatosalata]

potato salad

ΠΑΤΖΑΡΙΑ πατζάρια [patzaria] beetroot

ΠΑΤΣΑΣ πατσάς [patsas] tripe; soup made from lambs' intestines

ΠΑΤΣΑΣ ΣΟΥΠΑ πατσάς σούπα [patsas soopa] tripe soup

ΠΕΠΟΝΙ πεπόνι [peponi] melon

ΠΕΣΤΡΟΦΑ πέστροφα [pestrofa] trout

ΠΕΣΤΡΟΦΑ ΨΗΤΗ πέστροφα ψητή [pestrofa psiti] grilled trout

ΠΗΧΤΗ πηχτή [pikhti] potted meat

ΠΙΛΑΦΙ πιλάφι [pilafi] rice

ΠΙΛΑΦΙ ΜΕ ΓΑΡΙΔΕΣ πιλάφι με γαρίδες [pilafi meh garithes] shrimp pilaf

ΠΙΛΑΦΙ ΜΕ ΜΥΔΙΑ πιλάφι με μύδια [pilafi meh mithia] pilaf with mussels

ΠΙΛΑΦΙ ΜΕ ΣΑΛΤΣΑ ΝΤΟΜΑΤΑ πιλάφι με σάλτσα ντομάτα [pilafi meh saltsa domata] pilaf with tomato sauce

ΠΙΛΑΦΙ ΤΑΣ-ΚΕΜΠΑΠ πιλάφι τας-κεμπάπ [pilafi tas kebab] rice with cubes of beef in tomato sauce

ΠΙΠΕΡΙ πιπέρι [piperi] pepper (spice)

ΠΙΠΕΡΙΕΣ πιπεριές [piperi-es] peppers

ΠΙΠΕΡΙΕΣ ΓΕΜΙΣΤΕΣ ΜΕ

ΚΙΜΑ πιπεριές γεμιστές με κιμά [piperi-es yemistes meh kima] peppers stuffed with minced meat

ΠΙΠΕΡΙΕΣ ΓΕΜΙΣΤΕΣ ΜΕ ΡΥΖΙ πιπεριές γεμιστές με ρύζι [piperi-es yemistes meh rizi] peppers stuffed with rice

ΠΙΠΕΡΙΕΣ ΓΕΜΙΣΤΕΣ πιπεριές γεμιστές [piperi-es yemistes] stuffed peppers

ΠΙΠΕΡΙΕΣ ΚΟΚΚΙΝΕΣ πιπεριές κόκκινες [piperi-es kokines] red peppers

ΠΙΠΕΡΙΕΣ ΠΡΑΣΙΝΕΣ πιπεριές πράσινες [piperi-es prasines] green peppers

ΠΙΡΟΣΚΙ πιροσκί [piroski] minced meat or sausage rolls

ΠΙΤΣΑ πίτσα [pizza] pizza

ΠΙΤΣΑ ΜΕ ΖΑΜΠΟΝ πίτσα με ζαμπόν [pizza meh zabon] ham pizza

ΠΙΤΣΑ ΜΕ ΜΑΝΙΤΑΡΙΑ πίτσα με μανιτάρια [pizza meh manitaria] mushroom pizza

ΠΙΤΣΑ ΜΕ ΝΤΟΜΑΤΑ ΤΥΡΙ πίτσα με ντομάτα τυρί [pizza meh domata tiri] cheese and tomato pizza

ΠΙΤΣΑ ΣΠΕΣΙΑΛ πίτσα σπέσιαλ [pizza special] special pizza

ΠΙΤΤΑ πίττα [pita] pie

ΠΙΤΤΑ ΜΕ ΚΙΜΑ πίττα με κιμά [pita meh kima] minced meat pie

ΠΛΑΚΙ πλακί [plaki] baked in

the oven in a tomato sauce
πολύ ψημένο [poli psimeno]
overdone
ΠΟΡΤΟΚΑΛΙ πορτοκάλι
[portokali] orange
ΠΟΥΛΕΡΙΚΑ πουλερικά
[poulerika] poultry
ΠΟΥΤΙΓΚΑ πουτίγκα [pootiga]
pudding
ΠΟΥΤΙΓΚΑ ΜΕ ΑΝΑΝΑ
πουτίγκα με ανανά [pootiga meh
anana] pineapple pudding
ΠΟΥΤΙΓΚΑ ΜΕ ΚΑΡΥΔΙΑ
πουτίγκα με καρύδια [pootiga
meh karithia] walnut pudding
ΠΟΥΤΙΓΚΑ ΜΕ ΣΤΑΦΙΔΕΣ
πουτίγκα με σταφίδες [pootiga
meh stafithes] sultana pudding
ΠΡΑΣΑ πράσα [prasa] leeks
ΠΡΑΣΟΠΙΤΤΑ πρασόπιττα
[prasopita] leek pie
ΠΡΩΤΟ ΠΙΑΤΟ πρώτο πιάτο
[proto piato] starter

ΡΑΒΑΝΙ ραβανί [ravani] very
sweet sponge cake
ΡΑΒΙΟΛΙΑ ραβιόλια [raviolia]
ravioli
ΡΙΓΑΝΗ ρίγανη [rigani]
oregano
ΡΟΔΑΚΙΝΟ ροδάκινο
[rothakino] peaches
ΡΟΣΜΠΙΦ ΑΡΝΙ ΜΟΣΧΑΡΙ
ροσμπίφ αρνί μοσχάρι [rozbif
arni moskhari] roast beef, veal
or lamb
ΡΥΖΙ ρύζι [rizi] rice
ΡΥΖΟΓΑΛΟ ρυζόγαλο
[rizogalo] rice pudding

ΡΩΣΙΚΗ ΣΑΛΑΤΑ ρώσικη
σαλάτα [rosiki salata] Russian
salad

ΣΑΛΑΜΙ σαλάμι [salami]
salami
ΣΑΛΑΤΑ σαλάτα [salata] salad
ΣΑΛΑΤΑ
ΑΜΠΕΛΟΦΑΣΟΥΛΑ σαλάτα
αμπελοφάσουλα [salata
abelofasoola] runner bean
salad
ΣΑΛΑΤΑ ΚΟΥΝΟΥΠΙΔΙ
ΒΡΑΣΤΟ σαλάτα κουνουπίδι
βραστό [salata koonoopithi
vrasto] boiled cauliflower
salad
ΣΑΛΑΤΑ ΜΑΡΟΥΛΙΑ
σαλάτα μαρούλια [salata
maroolia] lettuce salad
ΣΑΛΑΤΑ ΝΤΟΜΑΤΕΣ ΚΑΙ
ΑΓΓΟΥΡΙΑ σαλάτα ντομάτες
και αγγούρια [salata domates
keh agooria] tomato and
cucumber salad
ΣΑΛΑΤΑ ΝΤΟΜΑΤΕΣ-
ΠΙΠΕΡΙΕΣ σαλάτα ντομάτες-
πιπεριές [salata domates piperi-
es] tomato and green
pepper salad
ΣΑΛΑΤΑ ΣΠΑΡΑΓΓΙΑ
σαλάτα σπαράγγια [salata
sparagia] asparagus salad
ΣΑΛΑΤΑ ΦΑΣΟΛΙΑ ΞΗΡΑ
σαλάτα φασόλια ξηρά [salata
fasolia xira] butter bean salad
ΣΑΛΑΤΑ ΧΟΡΤΑ
ΒΡΑΣΜΕΝΑ σαλάτα χόρτα
βρασμένα [salata khorta

vrasmena] chicory salad

ΣΑΛΑΤΑ ΧΩΡΙΑΤΙΚΗ
σαλάτα χωριάτικη [salata khoriatiki] Greek salad –
tomatoes, cucumber, peppers, feta, olives and boiled eggs with olive oil and vinegar dressing

ΣΑΛΙΓΚΑΡΙΑ σαλιγκάρια [saligaria] snails

ΣΑΛΤΣΑ σάλτσα [saltsa] sauce

ΣΑΛΤΣΑ ΜΠΕΣΑΜΕΛ
σάλτσα μπεσαμέλ [saltsa besamel] béchamel sauce

ΣΑΛΤΣΑ ΝΤΟΜΑΤΑ σάλτσα
ντομάτα [saltsa domata] tomato sauce

ΣΑΜΑΛΙ σάμαλι [samali] semolina cake with honey

ΣΑΝΤΙΓΥ σαντιγύ [sandiyi] whipped cream

ΣΑΝΤΟΥΙΤΣ σάντουιτς [sandwich] sandwich

ΣΑΡΔΕΛΛΕΣ σαρδέλλες [sartheles] sardines

ΣΑΡΔΕΛΛΕΣ ΛΑΔΙΟΥ
σαρδέλλες λαδιού [sartheles lathioo] sardines in oil

ΣΕΛΙΝΟ σέλινο [selino] celery

ΣΙΜΙΓΔΑΛΙ σιμιγδάλι [simigthali] semolina

ΣΙΡΟΠΙ σιρόπι [siropi] syrup

ΣΚΟΡΔΑΛΙΑ σκορδαλιά [skorthalia] thick garlic sauce

ΣΚΟΡΔΑΛΙΑ ΜΕ ΨΩΜΙ
σκορδαλιά με ψωμί [skorthalia meh psomi] thick garlic sauce

made with bread

ΣΚΟΡΔΟ σκόρδο [skortho] garlic

ΣΟΚΟΛΑΤΑΚΙΑ
σοκολατάκια [sokolatakia] little chocolate cakes; milk chocolates

ΣΟΛΟΜΟΣ σολομός [solomos] salmon

ΣΟΛΟΜΟΣ ΚΑΠΝΙΣΤΟΣ
σολομός καπνιστός [solomos kapnistos] smoked salmon

ΣΟΥΒΛΑΚΙΑ σουβλάκια [soovlakia] meat grilled on a skewer, served in pitta bread

ΣΟΥΒΛΑΚΙΑ ΑΠΟ ΚΡΕΑΣ
ΑΡΝΙΣΙΟ σουβλάκια από κρέας αρνίσιο [soovlakia apo kreas arnisio] lamb souvlaki/kebab

ΣΟΥΒΛΑΚΙΑ ΑΠΟ ΚΡΕΑΣ
ΜΟΣΧΑΡΙΣΙΟ σουβλάκια από κρέας μοσχαρίσιο [soovlakia apo kreas moskharisio] veal souvlaki/kebab

ΣΟΥΒΛΑΚΙΑ ΑΠΟ ΚΡΕΑΣ
ΧΟΙΡΙΝΟ σουβλάκια από κρέας χοιρινό [soovlakia apo kreas khirino] pork souvlaki/kebab

ΣΟΥΒΛΑΚΙΑ ΝΤΟΝΕΡ ΜΕ
ΠΙΤΤΑ σουβλάκια ντονέρ με πίττα [soovlaki doner meh pita] donner kebab with pitta bread

ΣΟΥΒΛΑΚΙ ΚΑΛΑΜΑΚΙ
σουβλάκι καλαμάκι [soovlaki kalamaki] shish kebab

ΣΟΥΠΑ σούπα [**soo**pa] soup
ΣΟΥΠΑ ΠΑΤΣΑΣ σούπα
πατσάς [**soo**pa pats**as**] tripe
soup
ΣΟΥΠΑ ΡΕΒΥΘΙΑ σούπα
ρεβύθια [**soo**pa revi**THi**a]
chickpea soup
ΣΟΥΠΑ ΤΡΑΧΑΝΑΣ σούπα
τραχανάς [**soo**pa trakhan**as**]
milk broth with flour
ΣΟΥΠΑ ΦΑΚΕΣ σούπα
φακές [**soo**pa fak**es**] lentil
soup
ΣΟΥΠΑ ΦΑΣΟΛΙΑ σούπα
φασόλια [**soo**pa fas**oli**a] bean
soup
ΣΟΥΠΑ ΨΑΡΙ σούπα ψάρι
[**soo**pa ps**ari**] fish soup
ΣΟΥΠΑ ΨΑΡΙ
ΑΥΓΟΛΕΜΟΝΟ σούπα ψάρι
αυγολέμονο [**soo**pa ps**ari**
avgo**le**mono] fish soup with
egg and lemon
ΣΟΥΠΕΣ σούπες [**soo**pes]
soups
ΣΟΥΠΙΕΣ σουπιές [**soo**pi-**es**]
cuttlefish
ΣΟΥΠΙΕΣ ΜΕ ΣΠΑΝΑΚΙ
σουπιές με σπανάκι [**soo**pi-**es**
meh span**aki**] cuttlefish and
spinach stew
ΣΟΥΠΙΕΣ ΤΗΓΑΝΗΤΕΣ
σουπιές τηγανητές [**soo**pi-**es**
tigan**ites**] fried cuttlefish
ΣΟΥΣΑΜΙ σουσάμι [**soo**sami]
sesame
ΣΟΥΤΖΟΥΚΑΚΙΑ
σουτζουκάκια [**soot**zoo**kaki**a]
spicy meatballs in red sauce

ΣΟΥΦΛΕ σουφλέ [soof**leh**]
soufflé
ΣΠΑΓΓΕΤΟ ΜΕ ΦΡΕΣΚΟ
ΒΟΥΤΥΡΟ ΚΑΙ
ΠΑΡΜΕΖΑΝΑ σπαγγέτο με
φρέσκο βούτυρο και
παρμεζάνα [spa**geto** meh fr**esko**
vootiro keh parme**zana**] spaghetti
with butter and parmesan
cheese
ΣΠΑΝΑΚΙ σπανάκι [span**aki**]
spinach
ΣΠΑΝΑΚΟΠΙΤΤΑ
σπανακόπιττα [spana**kopita**]
spinach (and sometimes
feta) in filo pastry
σπάνιος [sp**anios**] rare
(steak)
ΣΠΑΡΑΓΓΙΑ ΣΑΛΑΤΑ
σπαράγγια σαλάτα [spar**agia**
sal**ata**] asparagus salad
ΣΠΕΣΙΑΛΙΤΕ σπεσιαλιτέ
[spesialit**eh**] speciality
ΣΠΛΗΝΑΝΤΕΡΟ
σπληνάντερο [splin**andero**]
intestines stuffed with
spleen
ΣΤΑΦΙΔΕΣ σταφίδες [staf**ithes**]
dried fruit
ΣΤΑΦΙΔΟΨΩΜΟ
σταφιδόψωμο [stafith**opsomo**]
bread with raisins
ΣΤΑΦΥΛΙΑ σταφύλια [staf**ilia**]
grapes
ΣΤΙΦΑΔΟ στιφάδο [stif**atho**]
chopped meat with onions;
hare or rabbit stew with
onions
ΣΤΟ ΦΟΥΡΝΟ στο φούρνο

[sto **foorno**] baked in the oven

ΣΤΡΕΙΔΙΑ στρείδια [**stri**thia] oysters

ΣΥΚΑ σύκα [**sika**] figs

ΣΥΚΩΤΑΚΙΑ συκωτάκια [si**kotakia**] liver

ΣΥΚΩΤΑΚΙΑ ΜΑΡΙΝΑΤΑ συκωτάκια μαρινάτα [si**kotakia** mari**nata**] liver cooked in rosemary

ΣΥΚΩΤΑΚΙΑ ΠΙΛΑΦΙ συκωτάκια πιλάφι [si**kotakia pilafi**] liver pilaf

ΣΥΚΩΤΑΚΙΑ ΣΤΗ ΣΧΑΡΑ συκωτάκια στη σχάρα [si**kotakia** sti s**khara**] liver

ΣΥΚΩΤΑΚΙΑ ΤΗΓΑΝΗΤΑ συκωτάκια τηγανητά [si**kotakia** tiga**nita**] fried liver

ΣΥΚΩΤΙ ΨΗΤΟ συκώτι ψητό [si**koti** psi**to**] charcoal-grilled liver

ΣΥΝΑΓΡΙΔΑ ΨΗΤΗ συναγρίδα ψητή [sina**gritha** psi**ti**] grilled sea bream

ΣΦΥΡΙΔΑ ΒΡΑΣΤΗ σφυρίδα βραστή [s**ritha** vra**sti**] boiled pike

ΣΩΤΕ σωτέ [so**teh**] lightly fried, sautéed

ΤΑΡΑΜΑΣ ταραμάς [tara**mas**] cod roe

ΤΑΡΑΜΟΚΕΦΤΕΔΕΣ ταραμοκεφτέδες [taramokef**tethes**] roe pâté balls with spices

ΤΑΡΑΜΟΣΑΛΑΤΑ ταραμοσαλάτα [taramosa**lata**] cod roe dip

ΤΑΡΤΑ τάρτα [**tarta**] tart

ΤΑΡΤΑ ΜΕ ΚΕΡΑΣΙΑ τάρτα με κεράσια [**tarta** meh ke**rasia**] cherry tart

ΤΑΡΤΑ ΜΕ ΚΡΕΜΑ ΚΑΙ ΑΜΥΓΔΑΛΑ τάρτα με κρέμα και αμύγδαλα [**tarta** meh **krema** keh a**migthala**] cream and almond tart

ΤΑΡΤΑ ΜΕ ΚΡΕΜΑ ΚΑΙ ΚΑΡΥΔΙΑ τάρτα με κρέμα και καρύδια [**tarta** meh **krema** keh ka**rithia**] walnut and cream tart

ΤΑΡΤΑ ΜΕ ΦΡΑΟΥΛΕΣ τάρτα με φράουλες [**tarta** meh fra**ooles**] strawberry tart

ΤΑΡΤΑ ΜΗΛΟΥ τάρτα μήλου [**tarta miloo**] apple tart

ΤΑΣ-ΚΕΜΠΑΠ τας-κεμπάπ [tas **kebab**] spicy lamb cutlets

ΤΑΣ-ΚΕΜΠΑΠ ΠΙΛΑΦΙ τας-κεμπάπ πιλάφι [tas kebab **pilafi**] spicy lamb cutlets pilaf

ΤΖΑΤΖΙΚΙ τζατζίκι [**dzadziki**] yoghurt, cucumber and garlic dip

ΤΗΓΑΝΗΤΟΣ τηγανητός [tiga**nitos**] fried

ΤΗΓΑΝΙΤΕΣ τηγανίτες [tiga**nites**] pancakes

ΤΗΣ ΚΑΤΣΑΡΟΛΑΣ της κατσαρόλας [tis katsa**rolas**] casseroled

ΤΗΣ ΣΟΥΒΛΑΣ της σούβλας [tis **soovlas**] roast on a spit

ΤΗΣ ΣΧΑΡΑΣ της σχάρας [tis skharas] grilled over charcoal

ΤΟΝΝΟΣ τόννος [tonos] tuna

ΤΟΝΝΟΣΑΛΑΤΑ τοννοσαλάτα [tonosalata] tuna salad

ΤΟΣΤ τοστ [tost] toasted sandwich

ΤΟΣΤ ΚΛΑΜΠ τοστ κλαμπ [tost club] toasted club sandwich

ΤΟΣΤ ΜΕ ΑΥΓΟ τοστ με αυγό [tost meh avgo] toasted egg sandwich

ΤΟΣΤ ΜΕ ΖΑΜΠΟΝ τοστ με ζαμπόν [tost meh zabon] toasted ham sandwich

ΤΟΣΤ ΜΕ ΚΟΤΟΠΟΥΛΟ τοστ με κοτόπουλο [tost meh kotopoolo] toasted chicken sandwich

ΤΟΣΤ ΜΕ ΚΡΕΑΣ τοστ με κρέας [tost meh kreas] toasted meat sandwich

ΤΟΣΤ ΜΕ ΜΠΙΦΤΕΚΙ τοστ με μπιφτέκι [tost meh bifteki] toasted hamburger

ΤΟΣΤ ΜΕ ΤΥΡΙ τοστ με τυρί [tost meh tiri] toasted cheese sandwich

ΤΟΥ ΑΤΜΟΥ του ατμού [too atmoo] steamed

ΤΟΥΡΣΙ τουρσί [toorsi] pickled

ΤΟΥΡΤΑ τούρτα [toorta] gâteau

ΤΟΥΡΤΑ ΑΜΥΓΔΑΛΟΥ τούρτα αμυγδάλου [toorta amigthaloo] almond gâteau

ΤΟΥΡΤΑ ΚΡΕΜΑ ΜΕ ΦΡΑΟΥΛΕΣ τούρτα κρέμα με φράουλες [toorta krema meh fraooles] strawberry cream gâteau

ΤΟΥΡΤΑ ΜΟΚΚΑ τούρτα μόκκα [toorta moka] coffee gâteau

ΤΟΥΡΤΑ ΝΟΥΓΚΑΤΙΝΑ τούρτα νουγκατίνα [toorta noogatina] nougat gâteau

ΤΟΥΡΤΑ ΣΑΝΤΙΓΥ τούρτα σαντιγύ [toorta sandiyi] whipped cream gâteau

ΤΟΥΡΤΑ ΣΟΚΟΛΑΤΑΣ τούρτα σοκολάτας [toorta sokolatas] chocolate gâteau

ΤΡΟΥΦΑΚΙΑ τρουφάκια [troofakia] small chocolate fudge cake

ΤΣΙΠΟΥΡΕΣ τσιπούρες [tsipoores] sea bream

ΤΣΙΠΟΥΡΕΣ ΨΗΤΕΣ τσιπούρες ψητές [tsipoores psites] roast sea bream

ΤΣΙΠΣ τσιπς [tsips] crisps, (US) potato chips

ΤΣΟΥΡΕΚΙ τσουρέκι [tsooreki] light sponge

ΤΣΟΥΡΕΚΙΑ τσουρέκια [tsoorekia] sweet bread with fresh butter (Christmas/Easter dish)

ΤΥΡΙ τυρί [tiri] cheese

ΤΥΡΙΑ τυριά [tiria] cheese

ΤΥΡΟΠΙΤΤΑ τυρόπιττα [tiropita] cheese and egg in filo pastry

ΤΥΡΟΠΙΤΤΑΚΙΑ
τυροπιττάκια [tiropitakia] small
cheese pies

ΦΑΒΑ φάβα [fava] chick pea
soup
ΦΑΚΕΣ φακές [fakes] lentil
soup
ΦΑΣΟΛΑΔΑ φασολάδα
[fasolatha] bean soup with
celery, carrots and tomatoes
ΦΑΣΟΛΑΚΙΑ φασολάκια
[fasolakia] green beans
ΦΑΣΟΛΑΚΙΑ ΛΑΔΕΡΑ
φασολάκια λαδερά [fasolakia
lathera] green beans in olive
oil and tomato sauce
ΦΑΣΟΛΑΚΙΑ ΦΡΕΣΚΑ
ΓΙΑΧΝΙ φασολάκια φρέσκα
γιαχνί [fasolakia freska yakhni]
runner beans with onion
and tomato
ΦΑΣΟΛΑΚΙΑ ΦΡΕΣΚΑ
ΣΑΛΑΤΑ φασολάκια φρέσκα
σαλάτα [fasolakia freska salata]
runner bean salad
ΦΑΣΟΛΙΑ φασόλια [fasolia]
beans
ΦΑΣΟΛΙΑ ΓΙΓΑΝΤΕΣ
ΓΙΑΧΝΙ φασόλια γίγαντες
γιαχνί [fasolia yigandes yakhni]
butter beans with onion
and tomato
ΦΑΣΟΛΙΑ ΓΙΓΑΝΤΕΣ ΣΤΟ
ΦΟΥΡΝΟ φασόλια γίγαντες
στο φούρνο [fasolia yigandes sto
foorno] oven-cooked butter
beans
ΦΑΣΟΛΙΑ ΓΙΓΑΝΤΕΣ

φασόλια γίγαντες [fasolia
yigandes] large dried beans
in tomato sauce
ΦΑΣΟΛΙΑ ΣΟΥΠΑ φασόλια
σούπα [fasolia soopa] bean
soup
ΦΕΤΑ φέτα [feta] feta cheese
ΦΙΛΕ ΜΙΝΙΟΝ φιλέ μινιόν
[fileh minion] thin fillet steak
ΦΙΛΕΤΟ φιλέτο [fileto] fillet
steak
ΦΛΟΓΕΡΕΣ ΜΕ ΚΡΕΜΑ
φλογέρες με κρέμα [floyeres
meh krema] round sweets
filled with cream
ΦΟΝΤΑΝ φοντάν [fondan]
sweets
ΦΟΝΤΑΝ ΑΜΥΓΔΑΛΟΥ
φοντάν αμυγδάλου [fondan
amigthaloo] almond sweets
ΦΟΝΤΑΝ ΑΠΟ ΚΑΡΥΔΑ
φοντάν από καρύδα [fondan apo
karitha] coconut sweets
ΦΟΝΤΑΝ ΑΠΟ ΚΑΡΥΔΙΑ
φοντάν από καρύδια [fondan
apo karithia] walnut sweets
ΦΟΝΤΑΝ ΙΝΔΙΚΗΣ
ΚΑΡΥΔΑΣ φοντάν ινδικής
καρύδας [fondan inthikis karithas]
coconut sweets
ΦΟΝΤΑΝ ΠΟΡΤΟΚΑΛΙΟΥ
φοντάν πορτοκαλιού [fondan
portokali-oo] orange sweets
ΦΟΥΝΤΟΥΚΙΑ φουντούκια
[foondookia] hazelnuts
ΦΡΑΟΥΛΕΣ φράουλες [fra-
ooles] strawberries
ΦΡΑΟΥΛΕΣ ΜΕ ΣΑΝΤΙΓΥ
φράουλες με σαντιγύ [fra-ooles

meh sandiyi] strawberries
with whipped cream

ΦΡΙΚΑΣΕ ΑΡΝΙ φρικασέ αρνί
[frikaseh arni] lamb cooked in
lettuce with cream sauce

ΦΡΟΥΙ-ΓΚΛΑΣΕ φρουί-
γκλασέ [frooi-glaseh] dried
assorted fruits with sugar

ΦΡΟΥΤΑ φρούτα [froota]
fruit

ΦΡΟΥΤΟΣΑΛΑΤΑ
φρουτοσαλάτα [frootosalata]
fruit salad

ΦΡΥΓΑΝΙΑ φρυγανιά [frigania]
toast

ΦΡΥΓΑΝΙΕΣ φρυγανιές
[frigani-es] French toast

ΦΥΛΛΟ ΠΙΤΤΑΣ φύλλο
πίττας [filo pitas] filo pastry

ΦΥΣΤΙΚΙΑ φυστίκια [fistikia]
peanuts

ΦΥΣΤΙΚΙΑ ΑΙΓΙΝΗΣ
φυστίκια Αιγίνης [fistikia Eyinis]
pistachios

ΧΑΒΙΑΡΙ χαβιάρι [khaviari]
caviar

ΧΑΛΒΑΣ χαλβάς [khalvas]
halva, sweet made from
semolina, sesame seeds, nuts
and honey

ΧΑΜΠΟΥΡΓΚΕΡ
χάμπουργκερ [khamburger]
hamburger

ΧΗΝΑ χήνα [khina] goose

ΧΟΙΡΙΝΟ χοιρινό [khirino]
pork

ΧΟΙΡΙΝΟ ΜΕ ΣΕΛΙΝΟ
χοιρινό με σέλινο [khirino meh

selino] pork casserole with
celery

ΧΟΙΡΙΝΟ ΠΑΣΤΟ χοιρινό
παστό [khirino pasto] salted
pork

ΧΟΙΡΙΝΟ ΣΟΥΒΛΑΣ χοιρινό
σούβλας [khirino soovlas] pork
on the spit

ΧΟΙΡΙΝΟ ΣΤΗ ΣΧΑΡΑ
χοιρινό στη σχάρα [khirino sti
skhara] grilled pork

ΧΟΙΡΙΝΟ ΦΟΥΡΝΟΥ ΜΕ
ΠΑΤΑΤΕΣ χοιρινό φούρνου
με πατάτες [khirino foornoo meh
patates] roast pork with
potatoes

ΧΟΡΤΑ ΒΡΑΣΜΕΝΑ
ΣΑΛΑΤΑ χόρτα βρασμένα
σαλάτα [khorta vrasmena salata]
boiled chicory salad

ΧΟΡΤΑΡΙΚΑ χορταρικά
[khortarika] vegetables

ΧΟΡΤΟΣΟΥΠΑ χορτόσουπα
[khortosoopa] vegetable
soup

ΧΤΑΠΟΔΑΚΙ ΞΥΔΑΤΟ
χταποδάκι ξυδάτο [khtapothaki
xithato] pickled octopus

ΧΤΑΠΟΔΙ χταπόδι [khtapothi]
octopus

ΧΤΑΠΟΔΙ ΒΡΑΣΤΟ χταπόδι
βραστό [khtapothi vrasto]
boiled octopus

ΧΤΑΠΟΔΙ ΚΡΑΣΑΤΟ
χταπόδι κρασάτο [khtapothi
krasato] octopus in wine

ΧΤΑΠΟΔΙ ΜΕ
ΜΑΚΑΡΟΝΑΚΙ χταπόδι με
μακαρονάκι [khtapothi meh

makaronaki] octopus with macaroni

ΧΤΑΠΟΔΙ ΠΙΛΑΦΙ χταπόδι πιλάφι [khtapothi pilafi] octopus pilaf

ΧΤΑΠΟΔΙ ΣΤΙΦΑΔΟ χταπόδι στιφάδο [khtapothi stifatho] octopus with small onions

ΧΥΛΟΠΙΤΕΣ χυλοπίτες [khilopites] tagliatelle

ΧΥΛΟΠΙΤΕΣ ΜΕ ΒΟΥΤΥΡΟ ΚΑΙ ΤΥΡΙ χυλοπίτες με βούτυρο και τυρί [khilopites meh vootiro keh tiri] tagliatelle with butter and cheese

ΧΥΛΟΠΙΤΕΣ ΜΕ ΚΙΜΑ χυλοπίτες με κιμά [khilopites meh kima] tagliatelle with minced meat sauce

ΧΥΛΟΠΙΤΕΣ ΜΕ ΚΟΤΟΠΟΥΛΟ χυλοπίτες με κοτόπουλο [khilopites meh kotopoolo] tagliatelle with chicken

ΧΩΡΙΑΤΙΚΗ ΣΑΛΑΤΑ χωριάτικη σαλάτα [khoriatiki salata] Greek salad – tomatoes, cucumber, peppers, feta, olives and boiled eggs with olive oil and vinegar dressing

ΨΑΡΙ ψάρι [psari] fish

ΨΑΡΙ ΒΡΑΣΤΟ ΜΑΓΙΟΝΕΖΑ ψάρι βραστό μαγιονέζα [psari vrasto mayoneza] steamed fish with mayonnaise

ΨΑΡΙΑ ψάρια [psaria] fish

ΨΑΡΙΑ ΓΛΩΣΣΕΣ ΒΡΑΣΤΕΣ

ΜΕ ΑΥΓΟΛΕΜΟΝΟ ψάρια γλώσσες βραστές με αυγολέμονο [psaria gloses vrastes meh avgolemono] steamed sole with oil and lemon

ΨΑΡΙΑ ΜΑΡΙΝΑΤΑ ψάρια μαρινάτα [psaria marinata] marinated fish

ΨΑΡΙΑ ΤΗΓΑΝΗΤΑ ψάρια τηγανητά [psaria tiganita] fried fish

ΨΑΡΙΑ ΨΗΤΑ ΣΤΗ ΣΧΑΡΑ ψάρια ψητά στη σχάρα [psaria psita sti skhara] charcoal-grilled fish

ΨΑΡΟΣΟΥΠΑ ψαρόσουπα [psarosoopa] fish soup

ΨΗΤΟ ψητό [psito] grilled over charcoal; oven-roasted

ΨΗΤΟ ΣΤΗ ΣΧΑΡΑ ψητό στη σχάρα [psito sti skhara] grilled

ΨΩΜΑΚΙ ψωμάκι [psomaki] roll

ΨΩΜΙ ψωμί [psomi] bread

ΨΩΜΙ ΑΣΠΡΟ ψωμί άσπρο [psomi aspro] white bread

ΨΩΜΙ ΓΙΑ ΤΟΣΤ ψωμί γιά τοστ [psomi ya tost] sliced bread

ΨΩΜΙ ΜΑΥΡΟ ψωμί μαύρο [psomi mavro] brown bread

ΩΜΟΣ ωμός [omos] raw

Α
Β
Γ
Δ
Ε
Ζ
Η
Θ
Ι
Κ
Λ
Μ
Ν
Ξ
Ο
Π
Ρ
Σ
Τ
Υ
Φ
Χ
Ψ
Ω

Menu
Reader:
Drink

Essential Terms

beer i bira
bottle to bookali
brandy to koniak
coffee o kafes
cup: a cup of ... ena flidzani ...
fruit juice o khimos frooton
gin to tzin
 a gin and tonic ena tzin meh tonik
glass: a glass of ... ena potiri ...
milk to gala
mineral water to emfialomeno nero
orange juice i portokalatha
red wine to kokino krasi
rosé to rozeh
soda (water) i sotha
soft drink to anapsiktiko
sugar i zakhari
tea to tsa-i
tonic (water) to tonik
vodka i votka
water to nero
whisky to whisky
white wine to aspro krasi
wine to kras
wine list o katalogos ton krasion

another ..., please ali mia ..., parakalo

ΑΕΡΙΟΥΧΟ αεριούχο
[aeriookho] fizzy

ΑΛΚΟΟΛ αλκοόλ [alko-ol]
alcohol

ΑΝΑΝΑΣ ΧΥΜΟΣ ανανάς
χυμός [ananas khimos]
pineapple juice

ΑΝΑΨΥΚΤΙΚΟ αναψυκτικό
[anapsiktiko] soft drink

ΑΠΕΡΙΤΙΦ απεριτίφ [aperitif]
aperitif

ΑΣΠΡΟ ΚΡΑΣΙ άσπρο κρασί
[aspro krasi] white wine

ΒΟΤΚΑ βότκα [votka] vodka

ΒΥΣΣΙΝΑΔΑ βυσσινάδα
[visinatha] black cherry juice

ΓΑΛΑ γάλα [gala] milk
ΓΑΛΑ ΚΑΚΑΟ γάλα κακάο
[gala kakao] chocolate milk

ΓΑΛΛΙΚΟΣ ΚΑΦΕΣ γαλλικός
καφές [galikos kafes] filter
coffee; French coffee

ΓΛΥΚΟ ΚΡΑΣΙ γλυκό κρασί
[gliko krasi] sweet wine

ΕΛΛΗΝΙΚΟΣ ΚΑΦΕΣ
ελληνικός καφές [elinikos
kafes] Greek coffee

ΖΕΣΤΗ ΣΟΚΟΛΑΤΑ ζεστή
σοκολάτα [zesti sokolata] hot
chocolate

ΚΑΚΑΟ κακάο [kakao] cocoa

ΚΑΤΑΛΟΓΟΣ ΚΡΑΣΙΩΝ
κατάλογος κρασιών [katalogos
krasion] wine list

ΚΑΦΕΣ καφές [kafes] coffee
ΚΑΦΕΣ ΜΕΤΡΙΟΣ καφές
μέτριος [kafes metrios]
medium-sweet Greek
coffee

ΚΑΦΕΣ ΒΑΡΥΣ ΓΛΥΚΟΣ
καφές βαρύς γλυκός [kafes
varis glikos] sweet Greek
coffee

ΚΑΦΕΣ ΜΕ ΓΑΛΑ καφές με
γάλα [kafes meh gala] coffee
with milk

ΚΟΚΑ ΚΟΛΑ κόκα κόλα
[koka kola] Coca-Cola®

ΚΟΚΚΙΝΟ ΚΡΑΣΙ κόκκινο
κρασί [kokino krasi] red wine

ΚΟΚΤΕΗΛ κοκτέηλ [kokteil]
cocktail

ΚΟΝΙΑΚ κονιάκ [koniak]
brandy

ΚΡΑΣΙ κρασί [krasi] wine
ΚΡΑΣΙ ΑΣΠΡΟ κρασί άσπρο
[krasi aspro] white wine

ΚΡΑΣΙ ΚΟΚΚΙΝΟ κρασί
κόκκινο [krasi kokino] red
wine

ΚΡΑΣΙ ΜΑΥΡΟΔΑΦΝΗ
κρασί μαυροδάφνη [krasi
mavrothafni] sweet red wine

ΚΡΑΣΙ ΡΕΤΣΙΝΑ κρασί
ρετσίνα [krasi retsina] retsina

ΚΡΑΣΙ ΡΟΖΕ κρασί ροζέ
[krasi rozeh] rosé wine

ΚΡΑΣΙ ΤΟΥ ΜΑΓΑΖΙΟΥ
κρασί του μαγαζιού [krasi too
magazi-oo] house wine

ΛΕΜΟΝΑΔΑ λεμονάδα
[lemonatha] lemonade

ΛΙΚΕΡ λικέρ [**liker**] liqueur

ΜΕΤΑΛΛΙΚΟ ΝΕΡΟ
μεταλλικό νερό [**metaliko nero**]
mineral water

ΜΗΛΟΧΥΜΟΣ μηλοχυμός
[**milokhimos**] apple juice

ΜΠΥΡΑ μπύρα [**bira**] beer,
lager

ΝΕΣΚΑΦΕ νέσκαφέ [**neskafeh**]
Nescafé®, instant coffee

ΝΕΣΚΑΦΕ ΦΡΑΠΕ νέσκαφέ
φραπέ [**neskafeh frapeh**] iced
coffee

ΝΕΡΟ νερό [**nero**] water

ΝΤΟΜΑΤΑ ΧΥΜΟΣ ντομάτα
χυμός [**domata khimos**] tomato
juice

ΟΥΖΟ ούζο [**oozo**] ouzo

ΟΥΙΣΚΥ ουίσκυ whisky,
scotch

ΠΑΓΑΚΙ παγάκι [**pagaki**] ice
cube

ΠΑΓΟΣ πάγος [**pagos**] ice

ΠΟΡΤΟΚΑΛΑΔΑ
πορτοκαλάδα [**portokalatha**]
orange juice

ΠΟΡΤΟΚΑΛΙ ΧΥΜΟΣ
πορτοκάλι χυμός [**portokali
khimos**] orange juice

ΠΟΤΑ ποτά [**pota**] drinks

ΡΑΚΙ ρακή [**raki**] strong
spirit, eau-de-vie

ΡΕΤΣΙΝΑ ρετσίνα [**retsina**]
retsina

ΡΟΖΕ ΚΡΑΣΙ ροζέ κρασί
[**rozeh krasi**] rosé wine

ΡΟΥΜΙ ρούμι [**roomi**] rum

ΣΤΑΦΥΛΙ ΧΥΜΟΣ σταφύλι
χυμός [**stafili khimos**] grape
juice

ΤΖΙΝ τζιν [**tzin**] gin

ΤΖΙΝ ΜΕ ΤΟΝΙΚ τζιν με
τόνικ [**tzin meh tonik**] gin and
tonic

ΤΣΑΙ τσάι [**tsa-i**] tea

ΤΣΑΙ ΜΕ ΛΕΜΟΝΙ τσάι με
λεμόνι [**tsa-i meh lemoni**]
lemon tea

ΤΣΙΠΟΥΡΟ τσίπουρο [**tsipooro**]
type of ouzo

ΦΡΑΠΕ φραπέ [**frapeh**] iced
coffee

ΧΥΜΟΣ χυμός [**khimos**] juice

ΧΩΡΙΣ ΚΑΦΕΪΝΗ χωρίς
καφεΐνη [**khoris kafeini**]
decaffeinated